First Dictionary

DK PUBLISHING, INC.

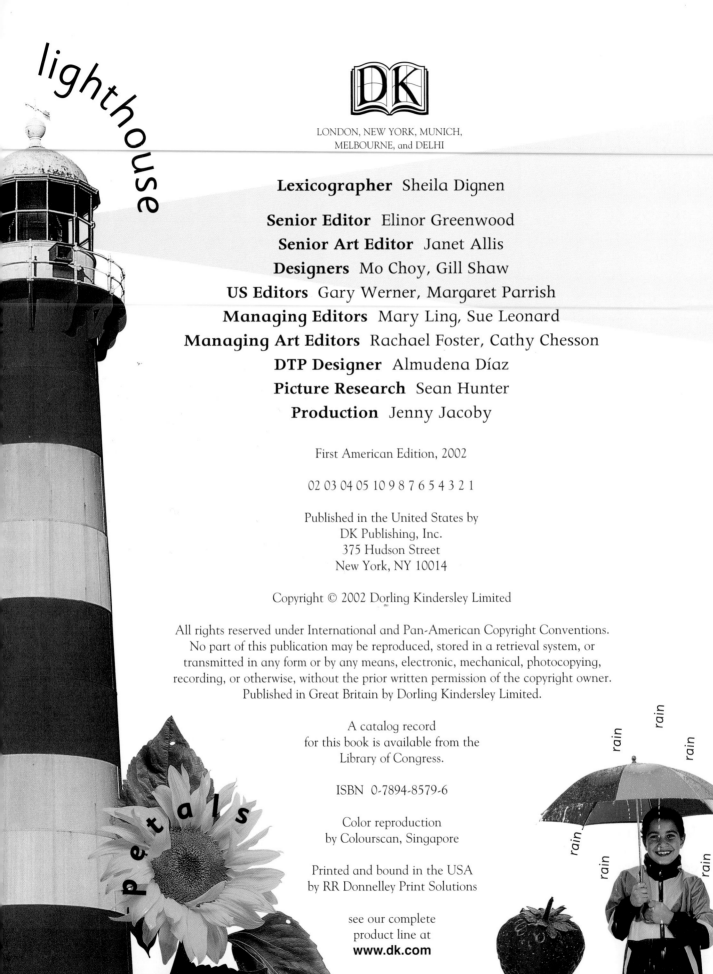

DK

LONDON, NEW YORK, MUNICH,
MELBOURNE, and DELHI

Lexicographer Sheila Dignen

Senior Editor Elinor Greenwood
Senior Art Editor Janet Allis
Designers Mo Choy, Gill Shaw
US Editors Gary Werner, Margaret Parrish
Managing Editors Mary Ling, Sue Leonard
Managing Art Editors Rachael Foster, Cathy Chesson
DTP Designer Almudena Díaz
Picture Research Sean Hunter
Production Jenny Jacoby

First American Edition, 2002

02 03 04 05 10 9 8 7 6 5 4 3 2 1

Published in the United States by
DK Publishing, Inc.
375 Hudson Street
New York, NY 10014

A catalog record
for this book is available from the
Library of Congress.

ISBN 0-7894-8579-6

Color reproduction
by Colourscan, Singapore

Printed and bound in the USA
by RR Donnelley Print Solutions

see our complete
product line at
www.dk.com

Introduction

butterfly

DK First Dictionary is a stunning and entertaining
new wordfinder for young children.

An interactive dictionary
DK First Dictionary provides a valuable
and fascinating insight into the world of
words. The striking design and interactive
features stimulate children's natural
curiosity and appetite for words.

Dictionary skills
The clear design and layout help children
to learn important dictionary skills. *DK
First Dictionary* helps to widen vocabulary
and improve spelling and grammar as well
as develop children's awareness of words.

Over 3,000 entries
Each word is clearly defined with simple,
age-related vocabulary. The definitions are
written in full sentences, making them easy
to understand. Example sentences illustrate
use and meaning.

Over 800 illustrations
The eye-catching color graphics and
photographs bring the definitions to life.

More than just a dictionary
While *DK First Dictionary* acts as a tool to
look up spellings and meanings of words,
there is more to it than that:

☞ **Similar words** and **Opposites**—the
dictionary can also be used as a thesaurus.
☞ **Say**—words that are hard to pronounce
are respelled as they are spoken.
☞ **Question circles**—questions about
words on the page stimulate interest.
☞ **Word collections**—fun-filled pages
of words under one theme are
valuable aids to creative writing.
☞ **Word histories**—fascinating
insights into how many of the
words came to be.

Contents

hisssssss

a
b
c
d
e
f
g
h
i
j
k
l
m
n
o
p
q
r
s
t
u
v
w
x
y
z

Alphabetical order

To look up a word, you need to find where it belongs among all the other words in the English language. This is why a dictionary arranges words in **alphabetical order**.

Get in order!

Here is the alphabet in the correct order. Remember this and using a dictionary will be easy!

a b c d e f g h i j k l m n o p q r s t u v w x y z

Putting words in order

To put words into alphabetical order, you compare their first letters, then their second letters, then their third, and so on.
For example, look at this list of animals.

1 Ant	A comes before C
2 Cat	Ca comes before Cr
3 Crab	Cra comes before Cre
4 Creature	Cre comes before Cro
5 Crocodile	Cr comes before Cu
6 Cub	

Cupboard chaos

Sam and Sophie are very neat, and they want to rearrange their shelves with their toys in alphabetical order. Can you put their toys into alphabetical order for them?
(Answers on page 256)

ball

tractor

drum

teddy bear

soldier

4

It's nonsense! ?

Make sense of nonsense by putting the letters of these mixed-up words into alphabetical order. Follow the example.
(Answers on page 256)

Silly sentence ?

Correct this nonsense sentence by putting the words into the correct alphabetical order.
(Answers on page 256)

a
b
c
d
e
f
g
h

tesb best

1. woc

2. awoll

3. poyc

4. rreby

5. atecnc

6. tleb

7. inf

An his incredible astronaut journey began.

shovel

doll

train

bucket

car

u
v

5

a
b
c
d
e

All about words

To make a sentence we use different types of words. Each word in a sentence has its own name and its own job to do.

f
g
h
i
j
k
l

Nouns

A **noun** is a word that names a thing, a person, or a place. **Cat**, **teacher**, **spoon,** and **city** are all nouns. Nouns do not have to be things that you can see—words such as **truth** and **geography** are also nouns.

One or two?

One of something is called the **singular**. More than one of something is called the **plural**. Nouns in the singular are sometimes spelled differently from nouns in the plural.

s o c k **s**

s o c k

*Often you make a noun plural by simply adding —s (or —es if the word ends in an —s, for example, "princess**es**.").*

*If a noun ends in —**y**, you can replace the —**y** with —**ies**.*

o
p
q
r

c h e r r **y**

c h e r r **i e s**

Curious plurals

A few nouns stay the same in the singular and the plural.
For example:
One **sheep**; three **sheep**

Some nouns change completely in the plural.
For example:
One **mouse**; two **mice**
One **man**; three **men**

s
t
u
v
w
x
y
z

Adjectives

An **adjective** is a word that is used to describe a noun. **Big**, **yellow**, **sticky**, and **dark** are all adjectives.

This piglet is...

h a i r y

s m a l l

pink

Comparing things

To compare two or more people or things, the adjective can change. For example, "tall" becomes "tall**er**" or "**the** tall**est**".

Some adjectives do not change. Instead we add **more** and **most** before the adjective to show comparison.

taller

tall

This flower is **beautiful**.

This flower is **more beautiful**.

Verbs

A **verb** is sometimes called an **action word** because it is a word that describes what a person or a thing is doing. **Sit**, **think**, **sleep**, **sing**, and **climb** are all verbs. A sentence must contain a verb to make sense.

*The boy **kicks** the ball.*

Now and then

The **tense** of a verb shows when something happens. Some tenses need helping verbs like "is" and "will." Notice how the verb changes according to which tense it is in.

If the action happens **now**, the verb is in the **present tense**.
*The boy **kicks** the ball.*

If the action is happening **now** and **continues** to happen, the verb is in the **continuous present tense**:
*The boy **is kicking** the ball.*

If the action happened **before**, in the past, the verb is in the **past tense**.
*The boy **kicked** the ball.*

If the action happens **later**, in the future, a "helping verb," such as **will**, is added before the verb to make the **future tense**.
*The boy **will kick** the ball.*

the tallest

*This flower is the **most beautiful**.*

Adverbs

An adverb is a word that gives more information about a verb, an adjective, or another adverb. **Slowly**, **yesterday**, and **very** are all adverbs. Many adverbs end with the letters —**ly**.

Follow the arrows linking the verbs to the adverbs.

run loudly
throw merrily
snore far
laugh quickly

a
b
c
d
e
f
g
h
i
j
k
l
m
n
o
p
q
r
s
t
u
v
w
x
y
z

Using the dictionary

Read the information on these pages to get the most out of your dictionary. Most pages in the book look like this double page from the letter **R** section (below).

Getting directions

When you travel somewhere, there are usually signs to help point you in the right direction. It's the same when you are looking up words in this dictionary. Look at this double-page example.

Top left
This is the first word on this page.

A new letter
This big "R" shows that you are starting the section of words that all begin with "R."

Top right
This is the last word on this page.

Test yourself
You can test your word know-how by answering the questions in the circles. If you don't know the answer, look on one of the two facing pages.

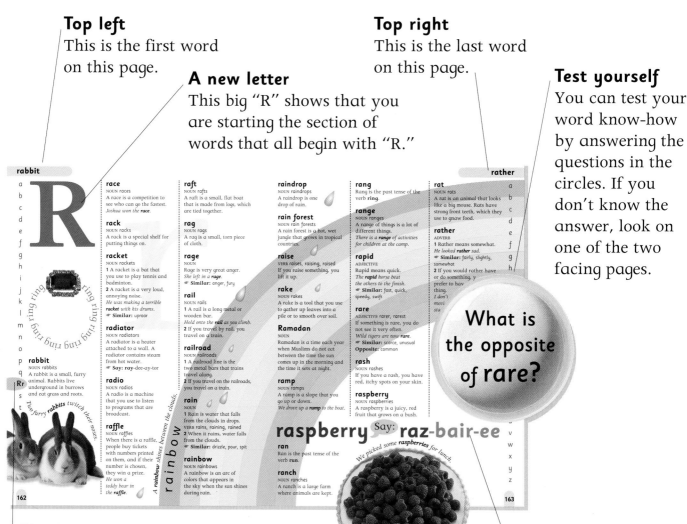

What is the opposite of rare?

Check your alphabet
The alphabet running down the edge of each page helps you to put words into alphabetical order. The highlighted letter tells you which letter section you are in.

Picture it
Pictures illustrate words.

Pronunciation
Look out for words that are respelled to help you pronounce them.

Looking at a word

This dictionary tells you lots of things about words and how to use them.

What does it mean?

The meaning of the word is given for each entry. If a word has more than one meaning or part of speech, it is listed below the headword.

Extra information

Follow the pointing hand symbol ☞ to find out more about words.
(See pages 10–11)

Headword
The big, bold word at the head of each entry is the word you are looking up.

email
NOUN emails
1 An email is a message that you send to someone from your computer to their computer.
VERB emails, emailing, emailed
2 When you email someone you send them a message in an email.
*I **emailed** Jessica about the party.*
☞ **Word history:** The word **email** is short for "electronic mail."

Part of speech
This tells you whether the headword is a **noun**, **verb**, **adjective**, or **adverb**.
(See pages 6–7)

Example sentence
Example sentences use the headword as it might be used in everyday life. The headword is in heavy black type.

Parts of speech

The dictionary entries for nouns, verbs, and adjectives include different information.

Nouns

If the word you are looking at is a **noun**, you can find out what its plural is.

man
NOUN men
A man is an adult male person.

If a noun doesn't have a plural, or doesn't change in the plural, nothing is listed.

Verbs

If the word is a verb, you are given the verb tenses.

present tense continuous present tense

clap
VERB claps, clapping, clapped_____*past tense*
When people clap, they hit their hands together to make a loud sound.

Adjectives

If the entry word is an adjective, the line below may show the forms used for comparing a person or thing with another or others.

friendly
ADJECTIVE friendlier, friendliest
Someone who is friendly is kind and helpful and shows that they like you.

If an adjective has no comparative form, or its comparative form is rarely used, nothing is listed.

a
b
c
d
e
f
g
h
i
j
k
l
m
n
o
p
q
r
s
t
u
v
w
x
y
z

9

a
b
c
d
e
f
g
h
i
j
k
l
m
n
o
p
q
r
s
t
u
v
w
x
y
z

Find out more

Here is an outline of the extra information you can find. From pronunciations to word histories, there is more to this dictionary than meanings and spellings.

☞ Say and Rhymes

Words that are tricky to pronounce are respelled or given a simple rhyming word to make it easier.

The darker text is the part of the word that you say the loudest.

xylophone
NOUN xylophones
A xylophone is a musical instrument with bars on a frame. When you hit each bar it makes a different note.
☞ **Say: zye**-le-fown

guest
NOUN guests
A guest is someone who stays at a house or a hotel.
☞ **Rhymes:** best

Can you pronounce these words? Use the **?** dictionary to help you.

vaccination
wriggle
rhinoceros
tough

☞ Similar and Opposite words

In this dictionary, you can find words that mean the same thing, or the opposite thing, to the word you are looking up. For example, "big."

big
ADJECTIVE bigger, biggest
Something that is big is large because it is high or wide.
☞ **Similar:** enormous, great, huge, large, massive
Opposite: small

Follow the yellow **?** arrows to find similar words and the blue arrows to find words of opposite meaning.
(Answers on page 256)

enormous, great, huge, large, massive

big

little, minute, tiny

small

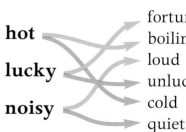

hot fortunate
 boiling
 loud
lucky unlucky
 cold
noisy quiet

☞ Word histories

Many English words have ancient histories. Often their origins can be found in different languages, especially Latin and Greek, which were spoken thousands of years ago. "Dinosaur" is one example.

Look up these words in the ❓ dictionary and find out their word histories.

alphabet **nectar**
bus **teddy bear**
denim **turkey**

☞ **Word history:**
The word **dinosaur** comes from the Greek words *deinos sauros*, meaning "terrible lizard."

dinosaur

a
b

g
h
i

Word collections

Full-page and half-page word collections provide extra vocabulary on a variety of subjects.

m
n
o
p
q
r
s
t
u
v
w
x
y
z

mammal

a **mammal**
NOUN mammals
b A mammal is an animal that
c is warm-blooded and has
 hair or fur on its body.
d Female mammals feed their
e babies with milk. Cows, lions,
 and whales are all mammals.
f People are also mammals.

man
g NOUN men
h A man is an adult male
 person.
i
 manage
j VERB manages, managing,
 managed
k 1 The person who manages a
 store or business is in charge
l of it. This person is the
Mm **manager**.
 She manages a store, and has
n *two assistants to help her.*
o 2 If you manage to do
 something, you do it even
p though it is difficult.
 She managed to swim all the
 way across the bay.

manner
NOUN manners
1 The manner in which you
do something is the way in
which you do it.
She always greets us in a
friendly manner.
2 Your manners are the way
you behave when you are
with other people.

many
ADJECTIVE
Many means a large number
of people or things.
There were so many
people that I couldn't
find my sister.
☞ **Similar:** loads,
lots, plenty,
tons
Opposite: few

map
NOUN maps
A map is a drawing of a
place. Maps show where
towns, roads, rivers, and
mountains are.

marathon
NOUN marathons
A marathon is a very long
running race. A marathon is
26 miles 385 yards (42.19 km)
long.
☞ **Word history:** When the
Greek army defeated its
enemies near the town of
Marathon in 490 BC, a runner
was sent to Athens with the
good news. The modern
marathon race is the same
distance as the distance
that ancient messenger ran.

I won lots of multicolored marbles.

marble
NOUN marbles
1 Marble is a hard stone that
people sometimes use for
building.
2 Marbles are small, glass
balls that children play with.

march
VERB marches, marching,
marched
When you march, you walk
with quick, regular steps, like
a soldier.
The band marched in time to
the music.

margarine
NOUN
Margarine is a soft substance
made from vegetable oils.
You spread it on bread like
butter.

marine Say:
mar-een

marine
ADJECTIVE
Marine animals live in the
sea. Marine life is life in
the sea.

ma
NOU
A m
stai
☞ S
smu

ma
NOU
A m
you
We
the

ma
NOU
Mar
from

ma
ADJE
Som
a hu

ma
VERB
Whe
you
or w

At the beach
There are lots of things to see
and do at the beach.

You can... fish, fly a kite, paddle, sail, surf, swim

sun sun sun
sunny sun
sun sun
boiling burning bright

windy, breezy, gusty

mask

beach ball bouncing
bouncing beach ball

seagulls seagulls seagulls seagulls

The sea can be... blue, calm, cool, rough, stormy, wavy

waves CRASH!

You can see... FiSH> FiSH>
splash!
FiSH>

sunglasses

ice pop

sand castle

T-shirt

bucket and shovel

shorts

pinch crab

sandals

... jellyfish, seaweed, shells, starfish

Marine life
Spectacular marine life
makes its home in the sea.

clown fish

angel fish

jellyfish

hermit crab

turtle

mullet fish

lobster

sea cucumber

sea horse

sea anemone

124

125

b
c
d
e
f
g
h
i
j
k
l
m
n
o
p
q
r
s
t
u
v
w
x
y
z

abbreviation
NOUN abbreviations
An abbreviation is a short way of writing a word. For example, "TV" is an abbreviation of "television."

able
ADJECTIVE
If you are able to do something, you can do it.
*He is **able** to ice-skate very well.*
☛ **Similar:** capable, competent

abroad
ADVERB
If you go abroad, you go to another country.
*We went **abroad** for our holiday.*

absent
ADJECTIVE
If you are absent, you are not in a place.
*He was **absent** from school because he was ill.*

absorb
VERB absorbs, absorbing, absorbed
If something absorbs water, it soaks it up.
*The cloth **absorbed** the water.*

abuse
VERB abuses, abusing, abused
To abuse someone means to hurt or treat a person badly.

accent
NOUN accents
Your accent is the way you say words when you speak. People from different places speak with different accents.

accept
VERB accepts, accepting, accepted
If you accept something, you take it when someone offers it to you.
*She **accepted** the prize for the best essay.*

accident
NOUN accidents
1 An accident is when something bad happens and someone is hurt.
*There was an **accident** on the freeway.*
2 If something was an accident, it happened by chance and no one did it deliberately.
*I didn't mean to break your pencil—it was an **accident**.*

accordion
NOUN accordions
An accordion is a musical instrument that you hold in both hands and squeeze in and out to make a sound.

accurate
ADJECTIVE
Something that is accurate is exactly right.
*She made an **accurate** copy of the picture.*
☛ **Say:** ak-yoo-rut
Similar: correct, precise, right
Opposite: inaccurate

accuse
VERB accuses, accusing, accused
If you accuse someone of doing something, you say that person did it.
*She **accused** him of stealing her money.*
☛ **Say:** a-**kyooz**
Similar: blame, charge

ache
VERB aches, aching, ached
If a part of your body aches, it hurts.
☛ **Rhymes:** cake
Similar: hurt, throb

achieve
VERB achieves, achieving, achieved
If you achieve something, you manage to do it.
*He **achieved** the highest score on the test.*
☛ **Similar:** accomplish, manage

acorn
NOUN acorns
An acorn is the seed of an oak tree.

Word history: The word **acrobat** comes from a Greek word, *akrobatos,* which means "walking on tiptoe."

acrobat
NOUN acrobats
An acrobat is a person who performs difficult gymnastic tricks on a stage or in a circus.

act
VERB acts, acting, acted
1 The way that you act is the way you behave.
*He was **acting** very strangely.*
2 When you act, you pretend to be a character in a play or film.
*If you enjoy **acting**, you should join a drama group.*

action
NOUN actions
An action is something that you do.
*You can do **actions** with your hands to a song.*

active
ADJECTIVE
If you are active, you are moving around, rather than being still.

activity
NOUN activities
An activity is something that you can do for fun.

actor
NOUN actors
An actor is someone who acts in plays, films, or television programs. A woman who is an actor is sometimes called an **actress**.

add
VERB adds, adding, added
1 If you add something, you put it with other things.
2 When you add up numbers, you count them together to find the total.

address
NOUN addresses
Your address is the number of the house and the name of the street where you live.

adjective
NOUN adjectives
An adjective is a word such as "big," "funny," or "old" that describes what something is like.

admire
VERB admires, admiring, admired
1 If you admire someone, you think very highly of them.
2 If you admire something, you enjoy looking at it.

admit
VERB admits, admitting, admitted
If you admit that you did something wrong, you tell the truth and say that you did it.
*He **admitted** that he had lied.*
☞ **Similar:** confess, own up
Opposite: deny

adopt
VERB adopts, adopting, adopted
When people adopt a child, they take the child into their home and become his or her parents.

adult
NOUN adults
An adult is a grown-up.
☞ **Opposite:** child

advantage
NOUN advantages
If you have an advantage, you have something good that will help you.
*Her long legs gave her an **advantage** in the high jump.*
☞ **Similar:** benefit, gain
Opposite: disadvantage

Aa b c d e f g h i j k l m n o p q r s

She admired her reflection in the mirror.

13

Aa

b
c
d
e
f
g
h
i
j
k
l
m
n
o
p
q
r
s
t
u
v
w
x
y
z

adventure

NOUN adventures
An adventure is something new and exciting that you do.

adverb

NOUN adverbs
An adverb is a word such as "quickly" or "cheerfully" that describes how you do something. Adverbs describe verbs or adjectives.

advertisement

NOUN advertisements
An advertisement is a picture or movie that shows you how good something is and tries to persuade you to buy it. You can shorten this word to **ad**.

advice

NOUN
If you give someone advice, you suggest to them what they should do.

afraid
Alice is afraid of the alligator.

aerobics

NOUN
Aerobics is fast, rhythmic exercise often done to music.
☞ **Say:** air-**roh**-biks

affectionate

ADJECTIVE
If you are affectionate, you show that you care for someone.

The yellow airplane loops the loop.

afford

VERB affords, affording, afforded
If you can afford something, you have enough money to buy it.
I can't afford a new bike.

afraid

ADJECTIVE
If you are afraid, you are scared.
Simon is afraid of the dark.
☞ **Similar:** frightened, scared, terrified

afternoon

NOUN afternoons
The afternoon is the time between midday and evening.
Farah went to the park at 2 o'clock in the afternoon.

again

ADVERB
If you do something again, you do it one more time.

age

NOUN
Your age is how old you are.

aggressive

ADJECTIVE
Someone who is aggressive often argues and fights.
☞ **Similar:** hostile, rough, violent
Opposite: gentle

airplane

ago

Ago means in the past.
He started school two years ago.

agree

VERB agrees, agreeing, agreed
If you agree with someone, you think the same as they do.
☞ **Opposite:** disagree

aim

VERB aims, aiming, aimed
If you aim at something, you point at it.

air

NOUN
Air is the mixture of gases around us that we breathe.
He opened a window to get some fresh air.

aircraft

NOUN
An aircraft is any vehicle that can fly.

b
c
d
e
f
g
h
i
j
k
l
m
n
o
p
q
r
s
t
u
v

air force
NOUN
The air force is the part of the military that fights from the air.

airplane
NOUN airplanes
An airplane is a vehicle that can travel through the air and carry people or goods.

airport
NOUN airports
An airport is where people go to travel by airplane.

alarm
NOUN
An alarm is a loud noise that warns you of something.
*They left the building quickly when the fire **alarm** went off.*

album
NOUN albums
An album is a book that you put stamps or photographs in so that you can look at them.

alien
NOUN aliens
An alien is a creature from another planet.
☞ **Say: ay**-lee-en
Word history: The word **alien** comes from the Latin word *alienus*, which means "coming from another place."

What is the opposite of agree?

Look around the page to find the answer.

alike
ADJECTIVE
Things that are alike are similar or the same.
*The two boys look very **alike**.*

alive
ADJECTIVE
People, animals, and plants that are alive are living.
☞ **Opposite:** dead

all
ADJECTIVE
All of something is every part of it.
*He ate **all** of the popcorn himself.*

alligator
NOUN alligators
An alligator is a large reptile that lives in swamps and rivers. Alligators eat fish and animals.

allow
VERB allows, allowing, allowed
If you allow someone to do something, you let them do it.
*Her parents don't **allow** her to stay up late.*
☞ **Similar:** let, permit

almost
ADVERB
Almost means nearly.
*The bottle is **almost** empty.*

alone
ADJECTIVE
If you are alone, you are by yourself and no one is with you.

aloud
ADVERB
If you say something aloud, you say it so that other people can hear it.

alphabet
NOUN alphabets
The alphabet is all the letters that are used for writing. The letters of the alphabet are usually written in order, called **alphabetical** order.
☞ **Word history:** The word **alphabet** comes from the names of the first two letters of the Greek alphabet, *alpha* and *beta*.

Word history:
The word **alligator** comes from the Spanish words *el lagarto*, which means "the lizard."

alligator

Aa
also

b

c

d

e

f

g

h

i

j

k

l

m

n

o

p

q

r

s

t

u

v

w

x

y

z

also
ADVERB
Also means as well.
Steven can play the piano and he can also sing very well.

alter
VERB alters, altering, altered
If you alter something, you change it.

altogether
ADVERB
Altogether means including everyone or everything.
There are eight eggs altogether.

always
ADVERB
If you always do something, you do it all the time or every time.
I always walk to school.
☞ **Opposite:** never

amazing
ADJECTIVE
Something that is amazing is very good or very surprising.
☞ **Similar:** astonishing, strange, surprising, unusual

ambulance
NOUN ambulances
An ambulance is a vehicle for taking sick or injured people to the hospital.

Here comes the ambulance!

amount
NOUN amounts
The amount of something is how much there is of it.
He ate a very large amount of chocolate.

amphibian
NOUN amphibians
An amphibian is an animal that can live in water and on land.
☞ **Say:** am-**fib**-ee-an
Word history: The word **amphibian** comes from the Greek words *amphi* and *bios*, meaning "both lives."

amuse
VERB amuses, amusing, amused
If something amuses you, it makes you laugh.
His jokes really amused them.

amusing
ADJECTIVE
Something that is amusing makes you laugh.
☞ **Similar:** comical, funny, hilarious

anchor
NOUN anchors
An anchor is a large, heavy, metal hook that digs into the seabed to stop a ship from drifting away.
☞ **Say:** **ang**-ker

ancient
ADJECTIVE
Something that is ancient is very old.
☞ **Say:** **ane**-shunt
Opposite: modern

angel
NOUN angels
An angel is a messenger from a god.

The size of an angle... ...is measured in degrees.

angle

90°

angle
NOUN angles
An angle is a corner where two lines meet.

angry
ADJECTIVE
If you are angry, you feel irritated and upset about something.
☞ **Similar:** annoyed, cross, furious, irritated

animal
NOUN animals
An animal is any living thing that breathes and moves around. Insects, fish, birds, mammals, and reptiles are all types of animals.

ambulance

Animal

Animals fall into these main groups.

Birds

Birds have wings and feathers.

Falcon

Parrot

Parakeet

fly

bill

Feathered friends take to the sky...

Hen and chicks

quack! quack!

Duck

Penguin

tall

Giraffe

Mammals

Mammals feed their young with milk.

striped

HUGE

furry, wild

Polar bear

Cat

meow!

Dog

Zebra

Elephant

Amphibians and reptiles

Amphibians live on land and in water. Reptiles have scaly skin and lay eggs.

Reptiles hide in the undergrowth...

Crocodile

scaly

Amphibian water-lovers

Newt

ribbit!

Frog

Tortoise

Lizard

Snake

Insects and arachnids

Insects are small animals with six legs. Arachnids have eight legs.

Scorpions and spiders are arachnids

antenna

Cardinal beetle

Butterfly

Scorpion

sting

spotted

beautiful

Ladybug

tiny, hurrying

Rhinoceros beetle

Ants

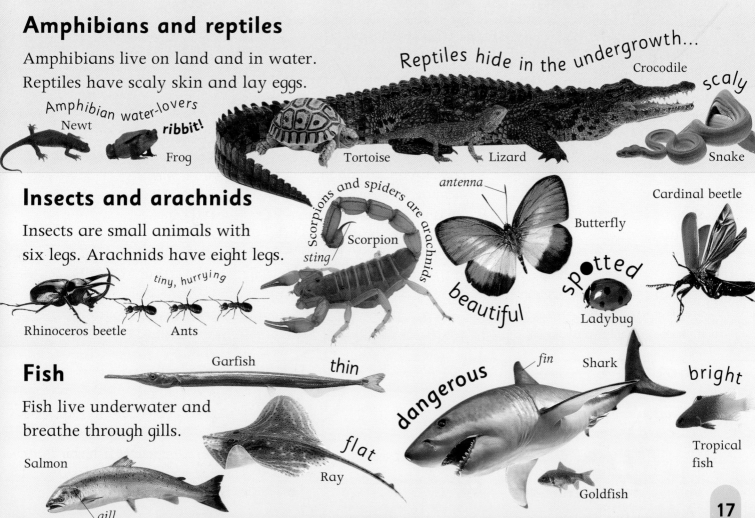

Fish

Fish live underwater and breathe through gills.

Garfish

thin

fin

Shark

bright

dangerous

flat

Salmon

Ray

Tropical fish

Goldfish

gill

Aa

b
c
d
e
f
g
j
k
l
r
s
t
u
v
w
x
y
z

ankle
NOUN ankles
Your ankle is the joint between your leg and your foot.

anniversary
NOUN anniversaries
An anniversary is a date that you remember because something important happened then.

announce
VERB announces, announcing, announced
If you announce something, you say it out loud so that everyone can hear it.

annoy
VERB annoys, annoying, annoyed
If something annoys you, it makes you feel irritated.
*Go away! You're **annoying** me!*
☞ **Similar:** bother, exasperate, infuriate, irritate, provoke

another
ADJECTIVE
1 Another means different.
*Do you have **another** pen? This one is broken.*
2 Another means one more.
*Do you want **another** cookie?*

answer
VERB answers, answering, answered
If you answer, you say something when someone has spoken to you or asked you a question. The thing that you say is your answer.

ant
NOUN ants
An ant is a type of insect. Ants live in very large groups.

*It's time to **announce** the winner.*

antelope
NOUN antelopes
An antelope is an animal like a large deer that lives on the plains in Africa and Asia. Antelopes eat grass and other plants.

antenna
NOUN antennae
The antennae on an insect or snail are the two long, thin parts on its head that it uses for feeling and touching things.

*An insect feels around with its **antenna**e.*

antiseptic
NOUN antiseptics
An antiseptic is a liquid or cream that you put on cuts to stop them from getting infected.

anxious
ADJECTIVE
If you feel anxious, you feel worried or nervous.
☞ **Say: ank**-shus
Similar: concerned, fretful, nervous, uneasy, worried,

any
ADJECTIVE
1 Any means some.
*Do you have **any** candy?*
2 Any means whichever one you want.
*You can choose **any** book you like from the library.*

anybody
Anybody or anyone means any person at all.
*It's a secret, so don't tell **anybody**.*

anything
Anything means a thing of any kind.
*We don't have **anything** to do.*

apart
ADVERB
If things are apart, they are away from each other.

apartment
NOUN apartments
An apartment is a home that is on one floor of a large building.

ape

*A chimpanzee is a type of **ape**.*

ape
NOUN apes
An ape is an animal, like a monkey, that lives in forests in various countries, and feeds on insects and fruit.

apologize
VERB apologizes, apologizing, apologized
If you apologize, you say you are sorry.

appear
VERB appears, appearing, appeared
If something appears, you can suddenly see it.
*The sun **appeared** from behind the clouds.*
☛ **Opposite:** disappear

appetite
NOUN appetites
Your appetite is your desire to eat food.
*He has a huge **appetite**.*

applause
NOUN
Applause is clapping and cheering.

apple
NOUN apples
An apple is a round fruit with a smooth skin and crisp, sweet flesh.

appointment
NOUN appointments
If you have an appointment with someone, you have arranged to meet them at a certain time.

appreciate Say:
a-pree-shee-ate

*I really **appreciate** all your help.*

appreciate
VERB appreciates, appreciating, appreciated
If you appreciate something, you are glad to have it and grateful for it.
☛ **Similar:** value, welcome

approach
VERB approaches, approaching, approached
When you approach a place, you come near to it.
*The train slowed down as it **approached** the station.*

approximately
ADVERB
Approximately means more or less, but not exactly.
*There are **approximately** 30 children in each class.*
☛ **Similar:** about, around, close to, more or less, roughly

apricot
NOUN apricots
An apricot is a small orange fruit with soft, sweet flesh and a pit in its center.

aquarium
NOUN aquariums or aquaria
An aquarium is a glass tank that you keep fish in.
☛ **Word history:** The word **aquarium** comes from the Latin word *aquarius*, which means "to do with water."

arch
NOUN arches
An arch is a curved part of a building or bridge that you can sometimes walk under.

arch

*Many bridges are shaped like an **arch**.*

Aa

b
c
d
e
f
g
h
i
j
k
l
m
n
o
p
q
r
s
t
u
v
w
x
y
z

architect

NOUN architects

An architect is a person who designs buildings.

☞ **Say: ar**-ki-tekt

area

NOUN areas

An area is a piece of land or ground.

This is a play **area**.

argue

VERB argues, arguing, argued

When people argue, they talk or shout at each other in an angry way because they do not agree about something. When people do this, you can say that they are having an **argument**.

Sandy and Steve are always **arguing**!

☞ **Similar:** bicker, disagree, fight, quarrel

arithmetic

NOUN

Arithmetic is adding, subtracting, multiplying, and dividing numbers.

arm

NOUN arms

Your arm is the part of your body between your shoulder and your hand.

armor

NOUN

Armor is metal clothing that knights used to wear to protect themselves in battle.

army

NOUN armies

An army is a large group of soldiers who fight on land.

arrange

VERB arranges, arranging, arranged

1 If you arrange to do something, you plan to do it.

She **arranged** *to meet me at 10 o'clock.*

2 When you arrange things, you put them neatly in a special order.

arrest

VERB arrests, arresting, arrested

When the police arrest someone, they catch them and take them into custody.

arrive

VERB arrives, arriving, arrived

When you arrive at a place, you get there.

We **arrived** *in the city at noon.*

armor

Knights wore suits of shining **armor** *in battle.*

arrow

NOUN arrows

1 An arrow is a pointed stick that you shoot from a bow.

2 An arrow is a pointed shape that shows you which way to go.

art

NOUN

Art is drawing, painting, and sculpture.

What is the opposite of asleep?

Look around the page to find the answer.

artist

NOUN artists

An artist is someone who draws or paints pictures, or makes sculptures.

ashamed

ADJECTIVE

If you feel ashamed, you feel guilty about something you have done.

ask

VERB asks, asking, asked

1 If you ask a question, you say it to someone because you want to know the answer.

Sarah is always **asking** *questions.*

2 If you ask for something, you say that you would like it.

astronaut

Word history:
The word **astronaut** comes from the Greek words *aster* meaning "star" and *nautes* meaning "sailor." So an astronaut is a "sailor of the stars."

asleep
ADJECTIVE
If you are asleep, you are resting and your eyes are closed.
☞ **Opposite:** awake

assistant
NOUN assistants
An assistant is someone who helps another person.

asthma
NOUN
Asthma is an illness that makes it difficult for you to breathe. Someone who suffers from asthma is **asthmatic**.
☞ **Say: az**-ma
Word history: The word **asthma** comes from the Greek word *asthma,* which means "breathing hard."

astonished
ADJECTIVE
If you are astonished, you are very surprised.
☞ **Similar:** amazed, shocked, surprised

astronaut
NOUN astronauts
An astronaut is a person who is trained to travel into space.

astronomy
NOUN
Astronomy is the scientific study of stars and planets.

ate
Ate is the past tense of the verb **eat**.

athlete
NOUN athletes
An athlete is a person who takes part in sports, exercises, or games. These sports and games are called **athletics**.

atlas
NOUN atlases
An atlas is a book of maps.

attach
VERB attaches, attaching, attached
When you attach something, you fasten it to something else.

attack
VERB attacks, attacking, attacked
If you attack someone, you hit them or try to hurt them in some way.

attempt
VERB attempts, attempting, attempted
If you attempt to do something, you try to do it.
☞ **Similar:** seek, struggle, try

attention
NOUN
If you pay attention, you listen or watch carefully.

athlete
The **athlete** takes his mark for the race...

...Get set!

...Go!

Aa
b
c
d
e
f
g
h
i
j

n
o
p
q
r
s
t
u
v
w
x
y
z

attitude
NOUN attitudes
Your attitude toward something is what you think of it and how you behave.
If you want to do well at school, you must have a good **attitude** *toward your work.*

attract
VERB attracts, attracting, attracted
If something attracts an object, it makes it come nearer.

Magnets **attract** *metal pins.*

attractive
ADJECTIVE
An attractive person or thing is good-looking or pretty.

audience
NOUN audiences
The people who come to watch a show or concert are called the audience.

aunt
NOUN aunts
Your aunt is the sister of one of your parents, or the wife of your uncle.

author
NOUN authors
An author is a person who writes books, poems, or plays.

autograph
NOUN autographs
A famous person's autograph is their signature. Some people collect autographs as a hobby.

autograph
Say: aw-teh-graf

automatic
ADJECTIVE
Something that is automatic works by itself, without anyone touching it or controlling it.

a t t r a c t

autumn
NOUN autumns
Autumn is one of the four seasons. Also called fall, autumn follows summer and comes before winter. It is the time when the leaves on some trees change color and fall to the ground.

avalanche
NOUN avalanches
An avalanche is a large amount of snow, rocks, and ice that suddenly slides down a mountain.

average
ADJECTIVE
An average amount or size is normal and usual.
He was of **average** *height for his age.*

avocado
NOUN avocados
An avocado is a fruit that is shaped like a pear. It has a tough, green skin and smooth, creamy flesh.

avoid
VERB avoids, avoiding, avoided
If you avoid something, you stay away from it.

awake
ADJECTIVE
When you are awake, you are not asleep.
I stayed **awake** *all night.*
☞ **Opposite:** asleep

aware
ADJECTIVE
If you are aware of something, you know about it.

awful
ADJECTIVE
Something that is awful is very bad.
☞ **Similar:** dreadful, horrible, terrible

awkward
ADJECTIVE
If something is awkward, it is slightly difficult to do.

ax
NOUN axes
An ax is a tool that you use for chopping wood.

B

BANG!

baboon
NOUN baboons
A baboon is a large monkey that lives in Africa. Baboons live on the ground and eat plants and small animals.

baby
NOUN babies
A baby is a very young child.

back
NOUN backs
1 Your back is the part of your body that is between your neck and your buttocks.
2 The back of something is the part opposite the front.
*Write your name on the **back** of the picture.*

backpack
NOUN backpacks
A backpack is a bag that you carry on your back.

backward
ADVERB
If you move backward, you move in the direction that is behind you.
*I fell **backward** into a prickly bush.*

bacteria
NOUN
Bacteria are very small organisms that live inside you and all around you. Some cause disease, while others help your body.
☞ **Say:** bac-**tee**-ree-a

bad
ADJECTIVE worse, worst
1 Something that is bad is wrong, and you should not do it.
*Stealing is **bad**.*
☞ **Similar:** criminal, illegal, naughty
Opposite: good
2 Something that is bad is serious.
*She has a **bad** cold.*
☞ **Similar:** awful, dreadful, terrible
3 Food that is bad is rotten.
*The meat had gone **bad**.*
☞ **Similar:** moldy, rancid

badge
NOUN badges
A badge is a small picture or sign that you pin or sew onto your clothes.
*He was awarded a **badge** for community service.*

badminton
NOUN
Badminton is a game in which you use a racket to hit a birdie over a high net.
☞ **Word history:** The word **badminton** comes from the name of a house. "Badminton House" was where people first played the game.

badminton

a birdie

a badminton racket

baffle
VERB baffles, baffling, baffled
If something baffles you, you cannot understand it.
☞ **Similar:** bewilder, confuse

bag
NOUN bags
A bag is a container that you can carry things in.

a
Bb
c
d
e
f
g
h
i
j
k
l
m
n
o
p
q
r
s
t
u

baggy
ADJECTIVE
Baggy clothes fit loosely around your body.
*Tom likes to wear **baggy** pants.*
☞ **Opposite:** tight

bake
VERB bakes, baking, baked
When you bake something, you cook it in an oven. A **baker** is someone who bakes and sells bread and cakes.

balance
VERB balances, balancing, balanced
When you balance something, you keep it steady so that it does not fall.

bald
ADJECTIVE
Someone who is bald has no hair.

ball
NOUN balls
1 A ball is a round object that you use to play games and sports.
2 A ball is a big, grand party where there is dancing.

ballet
NOUN
Ballet is a type of dancing in which you dance on your toes and move very gracefully.
☞ **Say:** bal-**lay**

balloon
NOUN balloons
A balloon is a bag of very thin rubber that you can fill with air or other gases.

ban
VERB bans, banning, banned
If people ban something, they say that you are not allowed to do it.
*The teachers have **banned** soccer in the playground.*

banana
NOUN bananas
A banana is a long, thin fruit with a yellow skin that you peel off. Bananas grow in hot countries.

band
NOUN bands
1 A band is a group of people who play music together.
2 A band is a narrow strip of something that you use to hold things together.

bandage
NOUN bandages
A bandage is a strip of material that you wrap around a wound to keep it clean.

bang
NOUN bangs
1 A bang is a sudden, loud noise.
*The fireworks went off with a loud **bang**.*
☞ **Similar:** boom, crash, thud, thump
VERB bangs, banging, banged
2 When something bangs, it makes a loud noise.

bank
NOUN banks
1 The bank of a river is the ground along the edge of it.
2 A bank is a place where people can put their money to keep it safe. People can also borrow money from a bank.

bar
NOUN bars
1 A bar is a long, narrow piece of metal.
2 A large piece of chocolate is called a chocolate bar.

barbecue
NOUN barbecues
1 A barbecue is a grill that you use to cook food outside.
2 A party where you cook food outside is also called a barbecue.
*We all went to the **barbecue**.*
☞ **Say:** **bar**-bi-kew

barbecue

Word history:
The word **barbecue** comes from a word in a Caribbean language, *barbacoa*, which means "wooden frame."

bare

ADJECTIVE

If a part of your body is bare, it is not covered by clothes.

*She liked the feel of warm sand on her **bare** feet.*

bargain

NOUN bargains

A bargain is something that you buy for less money than it is really worth.

*I got these shoes on sale— they were a real **bargain**.*

bark

NOUN barks

1 Bark is the rough wood on the outside of a tree trunk.

VERB barks, barking, barked

2 When a dog barks, it makes a rough, loud noise.

woof! woof!

*Barney is **barking** at a basketball player.*

bark

barn

NOUN barns

A barn is a large building on a farm where animals are kept or things are stored.

barrel

NOUN barrels

A barrel is a large, round container that people keep liquids or food in.

base

NOUN bases

The base of something is the bottom part of it.

baseball

NOUN

Baseball is a game in which teams have to hit a ball with a long, narrow bat and then run around bases to score runs.

basket

NOUN baskets

A basket is a container that you use for carrying things. It is made of thin strips of cane or straw.

basketball

NOUN

Basketball is a game in which teams of players bounce a ball and throw it to each other, and score points by throwing it through a high hoop called the **basket**.

bat

NOUN bats

1 A bat is a special stick that you use to hit a ball in baseball and softball.

2 A bat is an animal that flies at night and lives in caves and dark places. Bats eat insects, fruit, or small animals, and rest hanging upside down.

bathtub

NOUN bathtubs

A bathtub is a large tub that you sit in to wash your body. The room in a house with a bathtub in it is called the **bathroom**.

basketball

*A **basketball** player jumps to put the ball in the basket.*

battery

NOUN batteries

A battery is a small, metal object that stores a small amount of electricity. You put batteries into things like flashlights and clocks to make them work.

battle

NOUN battles

A battle is a fight between two armies that are at war.

a
Bb
d
e
f
g
h
i
j
k
l
m
n
o
p
q
r
s
t
u
v
w
x
y
z

Bb

beach

NOUN beaches

A beach is an area of sand or pebbles next to water.
*We're going to the **beach** today.*

bead

NOUN beads

Beads are pieces of wood or glass that can be threaded on string.

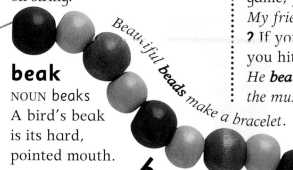

beak

NOUN beaks

A bird's beak is its hard, pointed mouth.

beam

NOUN beams

1 A long, narrow ray of light is called a beam of light.
2 A beam is a long, thick piece of wood.

bean

NOUN beans

A bean is a seed or pod that you can eat as a vegetable.
*They had string **beans** for dinner.*

bear

NOUN bears

1 A bear is a large animal with thick fur that lives in forests and mountain areas. All bears eat meat, but some also eat honey, roots, berries, and fruit.
VERB bears, bearing, bore, born, or borne
2 If something will bear your weight, it will support it.
3 If you cannot bear something, you hate it.

Beautiful beads make a bracelet.

beads

beard

NOUN beards

A man's beard is hair that grows on his face if he does not shave.

beat

VERB beats, beating, beat, beaten

1 If you beat someone at a game, you win and they lose.
*My friend **beat** me at chess.*
2 If you beat something, you hit it many times.
*He **beat** the drum in time to the music.*

beautiful

ADJECTIVE

Something that is beautiful is very pleasant to look at or hear.
*They played some **beautiful** music.*
☞ **Say: byoo**-ti-ful
Similar: attractive, fine, lovely, pleasant, pretty

beaver

NOUN beavers

A beaver is an animal with very strong teeth. Beavers cut down trees with their teeth to build dams in rivers.

become

VERB becomes, becoming, became, become

To become something means to change into it.
*A tadpole **becomes** a frog after four months.*

bed

NOUN beds

A bed is a piece of furniture that you sleep on. A room in a house with a bed in it is called a **bedroom**.

bee

NOUN bees

A bee is a flying insect with black and yellow stripes that makes honey. Bees live together in large groups and feed on nectar from flowers.

beef

NOUN

Beef is the meat from a cow or bull.

beehive

NOUN beehives

A beehive is a house for bees where a beekeeper collects honey.

beetle

NOUN beetles

A beetle is an insect with hard, shiny wings. Beetles eat small insects, wood, or plants.

beg

VERB begs, begging, begged

1 When a dog begs, it sits up on its back legs to ask for something.
2 If you beg for something, you ask for it very strongly.

begin

VERB begins, beginning, began, begun

When something begins, it starts.
*The story **begins** in a castle.*
☞ **Similar:** commence, start

At the beach

There are lots of things to see and do at the beach.

sun sun sun
sunny
uns uns
boiling burning bright

windy, breezy, gusty

You can... fish, fly a kite, paddle, sail, surf, swim

bouncing beach ball bouncing beach ball bouncing

seagulls
seagulls
seagulls
seagulls
seagulls

The sea can be... blue, calm, cool, rough, stormy, wavy

waves
CRASH!
splash!

You can see...
FISH> FISH>
FISH>
jellyfish, seaweed, shells, starfish

bucket and shovel

sand castle

pinch
crab

sunglasses
ice pop
T-shirt
shorts
sandals

a
Bb
c
d
e
f
g
h
i
j
k
l
o
p
q
r
s
t
u
v
w
x
y
z

behave

VERB behaves, behaving, behaved

The way you behave is how you speak and act in front of other people.
*All the children **behaved** well today.*

behavior

NOUN

Your behavior is how you behave.
*The teacher was pleased with our **behavior**.*

believe

VERB believes, believing, believed

If you believe something, you think that it is true.

bell
ding!
dong!

bell

NOUN bells

A bell is a piece of metal that makes a ringing sound when you hit it or shake it.

belong

VERB belongs, belonging, belonged

If something belongs to you, it is yours.
*That book **belongs** to me.*

belt

NOUN belts

A belt is a narrow strip of leather or material that you wear around your waist.

bench

NOUN benches

A bench is a long, wooden seat.

bend

NOUN bends

1 A bend in the road is a place where it goes around a corner and is not straight.
VERB bends, bending, bent
2 If you bend something, you press it or curve it so that it is not straight.
3 If you bend over, you lean forward so that your head goes toward the ground.
*She **bent** over to touch her toes.*

bent

ADJECTIVE

Something that is bent is not straight.
*It was hard to eat dessert with the **bent** spoon.*

berry

NOUN berries

A berry is a small, round, juicy fruit with seeds inside.
*Some wild **berries** are poisonous.*

best

ADJECTIVE

See **good**

The best person or thing is the one that is better than all the others.
*This chocolate cake tastes **best**.*
☞ **Similar:** excellent, finest, first-rate, outstanding, top

bet

VERB bets, betting, bet

If you bet that something is true, you believe that it is true.
*I **bet** it's going to rain later.*

better

ADJECTIVE

See **good**

1 A person or thing that is better than others is quicker, more clever, more useful, or more interesting.
☞ **Similar:** preferable, superior
2 If you are better, you are well again.
*I felt ill yesterday, but I feel **better** today.*

beware

VERB

If you tell someone to beware of something, you warn that person to be careful of it.
***Beware** of the dog.*

bicycle

NOUN bicycles

A bicycle is a vehicle with two wheels that you ride by turning the pedals with your feet. You can shorten the word bicycle to **bike**.
☞ **Word history:** The word **bicycle** comes from the Greek words *bi* and *cycle* meaning "two wheels."

big

ADJECTIVE bigger, biggest

Something that is big is large because it is high or wide.
☞ **Similar:** enormous, great, huge, large, massive

bike

A bike is a **bicycle**.

*Toucans have big, colorful **bills**.*

bikini
NOUN bikinis
A bikini is a swimsuit in two pieces that women and girls wear.

bill
NOUN bills
1 A bird's bill is its beak.
2 A bill is a piece of paper that shows you how much you have to pay for something.

billion
NOUN billions
A billion is a thousand million (1,000,000,000).

bin
NOUN bins
A bin is a box or container used to store things.

bird
NOUN birds
A bird is an animal that has wings and feathers on its body.

birthday
NOUN birthdays
Your birthday is the day you were born on, which you celebrate each year.

Happy birthday!

bison
NOUN
A bison is a large animal with a shaggy mane. It is also known as a buffalo.

bit
NOUN bits
A bit is a small piece of something.
☛ **Similar:** chunk, lump, piece, scrap

bite
VERB bites, biting, bit, bitten
If you bite something, you cut it with your teeth.
*Don't **bite** your nails!*
☛ **Similar:** chew, chomp, gnaw

bitter
ADJECTIVE
Something that is bitter tastes sour and not sweet.
*Lemons taste very **bitter**.*
☛ **Similar:** acidic, sharp, sour

black
ADJECTIVE
Something that is black is the color of night.
☛ **Similar:** dark, inky

blackberry
NOUN blackberries
A blackberry is a small, black fruit that grows on prickly stems called brambles.

blackbird
NOUN blackbirds
A blackbird is a bird that lives in gardens and fields. The male has black feathers and a yellow beak, and the female has brown feathers.

blackboard
NOUN blackboards
A blackboard is a large board that has been painted black. You write on a blackboard with chalk.

blade
NOUN blades
1 The blade of a knife or sword is the long, sharp part.
2 One stem of grass is called a blade of grass.

blame
VERB blames, blaming, blamed
If you blame someone for something, you say that they did it or it is their fault.

blank
ADJECTIVE
A blank space has nothing written or recorded on it.
☛ **Similar:** empty, vacant

blanket
NOUN blankets
A blanket is a thick, soft cover that you put on a bed.

a
Bb
h
i
j
k
l
m
n
o
p
q
r
s
t
u
v
w
x
y
z

29

a

Bb

c

d

e

f

g

h

i

Five, four, three, two, one... Blast off!

Blast off!

blast

NOUN blasts

1 A blast is a powerful explosion.

☞ **Similar:** bang, explosion

VERB blasts, blasting, blasted

2 When a rocket blasts off, it leaves the ground and goes up into the air.

bleed

VERB bleeds, bleeding, bled

When you bleed, blood comes out of your body.

o

blew

Blew is the past tense of the verb **blow**.

p

q

blind

ADJECTIVE

Someone who is blind is unable to see.

r

s

blindfold

NOUN blindfolds

A blindfold is a piece of cloth that you put over someone's eyes so that they cannot see.

t

u

v

w

blink

VERB blinks, blinking, blinked

When you blink, you shut your eyes and then open them again quickly.

x

y

z

blister

NOUN blisters

A blister is a bubble of watery liquid that forms under your skin when it has been burned or rubbed.

blizzard

NOUN blizzards

A blizzard is a very heavy snowstorm.

blob

NOUN blobs

A blob is a small lump of something with no shape.

block

NOUN blocks

1 A block is a solid piece of something.

VERB blocks, blocking, blocked

2 If something is blocking a road or path, it is in the way and people cannot get past.

*The fallen tree **blocked** the road.*

blond/blonde

ADJECTIVE

Someone who is blond has light-colored hair. **Blond** is used for boys and men, and **blonde** is used for girls and women.

blood

NOUN

Blood is the red liquid that flows around your body.

blossom

NOUN blossoms

A blossom on a tree is the flower that appears before the fruit.

blouse

NOUN blouses

A blouse is a shirt that a girl or woman wears.

blow

VERB blows, blowing, blew, blown

1 When you blow, you push air out of your mouth.

2 When the wind blows, it moves.

3 When something blows in the air, the air moves it around.

blue

ADJECTIVE

Something that is blue is the color of the sky on a sunny day.

☞ **Similar:** sapphire, turquoise

What is the opposite of blunt?

Look around the page to find the answer.

blunt

ADJECTIVE

Something that is blunt has a round end and is not sharp.

☞ **Opposite:** sharp

blurry

ADJECTIVE

If something is blurry, you cannot see it clearly.

blush

VERB blushes, blushing, blushed

When you blush, your face turns red because you are embarrassed or shy.

board

NOUN boards

A board is a flat piece of wood or very stiff paper.

boast

VERB boasts, boasting, boasted

If you boast, you tell people about something in a proud and annoying way.

*He **boasted** about all his money.*

☞ **Similar:** brag, show off

boat

NOUN boats

A boat is a vehicle that can travel on water and carry people or goods.

☞ **Similar:** craft, ship, vessel

body

NOUN bodies

Your body is all the physical parts that you are made of.

boil

VERB boils, boiling, boiled

When a liquid boils, it becomes very hot and starts to bubble.

☞ **Similar:** bubble, simmer, stew

bold

ADJECTIVE bolder, boldest

Someone who is bold is very brave.

☞ **Similar:** brave, courageous, fearless

Opposite: cowardly

bomb

NOUN bombs

A bomb is a weapon that explodes and damages buildings and other things around it.

☞ **Say:** bom

Word history: The word **bomb** comes from the Greek word *bombos* – a word for a booming or buzzing sound.

bone

NOUN bones

Your bones are the hard, white parts of your body that make up your skeleton.

bonfire

NOUN bonfires

A bonfire is a large, outdoor fire.

☞ **Word history:** A bonfire was originally a "bone-fire," a fire on which bones were burned.

book

NOUN books

A book is a set of pages filled with words or pictures that are joined together inside a cover.

boom

VERB booms, booming, boomed

If something booms, it makes a deep, loud sound.

☞ **Similar:** bang, crash, roar, rumble

boomerang

NOUN boomerangs

A boomerang is a curved piece of wood that comes back to you when you throw it through the air. Boomerangs were used in the past as a weapon by people in Australia.

A boomerang flies through the sky.

boot

NOUN boots

A boot is a type of shoe that covers your foot and part of your leg.

border

NOUN borders

1 The border between two countries is the line that divides them from each other.

☞ **Similar:** boundary, frontier

2 A border is a strip of a different color around the edge of something.

a
Bb
c
d
e
f
g
h
i
j
k
l
m
n
o
p
q
r
s
t
u
v
w
x
y
z

31

a
Bb
c
d
e
f
g
h
i
j
k

boring

ADJECTIVE

If something is boring, it is not exciting or interesting.
☞ **Similar:** dull, tedious, uninteresting

born

VERB

When a person or animal is born, they come into the world as a baby.

This ball can bounce very high.

bounce

o
p
q
r
s
t
u
v
w
x
y
z

borrow

VERB borrows, borrowing, borrowed

If you borrow something, you take it for awhile and then give it back.
May I please borrow your pen?

boss

NOUN bosses

The boss is the person who is in charge at work.

both

ADJECTIVE

Both means not just one thing, but two.
Both pens are broken.

bottle

NOUN bottles

A bottle is a tall container for liquids.

bottom

NOUN bottoms

The bottom of something is the lowest part of it.
*The boat sank to the **bottom** of the sea.*
☞ **Opposite:** top

bought

Bought is the past tense of the verb **buy**.
☞ **Say: bawt**

bounce

VERB bounces, bouncing, bounced

If something bounces, it springs back when it hits something.

bow

NOUN bows

1 When you tie a bow, you tie a piece of string or ribbon so that it has two loops.
*She wore a pretty **bow** in her hair.*
2 A bow is a curved piece of wood with a string attached to each end that you use for shooting arrows.
☞ **Rhymes:** go

bow

VERB bows, bowing, bowed

When you bow, you bend forward from the waist as a greeting or a sign of respect.
☞ **Rhymes:** now

bowl

NOUN bowls

1 A bowl is a round, deep container that you use for food.
VERB bowls, bowling, bowled
2 When you bowl, you roll a ball and try to knock down bowling pins.

box

NOUN boxes

A box is a container.

boy

NOUN boys

A boy is a child who will become a man when he grows up.

bracelet

NOUN bracelets

A bracelet is a piece of jewelry that you wear around your wrist.

braces

NOUN

Braces are pieces of wire that you wear over your teeth to straighten them.

Braille

NOUN

Braille is a type of writing where letters are represented by raised dots. People who are blind read the dots by feeling them with their fingers.

B r a i l l e

Braille Say: **brayl**

Word history: Braille was named after the man who invented it, Louis Braille.

brain
NOUN brains
Your brain is the part of your body inside your head that controls how you think and move.

What is the past tense of buy?

Look around the page to find the answer.

brake
NOUN brakes
1 The brake is the part on a vehicle that slows it down and stops it.
VERB brakes, braking, braked
2 When you brake, you slow down and stop a vehicle by using the brakes.

branch
NOUN branches
The branches on a tree are the parts that grow out of the trunk.

brass
NOUN
Brass is a shiny, yellow metal.

brave
ADJECTIVE braver, bravest
Someone who is brave does not show that they are afraid even when they have to do difficult or dangerous things.
*The **brave** firefighter climbed up the ladder to rescue a child.*
☞ **Similar:** bold, courageous, daring, tough, unafraid
Opposite: cowardly

bread
NOUN
Bread is a food that is made from flour, yeast, and water and baked in an oven.

break
NOUN breaks
1 A break is a short time when you stop working and rest or relax.
VERB breaks, breaking, broke, broken
2 If you break something, you damage it so that it is in lots of pieces or does not work any more.
☞ **Similar:** crack, damage, destroy, smash, snap, split, tear

break

*How did you **break** my beautiful plate?*

breakfast
NOUN breakfasts
Breakfast is the meal that you eat in the morning.
☞ **Word history:** A "fast" is a time when you do not eat. **Breakfast** comes from the words "break" and "fast," because in the morning you eat, and so you end, or "break," your "fast."

breathe
VERB breathes, breathing, breathed
When you breathe, you take air into your lungs through your nose or mouth, and then push it out again.

breeze
NOUN breezes
A breeze is a gentle wind.

brick
NOUN bricks
Bricks are blocks of baked clay that people use for building houses.

bride
NOUN brides
A bride is a woman on the day she gets married.

bridegroom
NOUN bridegrooms
A bridegroom is a man on the day he gets married.

a
Bb
c
d
e
f
g
h
i
j
k
l
r
s
t
u
v
w
x
y
z

a

Bb

c

d

e

f

g

h

i

j

k

l

m

n

o

p

q

r

bridge
NOUN bridges
A bridge is a structure that is built over a river, road, or railroad track so that you can cross it easily.

brief
ADJECTIVE
Something that is brief only lasts for a short time.

bright
ADJECTIVE brighter, brightest
1 Something that is bright shines strongly and gives off a lot of light.
☞ **Similar:** dazzling, gleaming, glowing, shiny, sparkling
2 A bright person is intelligent.

brilliant
ADJECTIVE
1 Something that is brilliant is bright and glittering.
☞ **Similar:** bright, dazzling, shining, sparkling
2 Someone who is brilliant is very intelligent.

Ribbons decorate the brim of her hat.

brim

x

y

z

brim
NOUN brims
1 The brim of a hat is the part that sticks out around the edge.
2 The brim of a cup is the top edge of it.

bring
VERB brings, bringing, brought
If you bring something with you, you take it with you when you go somewhere.
Bring your pajamas with you when you come to stay.

broad
ADJECTIVE broader, broadest
Something that is broad is very wide.
☞ **Opposite:** narrow

broke
Broke is the past tense of the verb **break**.

bronze
NOUN
Bronze is a shiny, brown-colored metal.

brooch
NOUN brooches
A brooch is a piece of jewelry that you pin onto your clothes.
☞ **Say: broach**

broom
NOUN brooms
A broom is a stiff brush with a long handle that you use for sweeping. In stories, witches ride through the air on **broomsticks**.

brother
NOUN brothers
Your brother is a boy who has the same mother and father as you do.

brought
Brought is the past tense of the verb **bring**.
☞ **Say: brot**

brown
ADJECTIVE
Something that is brown is the color of mud.

browse
ADJECTIVE browses, browsing, browsed
1 When you browse in a store, you look around but do not buy anything.
2 When you browse on a computer, you look for information.

brush
NOUN brushes
A brush is a tool that has a handle with stiff hairs attached to it. You use a brush to clean things or for painting.

bubble
NOUN bubbles
A bubble is a very light ball of air with a thin layer of liquid around it.

bucket
NOUN buckets
A bucket is a container with a handle that you use for carrying water or dirt.
*The window cleaner filled the **bucket** with clean water.*

bud
NOUN buds
A bud is a new flower or leaf on a plant, before it has opened.

buffalo
NOUN buffaloes
A buffalo is a large animal that lives on the plains and eats grass.

A bright bulb lights up the room.

bug
NOUN bugs
1 A bug is an insect.
2 If there is a bug in a computer program, there is a problem and the program does not work properly.

build
VERB builds, building, built
When you build something, you make it by putting things together.
The bird built a nest out of twigs.

building
NOUN buildings
A building is a structure such as a house, factory, or school.

built
Built is the past tense of the verb **build**.

bulb
NOUN bulbs
1 A bulb is the round glass part of an electric light.
There is a blue bulb in the night light.
2 A bulb is the rounded part of some plants that grows underground. You can plant bulbs in the soil to produce new plants.
He decided to plant some daffodil bulbs.

bulge
VERB bulges, bulging, bulged
If something is bulging, it is so full that it looks round and fat.
Her pockets were bulging with food.

bull
NOUN bulls
A bull is a male cow. A male elephant or whale is also called a bull.
The angry bull charged at us.

bulldozer
NOUN bulldozers
A bulldozer is a machine with a large, metal blade at the front for moving large amounts of heavy dirt and rocks.

bully
NOUN bullies
1 A bully is a mean person who hurts or frightens other people.
VERB bullies, bullying, bullied
2 If someone bullies you, that person is mean to you or hurts you.

bump
NOUN bumps
1 A bump on the road is a part that sticks up.
It was difficult to ride my bike over the bumps.
2 A bump on your body is a sore part where you have hit it.
VERB bumps, bumping, bumped
3 If you bump into something, you knock into it.
☛ **Similar:** bang, crash, hit, knock, ram, smash

bun
NOUN buns
1 A bun is the kind of bread that you eat with a burger.
2 A bun is a small, sweet roll.

bunch
NOUN bunches
A bunch is a group of things that are gathered together.

bundle
NOUN bundles
A bundle is a group of things that are loosely joined together.

bulldozer
A bulldozer clears land for building.

a
Bb
c
d
e
f
g
h
i
j
k
l
m
n
o
p
q
r
s
t
u
v
w
x
y

a
Bb
c
d
e
f
g
h
i
j
k
l
m
n
o
p
q
r
s
t
u
v
w
x
y
z

bungalow

NOUN bungalows
A bungalow is a house that has no upstairs, but has all its rooms on one level.
☞ **Word history:** The word **bungalow** comes from the Gujarati word *bangalo*, which means "a house in the style of Bengal" (an area in eastern India).

burglar

NOUN burglars
A burglar is a person who steals things from people's houses.
☞ **Similar:** robber, thief

burn

VERB burns, burning, burned
If you burn something, you damage it or destroy it by using fire.

burrow

NOUN burrows
A burrow is a hole under the ground where a small animal lives.

burst

VERB bursts, bursting, burst
If something bursts, it splits open.
*My balloon has **burst**!*
☞ **Similar:** explode, pop, puncture, split

bury

VERB buries, burying, buried
If you bury something, you put it in the ground and cover it over.
*The dog **buried** its bone in the backyard.*
☞ **Say:** ber-ee

bus

NOUN buses
A bus is a vehicle that carries passengers on the road.
☞ **Word history:** The word **bus** is short for the Latin word *omnibus*, which means "for everyone," because a bus can be used by everyone.

bush

NOUN bushes
A bush is a large plant with a lot of branches.

business

NOUN businesses
A business is an organization that makes and sells things.
☞ **Say: biz**-nis

busy

ADJECTIVE busier, busiest
If you are busy, you are doing lots of things.
☞ **Say: biz**-ee
Similar: active, occupied
Opposite: idle

butcher

NOUN butchers
A butcher is a person who cuts up and sells meat.

butter

NOUN
Butter is a soft, yellow food that is made from milk.

buttercup

NOUN buttercups
A buttercup is a small, yellow wildflower.

butterfly

NOUN butterflies
A butterfly is an insect with large, colorful wings.

button

NOUN buttons
Buttons are the small, round objects on your clothes that you fasten when you put your clothes on.

buy

VERB buys, buying, bought
When you buy something, you pay money for it and it becomes yours.
☞ **Opposite:** sell

buzz

VERB buzzes, buzzing, buzzed
When something buzzes, it makes a low, humming noise.

*Busy bees **buzz** around the buttercups.*

C

cabbage
NOUN cabbages
A cabbage is a vegetable with large, green leaves.

cabin
NOUN cabins
1 A cabin is a small hut made of logs.
2 A cabin is a room for passengers or crew on an airplane or ship.

cable
NOUN cables
A cable is a bundle of wires that carry electrical power or signals. **Cable television** is television signals that enter people's houses through wires or cables.

cafeteria
NOUN cafeterias
A cafeteria is a restaurant in which the customers serve themselves by carrying their food and drinks to their tables.
☞ **Say:** kaf-uh-**tir**-ee-uh

cage
NOUN cages
A cage is a small room with bars that you keep animals or birds in.

cake
NOUN cakes
A cake is a sweet food. You make a cake by mixing flour, sugar, eggs, and butter together and baking the mixture in an oven.

calculate
VERB calculates, calculating, calculated
When you calculate the answer to a math problem, you figure it out. The process of solving that problem is called a **calculation**.
☞ **Say: kal**-kew-late

calculator
NOUN calculators
A calculator is a small electronic machine for doing math quickly.

calculator
Say:
kal-kew-late-or

*I used my **calculator** to find the answer to the math problem.*

calendar
NOUN calendars
A calendar is a chart that lists the days, weeks, and months of the year.

calf
NOUN calves
1 A calf is a young cow or bull. A young elephant or whale is also called a calf.
2 Your calf is the back of your leg below your knee.

A cow with her **calf**

calf

call
VERB calls, calling, called
1 If you call to someone, you shout to them.
*They **called** for help.*
☞ **Similar:** scream, shout, yell
2 What you call someone is the name that you give them.
*We decided to **call** our dog Max.*
3 If you call someone, you phone them.

calm
ADJECTIVE calmer, calmest
1 If something is calm, it is still and quiet.
*The sea was **calm** after the storm had passed.*
2 If you feel calm, you feel peaceful and relaxed.
☞ **Similar:** quiet, untroubled

a
b
Cc
d
e
j
k
l
m
n
o
p
q
r
s
t
u
v
w
x
y
z

37

a
Cc
b
d
e
f
g
h
i
j
k
l
m
n
o
p
q
r
s
t

camcorder

NOUN camcorders
A camcorder is a video camera that records moving pictures and sounds.
☞ **Word history:** The word **camcorder** was formed by joining the words "camera" and "recorder" together.

camel

NOUN camels
A camel is an animal with one or two humps on its back. Camels live in hot deserts and store fat in their humps to help them go without water or food for long periods of time.

camera

NOUN cameras
A camera is a piece of equipment that you use for taking photographs, or for making videos or movies.

camouflage

NOUN
Camouflage is a color or pattern on an animal that makes it look like the things around it. This means it can hide from its enemies. Soldiers also use camouflage to hide themselves and their vehicles.

camp

VERB camps, camping, camped
When you camp, you sleep in a tent outdoors.
*We went **camping** in the forest for our vacation.*

can

NOUN cans
1 A can is a metal container for food or drink.
VERB can, could
2 If you can do something, you are able to do it.

canal

NOUN canals
A canal is a deep channel of water that people have built across the land for boats and ships to travel along.

candle

NOUN candles
A candle is a stick of wax with a wick running through the middle. Candles are burned to give light.

cannon

NOUN cannons
A cannon is a very large gun that fires heavy metal balls.

canoe

NOUN canoes
A canoe is a light, narrow boat that you move along using a paddle.

canoe

Sally went down the river in a blue canoe.

cap

NOUN caps
A cap is a hat with a stiff brim sticking out at the front.

capable

ADJECTIVE
If you are capable of doing something, you can do it.
☞ **Similar:** able, competent

*Chameleons use **camouflage** to hide from predators—they change color to match their surroundings.*

camouflage
kam-o-flaj
Say:

capacity

NOUN capacities

The capacity of a container or room is the amount that it will hold.

*The **capacity** of the concert hall is 500 people.*

capital

NOUN capitals

The capital of a country is the city where it has its government offices.

*Paris is the **capital** of France.*

captain

NOUN captains

1 A captain is the person in charge of a ship or airplane.
2 The captain of a team is the leader of the team.

capture

VERB captures, capturing, captured

To capture someone means to catch them.

What is the capital of France?

Look around the page to find the answer.

car

NOUN cars

A car is a vehicle with an engine that is used to carry people from place to place.

caravan

NOUN caravans

A caravan is a group of vehicles traveling together in a line.

☛ **Word history:** The word **caravan** comes from a Persian word *karwan*, which means a group of people traveling across the desert.

card

NOUN cards

1 A card is a piece of stiff paper with a picture or words on it. You send people cards for their birthday.
2 Playing cards are pieces of stiff paper, often with pictures on them, that you use for playing games.

cardboard

NOUN

Cardboard is strong, stiff paper that is used to make boxes.

care

VERB cares, caring, cared

1 If you care about something, you are interested in it and it is important to you.
*He **cares** about his appearance.*
2 If you care for someone, you look after them.
*She helped **care** for her sister when she was ill.*
3 If you care about someone, you like them or love them.

careless

ADJECTIVE

When you are careless, you do not think about what you are doing and so you make a mistake or do something silly or dangerous.

☛ **Similar:** clumsy, forgetful, sloppy
Opposite: careful

carnival

NOUN carnivals

1 A carnival is a traveling fun fair.
2 A carnival is a special event.

carol

NOUN carols

A carol is a special song that you sing at Christmas.

carpet

NOUN carpets

A carpet is a thick, soft covering for a floor.

carrot

*He grew juicy **carrots** in his garden.*

carrot

NOUN carrots

A carrot is a long, thin, orange vegetable.

a
b
Cc
d
e
f
g
h
i
j
k
l
v
w
x
y
z

39

a
b
Cc
d
e
f
g
h
i
j
k
l
m
n
o
p
q
r
s
t
u
v
w
x
y
z

carry
VERB carries, carrying, carried
If you carry something, you hold it and take it somewhere.
☞ **Similar:** bring, take, transport

carve
VERB carves, carving, carved
When you carve something, you cut it into a shape.

case
NOUN cases
1 A case is a container that you keep or carry things in.
2 A case of something is one time when it happens.
*There have been several **cases** of the flu at school.*

castle
NOUN castles
A castle is a large house with high stone walls and strong defenses to protect it against attacking armies.

cat
NOUN cats
A cat is an animal with soft fur that people often keep as a pet. Cats eat small animals and are fierce hunters. Animals such as lions and tigers are large wild cats.

*The fisherman **caught** a fish on his line.*

catch
VERB catches, catching, caught
1 If you catch something, you get hold of it while it is moving.
***Catch** this ball!*
☞ **Similar:** grab, grasp, snatch
2 When you catch a bus, train, or plane, you get on it.
3 If you catch an illness, you get it.
*I **caught** chicken pox from my brother.*

caterpillar
NOUN caterpillars
A caterpillar is the young form of a butterfly or moth. Caterpillars look like small, fat worms and some are furry or hairy.

Word history:
The word **caterpillar** comes from the Latin words *catta pilosa*, which mean "hairy cat."

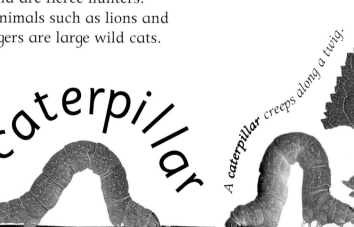
A caterpillar creeps along a twig.

cattle
NOUN
Cattle are cows and bulls.

caught
Caught is the past tense of the verb **catch**.
☞ **Say:** kawt

cause
NOUN causes
The cause of something is what makes it happen.
*What was the **cause** of the fire?*
☞ **Say:** koz
Similar: origin, reason, source

cautious
ADJECTIVE
If you are cautious, you are careful because you are slightly afraid that something might be dangerous.
*The **cautious** climber checked that his ropes were secure.*
☞ **Say:** kaw-shuss
Similar: careful, watchful

cave
NOUN caves
A cave is a hole under the ground or in the side of a mountain.

CD

NOUN CDs

A CD is a small plastic disc on which music or computer information can be stored. You play music CDs on a **CD player**. CD is short for **compact disc**. A **CD-ROM** is a CD for computers on which information, music, and pictures are stored.

caught

ceiling

NOUN ceilings

The ceiling is the surface of a room that is above your head.
☞ **Say: see**-ling

celebrate

VERB celebrates, celebrating, celebrated

When you celebrate, you do something enjoyable for a special reason.

center

NOUN centers

1 The center of something is the middle part.
*It took them an hour to find the **center** of the maze.*
2 A center is a building where particular events take place.

centimeter

NOUN centimeters

In the metric system, you measure how long something is by saying how many centimeters long it is. There are 100 centimeters in a **meter**.

century

NOUN centuries

A century is a period of a hundred years.
☞ **Say: sent**-choo-ree
Word history: The word **century** comes from the Latin word *centuria*, which means "a group of one hundred."

cereal

NOUN cereals

1 Cereal crops are crops such as wheat, barley, and oats that are grown on farms.
2 A breakfast cereal is a type of food that is made from the grains of a cereal crop.
☞ **Say: seer**-ree-al

certain

ADJECTIVE

If you are certain about something, you are sure about it.
*Are you **certain** this is the right train?*
☞ **Similar:** confident, sure
Opposite: uncertain

chain

NOUN chains

A chain is a line of metal loops that are joined together and used like a rope.
*The anchor has a very long **chain**.*

chair

NOUN chairs

A chair is a piece of furniture that you sit on.

chair

*She painted the **chair** a beautiful blue.*

chalk

NOUN chalks

Chalk is a type of soft, white rock. You use pieces of chalk to write on a chalkboard.

champion

NOUN champions

A champion is someone who has won a competition or shown that they are the best at a sport. *Michael was the school tennis **champion**.*

chance

NOUN chances

If you have the chance to do something, it is possible for you to do it.
*He got the **chance** to go to Disneyland.*

change

VERB changes, changing, changed

If something changes, it becomes different.
*Tadpoles slowly **change** into frogs.*
☞ **Similar:** alter, transform

m
n
o
p
q
r
s
t
u
v
w
x
y
z

41

a
b
Cc
d
e
f
g
h
i
j
k
l
m
n
o
p
q
r
s
t
u
v
w
x
y
z

channel

NOUN channels

1 A channel is a long, narrow stretch of water.
2 A channel is a television or radio station.

chapter

NOUN chapters

A chapter is one part of a book.

character

NOUN characters

1 A character is a person in a play, book, or film.
2 Your character is the type of person that you are.

charity

NOUN charities

A charity is an organization that raises money and gives it to people who need it.

chart

NOUN charts

A chart is a map or diagram that shows information.
☞ **Similar:** diagram, map, plan, table

chase

VERB chases, chasing, chased

To chase someone means to run after them.
*The cheetah **chased** a gazelle.*
☞ **Similar:** follow, pursue

cheap

ADJECTIVE cheaper, cheapest

Something that is cheap does not cost very much money.
☞ **Opposite:** expensive

cheat

VERB cheats, cheating, cheated

If you cheat at a game, you do something that is against the rules because you want to win.

check

NOUN checks

1 A check is a piece of paper from a bank that you can use to pay for things.
VERB checks, checking, checked
2 If you check something, you look at it to make sure it is all right.

cheek

NOUN cheeks

Your cheeks are the sides of your face.

cheer

VERB cheers, cheering, cheered

When people cheer, they shout to someone to encourage them or show that they like them.

cheerful

ADJECTIVE

If you are cheerful, you are happy.
☞ **Similar:** contented, happy, jolly, merry

cheese

NOUN cheeses

Cheese is a solid, salty food that is made from milk.

cheetah

NOUN cheetahs

A cheetah is a spotted animal that belongs to the cat family. Cheetahs live on the dry plains of Africa and hunt other animals. They are extremely fast runners.

cheetah

The cheetah is the fastest land animal.

chemist

NOUN chemists

A chemist is a person who is trained in the science of chemistry.
☞ **Say: kem**-ist

cherry

NOUN cherries

A cherry is a soft, red fruit with a pit in its center.

chess

NOUN

Chess is a board game for two people. The winner is the person who traps the other player's king.

chocolate

Word history:
The word **chocolate** comes from the Aztec word *chocolatl*, which means "a bitter drink."

chocolate
NOUN chocolates
Chocolate is a sweet, brown food made from crushed and roasted cocoa beans, milk, and sugar.

choke
VERB chokes, choking, choked
If you choke, you cannot breathe.

chest
NOUN chests
1 Your chest is the front of your body below your shoulders and above your stomach.
2 A chest is a wooden box with a lid for storing things.
I keep all of my toys in a large toy chest.

chew
VERB chews, chewing, chewed
When you chew food, you move your teeth up and down on it to break it up.
☞ **Say:** choo
Similar: bite, gnaw, munch

chicken
NOUN chickens
A chicken is a type of bird that is kept on farms for its eggs and meat.

chief
NOUN chiefs
A chief is a leader of a group of people.
The chief of police ordered his officers to patrol the streets.

child
NOUN children
A child is a boy or girl.
☞ **Opposite:** adult

chimney
NOUN chimneys
A chimney is a pipe above a fire that takes smoke out of a building.

chimpanzee
NOUN chimpanzees
A chimpanzee is a type of ape that lives in groups in forests in central Africa. Chimpanzees eat fruit and nuts, and sometimes small animals.

chin
NOUN chins
Your chin is the part at the bottom of your face.

china
NOUN
China is a type of pottery made from fine, white clay.

chip
NOUN chips
1 Chips are round, very thin pieces of fried potato.
2 A computer chip is the part inside a computer that stores information and makes the computer work.
3 A chip is a small piece that has been cut or broken off something.

choose
VERB chooses, choosing, chose, chosen
If you choose something, you decide that it is the thing you want.
☞ **Similar:** pick, prefer, select

chop
VERB chops, chopping, chopped
If you chop something, you cut it with a knife or an ax.

ch op

Christian
NOUN Christians
A Christian is a person who believes that Jesus Christ is the son of God, and follows his teachings. The Christian religion is called Christianity.

Christmas
NOUN
Christmas is the Christian celebration of the birth of Jesus Christ.

church
NOUN churches
A church is a building where Christian people go to pray.

a
b
Cc
d
e
f
g
h
i
j
k
l
m
n
o
p
q
r
s
t
u
v
w
x
y
z

43

In the city

There is a lot to see and do in the city.

modern, high, tall

Traffic...

buzzing

growls, hums, roars

busy

lively

noisy

rushing

Buildings... apartment buildings, city hall, department stores, office buildings, police station

HOTEL

dirt, pollution

SKYSCRAPERS

spectacular

crowded, exciting, fast

City life is... active,

Art gallery
Movie theater
Concert hall
Theater
Museum
Opera house

Park
Sports stadium
Ice-skating rink
Restaurant
Library
Mall

Downtown

circle

NOUN circles

A circle is a flat, round shape.

circus

NOUN circuses

A circus is a show with clowns, jugglers, and acrobats that travels around the country and is performed in a tent.

☞ **Word history:** The word **circus** comes from the Latin word *circus*, which means "ring" or "circle."

city

NOUN cities

A city is a very large town.

clap

VERB claps, clapping, clapped

When people clap, they hit their hands together to make a loud sound.

class

NOUN classes

A class is a group of people who learn something together.

classroom

NOUN classrooms

A classroom is a room in which you have lessons at school.

claw

NOUN claws

An animal's claws are its long, curved, pointed nails.

clay

NOUN

Clay is a type of earth used to make pots and bricks. It is made into the right shape when wet, then baked until it is hard.

clean

VERB cleans, cleaning, cleaned

1 If you clean something, you remove dirt from it.

☞ **Similar:** dust, polish, scrub, wash, wipe

ADJECTIVE cleaner, cleanest

2 Something that is clean has no dirt on it.

☞ **Opposite:** dirty

Scott's bedroom was so messy, it was impossible to **clean**.

clear

ADJECTIVE clearer, clearest

1 Something that is clear is easy to see through.

The water was so **clear** *that I could see the fish.*

2 If something is clear, it is easy to see, hear, or understand.

It is **clear** *that Silvia is going to win the tournament.*

3 If a place is clear, there is nothing in it so you can move through it easily.

The road was **clear***, so we got to the game quickly.*

clever

ADJECTIVE cleverer, cleverest

Someone who is clever is able to understand things quickly.

☞ **Similar:** crafty, cunning, ingenious, intelligent, quick-witted

Opposite: stupid

click

VERB clicks, clicking, clicked

If you click on something on a computer screen, you point to it using the mouse and then press the button on the mouse.

cliff

NOUN cliffs

A cliff is the high, steep side of a mountain.

climate

NOUN climates

The climate of a place is the type of weather that it usually has.

The **climate** *in southern Africa is hot and dry.*

climb

VERB climbs, climbing, climbed

When you climb, you move upward, using your hands and feet.

cling

VERB clings, clinging, clung

If you cling onto something, you hold onto it very tightly.

The climbers **clung** *to the rock.*

Daniel **clings** *to the rockface.*

cling

a
b
Cc
d
e
f
g
h
i
j
k
l
m
p
r
s
t
u
x
y
z

45

a b **Cc** d e f g h o p q r s t u v w x y z

clock
NOUN clocks
A clock is an instrument that shows the time.

clockwise
ADVERB
If something moves clockwise, it moves in a circle in the same direction as the hands on a clock.
☞ **Opposite:** counterclockwise

The clock's hands move in a clockwise direction.

clockwise

close
VERB closes, closing, closed
1 When you close something, you shut it.
☞ **Similar:** bolt, fasten, lock, shut, slam
Opposite: open
ADJECTIVE closer, closest
2 Something that is close to a place is near to it.
*I live **close** to my school.*

cloth
NOUN cloths
1 Cloth is material made from cotton or wool that is used to make clothes and other things.
2 A cloth is a piece of material that you use to wipe greasy or wet surfaces.

clothes
NOUN
Clothes are the things that you wear on your body.

cloud
cloud
Fluffy, white clouds float around the big, blue sky.

cloud

cloud
NOUN clouds
A cloud is a mass of tiny drops of water, or pieces of ice, floating high in the air.

clown
NOUN clowns
A clown is someone who performs in a circus. Clowns wear funny clothes and do silly things to make people laugh.

clue
NOUN clues
A clue is a piece of information that helps to solve a mystery.

clumsy
ADJECTIVE clumsier, clumsiest
If you are clumsy, you move in a rough, careless way.

coach
NOUN coaches
1 A coach is a horse-drawn carriage.
2 A coach is a railroad passenger car.
3 A coach is a person who teaches people how to play a sport.

coal
NOUN
Coal is a hard, black rock that is burned as a fuel. Coal is made from fossilized plants that died millions of years ago.

coast
NOUN coasts
The coast is the part of the land where it joins the sea.

coat
NOUN coats
1 A coat is a piece of clothing you wear over your other clothes to keep you warm outside.
2 An animal's coat is its fur.
*My dog has a thick **coat**.*

cobweb
NOUN cobwebs
A cobweb is a very fine, sticky net that is made by spiders to trap flies.

code
NOUN codes
A code is a set of signs, symbols, or letters for sending secret messages.

coin

NOUN coins

A coin is a piece of money made of metal.

cold

NOUN colds

1 A cold is an illness that makes you sneeze and cough.
ADJECTIVE colder, coldest
2 Something that is cold is not warm or hot.
☞ **Similar:** chilly, cool, freezing, frosty, frozen, icy
Opposite: hot

collect

VERB collects, collecting, collected

1 If you collect things, you get as many of them as you can and put them together. A group of things collected together is called a **collection**.
2 If you collect something, you go and pick it up.

color

NOUN colors

Red, yellow, and blue are the names of some colors.

colorful

ADJECTIVE

Something that is colorful is decorated with bright colors.

column

NOUN columns

1 A column is a tall, round post that supports a building.
2 A column is a list of words or numbers that are written underneath each other.

comb

NOUN combs

A comb is a piece of wood, metal, or plastic with teeth, used to make hair look neat.

come

VERB comes, coming, came

1 When you come to a place, you arrive there.
*Hurry up! The train is **coming**.*
☞ **Similar:** approach, arrive
2 If you ask someone to come along, you are asking them to go with you to a place.

comedy

NOUN comedies

A comedy is a movie, play, radio, or television program that makes you laugh. Someone who does funny things to make you laugh is called a **comedian**.

c o m e t

Word history:
The word **comet** comes from the Greek words *aster kometes*, which mean "a long-haired star." Comets were called this because of the long trail of gases that you can see behind them.

comet

NOUN comets

A comet is a huge ball of dust, ice, and gases that travels around the Sun, often followed by a trail of gases.

comfortable

ADJECTIVE

Something that is comfortable is pleasant to sit in or wear.
☞ **Similar:** comfy, relaxing, snug, soft
Opposite: uncomfortable

a
b
Cc
i
j
k
l
m
n
o
p
q
r
s
t

Colorful butterflies flutter around the yard.

47

a
b
Cc
d
e
f
g
h
i
j
k
l
m
n
o
p
q
r
s
t
u
v
w
x
y
z

comma

NOUN commas

A comma is the punctuation mark (,) that you use to divide different parts of the same sentence.

common

ADJECTIVE

If something is common, you see it very often.

compact disc

NOUN compact discs

A compact disc is a small, plastic disc on which music or computer information can be stored. Compact disc is often shortened to **CD**.

company

NOUN companies

1 A company is a group of people who work together to make or sell something.
He works for a computer company.
2 If you enjoy someone's company, you enjoy being with them.

compare

VERB compares, comparing, compared

If you compare two things, you look at them to see how they are similar and how they are different.

compass

NOUN compasses

1 A compass is an instrument that shows the direction you are facing. The magnetic needle on a compass always points north.
2 Compasses are tools that you use for drawing circles.

competition

NOUN competitions

A competition is an event where people race against each other or play games to see who is the best.
*Our team came in second in the swimming **competition**.*
☞ **Similar:** championship, contest, game, match, race, tournament

complain

VERB complains, complaining, complained

If you complain, you say that you are not happy about something.
*The passengers **complained** about the late train.*

complete

*Have you **completed** the jigsaw puzzle yet?*

complete

VERB completes, completing, completed

If you complete something, you finish it. Something that is finished and contains all the parts is complete.

complicated

ADJECTIVE

Something that is complicated has a lot of different parts and is very difficult to do or understand.
☞ **Opposite:** simple

computer

NOUN computers

A computer is an electronic machine that arranges information and stores it. Computers can also do difficult calculations, and you can play games on them.
☞ **Word history:** The word **computer** comes from the Latin word *computare*, which means "to work out together," because computers were originally used for working out mathematical calculations.

concentrate

VERB concentrates, concentrating, concentrated

When you concentrate, you think carefully about what you are doing.

concert

NOUN concerts

A concert is an event where people sing or play music for an audience to listen to.

concrete

NOUN

Concrete is a mixture of sand, cement, stones, and water, which is used for building.

cone

NOUN cones
A cone is a shape that has one round base and sides that come up to a point at the end.
*He put the ice cream into a **cone**.*

confident

ADJECTIVE
If you are confident, you believe that you are able to do something well.

confused

ADJECTIVE
If you feel confused, you do not know what to do because you do not understand what is going on.

connect

VERB connects, connecting, connected
If you connect things, you join them together.
☛ **Similar:** combine, join, link

conscious

ADJECTIVE
If you are conscious, you are awake and aware of what is happening around you.
☛ **Say:** kon-shus
Opposite: unconscious

conservation

NOUN
Conservation is protecting animals, plants, and the environment.

consider

VERB considers, considering, considered
If you consider something, you think about it carefully.
*She **considered** going out.*

considerate

ADJECTIVE
Someone who is considerate thinks about other people and does not do things that will upset or annoy other people.
☛ **Opposite:** inconsiderate

consonant

NOUN consonants
A consonant is any letter of the alphabet that is not a vowel.

constellation

NOUN constellations
A constellation is a group of stars.

construct

*A crane lifts blocks to **construct** a building.*

construct

VERB constructs, constructing, constructed
If you construct something, you build it. Something that you build is called a **construction**.

contain

VERB contains, containing, contained
If a box or bag contains things, it has those things inside it.
*The box **contains** tools.*

container

NOUN containers
A container is anything that you can put or keep things in.

content

ADJECTIVE
If you are content, you feel happy and satisfied.
☛ **Say:** kon-**tent**
Similar: cheerful, comfortable, happy, pleased, relaxed

contents

NOUN
The contents of an object, such as a box or bag, are the things that are inside it.
☛ **Say:** kon-tents

continent

NOUN continents
A continent is one of seven very large areas of land that make up the world. Most continents include several different countries.
*Africa is a **continent**.*

a
Cc
d
e
f
g
h
i
j
k
l
m
n
o
p
q
r
s
t
u
v
w
x
y
z

continue

VERB continues, continuing, continued

If you continue to do something, you keep on doing it.

*We **continued** to play even when it started raining.*

control

VERB controls, controlling, controlled

When you control something, you make it go where you want it to go or do what you want it to do.

*The driver **controls** the race car at high speeds.*

☞ **Similar:** direct, manage

conversation

NOUN conversations

A conversation is a talk between two or more people.

convince

VERB convinces, convincing, convinced

If you convince someone, you persuade them to believe something.

☞ **Say:** kon-**vins**

cook

*I **cooked** a meal for my family.*

cook

NOUN cooks

1 A cook is someone who prepares and cooks food.

VERB cooks, cooking, cooked

2 When you cook food, you prepare it and heat it so that you can eat it.

cool

ADJECTIVE cooler, coolest

1 Something that is cool is slightly cold.

*This box keeps drinks **cool**.*

☞ **Similar:** chilly, cold

Opposite: warm

2 Something that is cool is fashionable.

copy

NOUN copies

1 A copy is something that has been made to look exactly like something else.

VERB copies, copying, copied

2 If you copy someone, you do the same as them.

coral

NOUN corals

Coral is a hard substance that is made of the skeletons of small sea animals. Coral is found in warm seas.

core

NOUN cores

The core of something is the middle part of it.

cork

NOUN

A cork is a small object that is used to seal the top of a bottle.

cowboy hat

Western costume

lassoo

vest

chaps for riding

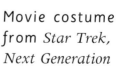

badge

Captain's uniform

Movie costume from *Star Trek, Next Generation*

tiara

tutu

tights

pointe shoe

Ballet costume

corn
NOUN
Corn is a name for small, hard seeds, or the kernels of sweet corn.

corner
NOUN corners
A corner is a point where two lines or edges meet at an angle.

correct
ADJECTIVE
Something that is correct is right and has no mistakes.
☞ **Similar:** accurate, right
Opposite: incorrect

correction
NOUN corrections
A correction is a change that you make to something so that it is correct.

corridor
NOUN corridors
A corridor is a passage inside a building that leads to other rooms.

cosmetics
NOUN
Lipstick and other types of makeup are called cosmetics.

cost
NOUN
1 The cost of something is the amount you have to pay for it.
VERB costs, cost
2 The amount that something costs is the amount that you have to pay for it.
*A computer **costs** hundreds of dollars.*

costume
NOUN costumes
1 A costume is a set of clothes that you wear when you are dressing up.
2 The costume of a time in history is the type of clothes that people wore then.

cot
NOUN cots
A cot is a portable bed.

cottage
NOUN cottages
A cottage is a small house in the country.
*The **cottage** was tiny.*

cotton
NOUN
Cotton is cloth that is made from the soft bloom of a cotton plant.

cough
VERB coughs, coughing, coughed
When you cough, you push air out of your lungs with a sharp noise.
☞ **Say: coff**

could
Could is the past tense of the verb **can**.

a
b
Cc
d
e
f
g
h
i
j
k
l
m
n
o
p

Costume

People dress in costumes for different activities or reasons.

Japanese kimono

National costume

shield

helmet

armor

sword

Historical costume

makeup

bow tie

boot

baggy pants

Clown costume

51

a
b
Cc
d
e
f
g
h
i
j
k
l
m
n
o
p
q
r
s
t
u
v
w
x
y
z

count

VERB counts, counting, counted
1 When you count, you say numbers in the right order.
2 When you count things, you figure out how many there are.

counter

NOUN counters
1 A counter is a work surface in a store or a kitchen.
2 A counter is a small object that you move around on a board when you are playing a game.

country

NOUN countries
1 A country is an area of land with its own borders, people, and laws.
2 The country is the land outside towns and cities.

couple

NOUN couples
1 When you talk about a couple of things, you mean two things.
2 A couple is two people who are married or going out with each other.

court

NOUN courts
1 A court is a place where judges and other people decide whether someone has done something wrong, and how they should be punished.
2 A court is a piece of ground with lines marked on it, where some sports are played.

*The **crabs** crawled across the sandy beach.*

cousin

NOUN cousins
Your cousin is related to you because their mother or father is the sister or brother of one of your parents.

crab

courage Say: kur-rij

*The fire fighters showed great **courage**.*

courage

NOUN
Courage is being brave when you are in danger or difficulty. Someone who is brave is **courageous.**
☞ **Similar:** boldness, bravery, daring, nerve
Opposite: cowardice

cover

NOUN covers
1 You put a cover over something to protect it.
VERB covers, covering, covered
2 When you cover something, you put something over it.
☞ **Similar:** conceal, hide
Opposite: uncover

cow

NOUN cows
A cow is a female animal that eats grass and is kept on a farm to produce milk and beef. A female elephant or whale is also called a cow.

coward

NOUN cowards
A coward is a person who is easily scared.

crab

NOUN crabs
A crab is a shellfish with 10 legs and a hard covering over its body. The front pair of legs end in claws, which the crab uses to catch its prey.

crack

NOUN cracks
1 A crack is a line or split on the surface of something where someone has broken it.
VERB cracks, cracking, cracked
2 If you crack something, you break it so that the surface is split or has lines on it, but it does not fall to pieces.
☞ **Similar:** break, chip, snap, split

cracker

NOUN crackers
A cracker is a thin, dry crispy bread that you sometimes eat with cheese.

cradle

NOUN cradle
A cradle is a baby's bed that can swing from side to side.

craft
NOUN crafts
1 A craft is an activity in which you make something.
*They enjoyed seeing all the arts and **crafts** at the show.*
2 A craft is a boat, airplane, or spaceship.

crafty
ADJECTIVE
Someone who is crafty is good at tricking people.

cramp
NOUN
When you get cramp, your muscles hurt because you have done too much exercise.

crane
NOUN cranes
1 A crane is a large machine that lifts heavy objects.
2 A crane is a large bird with long legs that lives near marshes and lakes.

crash
NOUN crashes
1 A crash is an accident in which cars or other vehicles bang into each other.
2 A crash is a loud noise.
VERB crashes, crashing, crashed
3 When cars crash, they bang into each other.
4 When a computer crashes, it stops working.
*My computer has **crashed** again!*

crawl
VERB crawls, crawling, crawled
When you crawl, you move along on your hands and knees.
*A baby **crawls** before it walks.*

crayon
Daisy loved drawing pictures with her crayons.

crayon
NOUN crayons
A crayon is a stick of colored wax that you use for drawing.

crazy
ADJECTIVE crazier, craziest
Crazy means very foolish or strange.
☞ **Similar:** insane, odd, zany

creak
VERB creaks, creaking, creaked
If something creaks, it makes a low, squeaking sound.
*The door **creaked** open.*

crease
NOUN creases
A crease is a line or fold in a piece of cloth or paper.
*There was a long **crease** in the piece of cloth.*

create
VERB creates, creating, created
When you create something, you design and make something new.
*She **created** a Halloween costume out of old clothes.*
☞ **Say:** kree-**ate**

creature
NOUN creatures
A creature is any living thing.

creep
VERB creeps, creeping, crept
When you creep along, you walk very slowly and quietly.
*The cat **crept** up on the birds.*

creepy
ADJECTIVE creepier, creepiest
Something that is creepy is slightly unpleasant and frightening.

crew
NOUN crews
A crew is a team of people who work together.
*The film **crew** set up the studio.*

cricket
NOUN crickets
A cricket is an insect with long legs that can jump high.

crime
NOUN crimes
A crime is something bad that is against the law.

Look around the page to find the answer.

Is creepy a noun or an adjective?

a
b
Cc
d
e
f
g
h
i
j
k
l
m
n
o
p
q
r
s
t
u
v
w
x
y
z

D

a
b
c
Dd
e
f
g
h
i
j
k
l
m
n
o
p
q
r
s
t
u
v
w
x
y
z

daffodil
NOUN daffodils
A daffodil is a yellow, trumpet-shaped flower that you see in the spring.

daily
ADVERB
Something that happens daily happens every day.

dairy
NOUN dairies
A dairy is a place where milk and cream are stored and butter and cheese are made.

daisy
NOUN daisies
A daisy is a small white or pink flower.

damage
VERB damages, damaging, damaged
If you damage something, you harm it. You can also say that you do damage to something.
*The collision **damaged** the front of the boat.*
☞ **Say: dam**-ij
Similar: break, spoil, wreck

damp
ADJECTIVE damper, dampest
Something that is damp is slightly wet.

dance
VERB dances, dancing, danced
When you dance, you move around to music.

dandelion
NOUN dandelions
A dandelion is a common, yellow wildflower. Dandelions produce seeds in a fluffy ball. The seeds are very light and blow away easily.

dandelion flower

dandelion seeds

Word history:
The word **dandelion** comes from the French phrase *dent-de-lion,* which means "lion's tooth." People think this is because the leaves are shaped like teeth.

danger
NOUN dangers
If there is danger, there is something that might hurt you.
***Danger**! – falling rocks.*

dangerous
ADJECTIVE
If something is dangerous, it could hurt you.

dare
VERB dares, daring, dared
1 If you dare someone to do something frightening, you tell them that they should do it to show they are not afraid.
2 If you dare to do something frightening, you are brave enough to do it.

daring
ADJECTIVE
Someone who is daring is brave enough to do frightening or dangerous things.
*Rock climbing is a **daring** sport.*

dandelion

seeds blowing away

dark

ADJECTIVE darker, darkest
1 When it is dark, there is no light.
☞ **Similar:** black, gloomy, shadowy
2 A dark color has a lot of black in it.
☞ **Opposite:** light

dash

VERB dashes, dashing, dashed
If you dash somewhere, you run there quickly.
☞ **Similar:** hurry, race, run, rush, speed, zoom

data

NOUN
Information and facts about something are called data.
☞ **Say: day**-ta

date

NOUN dates
1 The date is the day, month, and year.
2 A date is a sweet, sticky fruit with a pit in the middle.

daughter

NOUN daughters
Someone's daughter is their female child.
☞ **Say: daw**-ter

dawn

NOUN
Dawn is the very early part of the day when it starts to become light.
☞ **Opposite:** dusk

day

NOUN days
1 Day is the time when it is light.
☞ **Opposite:** night
2 A day is a period of 24 hours, starting and ending at midnight.

dazed

ADJECTIVE
If you are dazed, you feel shocked and you cannot think clearly.
☞ **Say: day**-zd
Similar: bewildered, confused, shocked, stunned

dazzle

VERB dazzles, dazzling, dazzled
If a bright light dazzles you, it shines into your eyes so that you cannot see.

dead

ADJECTIVE
Someone who is dead is no longer living.
☞ **Opposite:** alive

deadly

ADJECTIVE
Something that is deadly can kill you.
☞ **Similar:** fatal, lethal, poisonous

deaf

ADJECTIVE
Someone who is deaf cannot hear.

deal

VERB deals, dealing, dealt
When you deal cards, you give some to each person who is playing in a game.

dear

ADJECTIVE dearer, dearest
A dear person is someone you love very much.

death

NOUN deaths
Death is when someone dies.

debt

NOUN debts
A debt is an amount of money that you owe to someone.
☞ **Say: det**

decade

NOUN decades
A decade is a period of 10 years.

decay

VERB decays, decaying, decayed
If something decays it rots away.

dawn

Dawn is the start of a new day.

a
b
c
Dd
e
f
g
h
i
j
k
l
m
n
o
p
q
r
s
t
u
v
w
x
y
z

a
b
c

Dd

e
f
g
h
i
j
k
l
m
n
o
p

decide

VERB decides, deciding, decided
If you decide to do
something, you make
up your mind to do it.
*I **decided** to stay home
and do my homework.*

deck

NOUN decks
The deck on a ship is
an area without a roof.

decorate

VERB decorates, decorating,
decorated
If you decorate a place, you
paint the walls or put nice
things in it to make
it look pretty.

decorate

People like to decorate their houses.

t

decoration

NOUN decorations
A decoration is something
pretty that you put in a
place to make it look nice.
*They spent the afternoon
putting up party **decorations**.*

u
v
w

deep

ADJECTIVE deeper, deepest
Something that is deep goes
down a long way.
*The river is too **deep** to wade
across.*

x
y
z

☞ **Opposite:** shallow

deer

NOUN
A deer is an animal with
hooves that eats grass and
leaves. A male deer is called
a **stag** and has large,
branching horns called
antlers. A female deer is
called a **doe**.

defeat

VERB defeats, defeating,
defeated
If you defeat someone, you
win a game or a battle
against them.
☞ **Similar:** beat, conquer,
overcome

defend

VERB defends, defending,
defended
If you defend something,
you protect it or
guard it.

definitely

ADVERB
If something is definitely true,
it is certain that it is true.

definition

NOUN definitions
A definition explains
what a word means.

delay

VERB delays, delaying, delayed
To delay something means
to make it happen later
than people expected.
*The airplane's departure was
delayed for seven hours.*

delete

VERB deletes, deleting, deleted
If you delete writing, you
remove it.

deliberately

ADVERB
If you do something
deliberately, you do
it on purpose.
*He **deliberately** pushed me.*
☞ **Opposite:** accidentally

delicate

ADJECTIVE
If something is delicate,
it is not very strong and
will break easily.
☞ **Similar:** dainty, flimsy,
fragile

delicious

ADJECTIVE
Food that is delicious tastes
very nice.
*The ice cream was **delicious**.*
☞ **Similar:** scrumptious, tasty,
yummy

delighted

ADJECTIVE
If you are delighted, you are
very pleased.
☞ **Similar:** glad, happy,
overjoyed, pleased, thrilled

Where was **denim** first made?

Look around the page to find the answer.

deliver

VERB delivers, delivering,
delivered
If you deliver something to
someone, you take it to them.

demand

VERB demands, demanding, demanded

If you demand something, you ask for it very firmly.

den

NOUN dens

1 A den is a comfortable, usually quiet room.
2 An animal's den is its home.

denim

NOUN

Denim is a type of strong cloth that is often dyed blue and is used for making clothes.

☛ **Word history: Denim** was first made in the French town of Nîmes, and so in France was called *serge de Nîmes*, meaning "cloth from Nîmes." The phrase came into English as "serge de Nim", and this was shortened into our word "denim."

dent

NOUN dents

A dent is a hollow place in the surface of something after someone has hit it or pressed it.

dentist

NOUN dentists

A dentist is a person who examines and repairs your teeth.

deny

VERB denies, denying, denied

If you deny something, you say that it did not happen.
*He **denied** that he broke the window playing baseball.*

depth

NOUN

The depth of something is how deep it is.

describe

VERB describes, describing, described

When you describe something, you say what it is like.
***Describe** your house to me.*

desert

NOUN deserts

A desert is a large area of dry, sandy, or stony land with few plants.
☛ **Say: dez**-ert

deserve

VERB deserves, deserving, deserved

If you deserve something, it is fair that you should have it because of something that you have done.
*He **deserved** a rest after working so hard.*

design

VERB designs, designing, designed

When you design something, you draw it and plan what it will be like.

desk

NOUN desks

A desk is a table that you use for working on.

*This **dessert** is delicious and fruity.*

dessert

NOUN desserts

Dessert is a sweet dish that you eat at the end of a meal.
☛ **Say:** de-**zert**

destroy

VERB destroys, destroying, destroyed

To destroy something means to damage it so badly that it cannot be used again.
*The fire **destroyed** the hut.*

*She used shapes to **design** a pattern.*

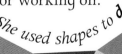

a
b
e
f
g
h
i
j
k
l
m
n
o
r
s
v
w

a
b
c
Dd
e
f
g
h
i
j
k
l
m
n
o
p
q
r

dew

NOUN

Dew is small drops of water that form outside at night.

diagonal

ADJECTIVE

A diagonal line goes across a square from one corner to the opposite corner.

diagram

NOUN diagrams

A diagram is a drawing that shows what something looks like or how it works.

☞ **Similar:** chart, drawing, illustration, picture, plan, sketch

diameter

NOUN diameters

The diameter of a circle is the distance through its center, measured by a straight line.

diamond

NOUN diamonds

A diamond is a jewel that looks like glass.

diary

NOUN diaries

A diary is a book in which you write down the things that you do and how you feel each day.

dice

NOUN dice

Dice are small cubes that have a different number of dots on each side. You roll dice in some games to see how far forward you should move. A single cube is called a **die**.

*They rolled the **dice** to see who would start the game.*

dictionary

NOUN dictionaries

A dictionary is a book that explains what words mean and shows the right spelling.

die

VERB dies, dying, died

When a living thing dies, it is no longer alive.

*The plant **died** because Toby forgot to water it.*

diesel

NOUN

Diesel is a type of fuel that is used in trucks and some cars.

diet

NOUN diets

1 Your diet is all the different kinds of food that you eat.
*You should try to eat a healthy **diet**.*

2 If you are on a diet, you eat less food because you want to become thinner.

different

ADJECTIVE

Things that are different are not the same.

Triceratops
Say: try-**ser**-a-tops

Tyrannosaurus rex
Say: ti-**ran**-oh-**saw**-rus **reks**

Corythosaurus
Say: kor-ith-oh-**saw**-rus

y
z

difficult
ADJECTIVE
Something that is difficult is hard to do.
*It was **difficult** to cut the string with blunt scissors.*
☛ **Similar:** complicated, hard, problematic, tough, tricky
Opposite: easy

dig
VERB digs, digging, dug
When you dig, you make a hole in the earth.

digest
VERB digests, digesting, digested
When you digest food, your stomach breaks it down so that your body can use it to give you energy.
☛ **Say:** die-**jest**

digit
NOUN digits
A digit is a number from zero to nine, shown as a numeral rather than written in words.

Is **different** a noun or an adjective?
Look around the page to find the answer.

digital
ADJECTIVE
A digital clock shows the time in numerals, rather than on a dial.

dilute
VERB dilutes, diluting, diluted
If you dilute a liquid, you add water to make it weaker.
*She **diluted** the juice with water.*

dim
ADJECTIVE dimmer, dimmest
A dim light is not very bright.
*The room was lit by a single **dim** light bulb.*

dinghy
NOUN dinghies
A dinghy is a small, open sailing boat.
*The children sailed their **dinghy** every morning.*
☛ **Say:** ding-ee

dining room
NOUN dining rooms
A dining room is a room in which you eat meals.
*Let's go and eat in the **dining room**.*

dinner
NOUN dinners
Dinner is the main meal of the day that is eaten in the evening.

dinosaur
NOUN dinosaurs
Dinosaurs were one of a group of land reptiles that lived on Earth for more than 150 million years. The last dinosaurs died out 65 million years ago.

a
b
c
Dd
e
f
g
h
i
j
k
l
m
n
o
p
q
r
s
t
u
v
w
x
y
z

Dinosaur

Word history:
The word **dinosaur** comes from the Greek words *deinos sauros,* meaning "terrible lizard."

Deinonychus
Say: die-no-**nike**-us

Stegosaurus
Say: steg-oh-**saw**-rus

Euoplocephalus
Say: yoo-oh-plo-**sef**-al-us

a
b
c
Dd
e
f
g
h
i
j
k
l
m
n
o
p
q
r
s
t
u
v
w
x
y
z

dip
NOUN dips
1 A dip is a sauce into which you can dunk snacks.
VERB dips, dipping, dipped
2 If you dip something into a liquid, you put it in and then take it out again.

direct
VERB directs, directing, directed
1 If you direct someone to a place, you tell them how to get there.
2 The person who directs a film or play is in charge of it and tells other people what they should do and how they should act.
ADJECTIVE
3 A direct way to a place is short and quick.

direction
NOUN directions
The direction you are moving in is the way you are going, or the place you are traveling toward.

disagree
VERB disagrees, disagreeing, disagreed
If you disagree with someone, you have different ideas from them and you think they are wrong.
☞ **Opposite:** agree

disappear
VERB disappears, disappearing, disappeared
If something disappears, it goes out of sight and you cannot see it any more.
☞ **Opposite:** appear

disappointed
ADJECTIVE
If you are disappointed, you are sad or upset because something is not as good as you thought it would be.

disaster
NOUN disasters
A disaster is a terrible event in which people are killed and things are damaged.

What is the opposite of dirty?
Look around the page to find the answer.

discover
VERB discovers, discovering, discovered
If you discover something, you find it or learn about it.
*They **discovered** some old coins in the attic.*

discuss
VERB discusses, discussing, discussed
If you discuss something, you talk about it with someone else.
*We **discussed** where to go for our vacation.*

disaster Say: di-za-ster

dirty
ADJECTIVE dirtier, dirtiest
Something that is dirty is not clean.
☞ **Similar:** dusty, filthy, messy, stained
Opposite: clean

disabled
ADJECTIVE
Someone who is disabled cannot use a part of their body very well because it is weak or injured.

disc
NOUN discs
A disc is a flat, circular object, for example one that you use in a computer or one that has music recorded on it.
*CD is short for compact **disc**.*

disc jockey
NOUN disc jockeys
A disc jockey is a person who puts on music at a party or on the radio. Disc jockey is often shortened to **DJ**.

disease
NOUN diseases
A disease is an illness.
☞ **Similar:** bug, illness, infection, sickness, virus

disguise
NOUN disguises
A disguise is a set of clothes or a mask that you wear to hide who you really are.

disgusting

ADJECTIVE
Something that is disgusting is very unpleasant and makes you feel a little sick.
☞ **Similar:** awful, gross, horrible, revolting, sickening

dish

NOUN dishes
1 A dish is a plate or bowl that you serve food in.
2 A dish is one type of food that you eat as part of a meal.
*We had chicken as the main **dish**.*

dishonest

ADJECTIVE
Someone who is dishonest tells lies or steals things.
☞ **Opposite:** honest

dishwasher

NOUN dishwashers
A dishwasher is a machine that washes dishes.

dislike

VERB dislikes, disliking, disliked
If you dislike something, you think that it is not very nice.
☞ **Opposite:** like

display

VERB displays, displaying, displayed
When you display something, you put it somewhere so that people can look at it.
*Ollie **displayed** his trophies on a shelf.*

disposable

ADJECTIVE
If something is disposable, you throw it away after you have used it.

disqualify

NOUN disqualifies, disqualifying, disqualified
If you are disqualified from a competition, you are not allowed to continue in the competition because you have broken the rules.

distance

NOUN distances
The distance between two places is how far apart they are.

distract

VERB distracts, distracting, distracted
If you distract someone, you take their attention away from what they are doing.

distribute

VERB distributes, distributing, distributed
If you distribute things, you give them out to people.
*The teacher **distributed** the books to the children.*

district

NOUN districts
A district is one area in a town, city, or country.

disturb

VERB disturbs, disturbing, disturbed
If you disturb someone, you interrupt them and stop them from doing what they are trying to do.
*Please don't **disturb** me while I'm working.*

dive

*He **dove** into the swimming pool.*

ditch

NOUN ditches
A ditch is a long, thin hole by the side of a road or field.

dive

VERB dives, diving, dove
When you dive, you jump headfirst into water.

diver

NOUN divers
A diver is a person who swims under the water with a tank of air on their back.

divide

VERB divides, dividing, divided
If you divide something, you split it into parts so that you can share it.

division

NOUN divisions
In math, division is the process of dividing one number by another.

divorce

VERB divorces, divorcing, divorced
When people get divorced, they end their marriage.

Diwali

NOUN
Diwali is the Hindu festival of light.

b
c
Dd
e
f
g
h
i
j
k
l
m
n
o
p
q
r
s
t
u
v
w
x
y
z

a
b
c

Dd

e
f
g
h
i
j
k
l
m
n
o
p
q
r
s
t
u
v
w
x
y
z

dizzy
ADJECTIVE
When you feel dizzy, your head spins and you feel as if you are going to fall over.

doctor
NOUN doctors
A doctor is a person who looks after people who are sick or injured.

dog
NOUN dogs
A dog is an animal that people often keep as a pet. Dogs eat mainly meat, and you can train them to do some types of work, such as herding sheep.

doll
NOUN dolls
A doll is a toy that looks like a baby or small person.

doll
Word history:
The word **doll** is a woman's name that was used in the past. It is a short form of the name **Dorothy**.

dolphin
NOUN dolphins
A dolphin is a sea animal that eats fish. Dolphins breathe air, so they must often swim to the surface. Dolphins are a type of small whale.
☞ **Say: doll**-fin

domino
NOUN dominoes
Dominoes are small, flat pieces of wood or plastic with dots marked on them. You use dominoes to play a game.

donkey
NOUN donkeys
A donkey is an animal like a small horse. Donkeys have long ears and a soft coat.

door
NOUN doors
A door is a piece of wood or metal that you open to go into a room or a car.

dot
NOUN dots
A dot is a very small, round spot.

double
VERB doubles, doubling, doubled
If you double an amount, you make it twice as big.
☞ **Say: dub**-ul

dough
NOUN
Dough is a mixture of flour and water that you use to make bread.
☞ **Say: doh**

doughnut Say:
doh-nut

doughnut
NOUN doughnuts
A doughnut is a small, round cake that is fried in oil and covered in sugar.

dove
NOUN doves
A dove is a pale-colored bird that looks like a pigeon. Doves are often used as a symbol of peace.

downstairs
ADVERB
If you go downstairs, you go to a lower floor in a building. *He ran **downstairs** to answer the phone.*

doze
VERB dozes, dozing, dozed
When you doze, you sleep lightly for a short time. *She was **dozing** in the chair.*

dozen
NOUN dozens
A dozen is 12 of something.

drag

VERB drags, dragging, dragged
If you drag something along, you pull it along the ground.
*He **dragged** his schoolbag along the ground.*
☞ **Similar:** haul, pull, tow, tug

dragon

NOUN dragons
A dragon is a fierce, imaginary animal in myths and fairy tales. Dragons can fly and usually breathe fire.
☞ **Word history:** The word **dragon** comes from the Greek word *drakon*, meaning "a snake."

A beautiful, bright dragonfly flies near water.

dragonfly

NOUN dragonflies
A dragonfly is an insect with large, brightly colored wings that you often see flying near water.

drain

NOUN drains
1 A drain is a pipe or ditch that takes away wastewater.
VERB drains, draining, drained
2 If water drains away, it flows away slowly.

drama

NOUN dramas
Drama is acting in plays.

drank

Drank is the past tense of the verb **drink**.

draw

NOUN draws
1 When a game ends in a draw, both people or teams have the same number of points.
VERB draws, drawing, drew, drawn
2 When you draw something, you make a picture of it with a pencil or crayon.
*She **drew** a beautiful picture.*

drawer

NOUN drawers
A drawer is a part of a piece of furniture that you can slide in and out and keep things in.

dreadful

ADJECTIVE
Something that is dreadful is very bad or very unpleasant.
☞ **Similar:** awful, disgusting, horrible, nasty, terrible

dream

VERB dreams, dreaming, dreamed
1 When you dream, you have thoughts and pictures in your mind while you are asleep.
2 If you dream of doing something, you hope that you will be able to do it one day.
*He **dreamed** of becoming a professional football player.*

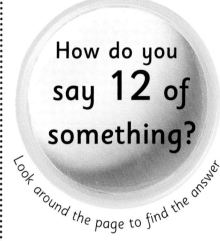

How do you **say 12 of** something?
Look around the page to find the answer.

dress

NOUN dresses
1 A dress is a piece of clothing that has a top and a skirt.
VERB dresses, dressing, dressed
2 When you get dressed, you put on clothes.
☞ **Opposite:** undress

drew

Drew is the past tense of the verb **draw**.

dried

Dried is the past tense of the verb **dry**.

d r e a m

*She **dreamed** about a dozen doughnuts.*

a b c **Dd** e f g h i j k l m n o p q r s t u

65

drift
VERB drifts, drifting, drifted
If something drifts along, water or air carries it slowly along.

drill
NOUN drills
A drill is a tool that makes holes in wood or metal.

*Water **dripped** from the faucet.*

d r i p

d r i n k

drink
NOUN drinks
1 A drink is a liquid, such as milk, that you take into your mouth and swallow.
VERB drinks, drinking, drank, drunk
2 When you drink, you take liquid into your mouth and swallow it.
☞ **Similar:** gulp, guzzle, sip

drip
VERB drips, dripping, dripped
When water drips, it falls slowly, drop by drop.

drive
VERB drives, driving, drove, driven
When you drive a car or train, you make it move along.
*Have you ever **driven** a car?*

driver
NOUN drivers
A person who drives a vehicle is called a driver.

droop
VERB droops, drooping, drooped
If something droops, it hangs down in a weak or tired way.

drop
NOUN drops
1 A drop is a small amount of liquid.
VERB drops, dropping, dropped
2 If you drop something, you let it fall out of your hands.
*Catch the ball, don't **drop** it!*

drought
NOUN droughts
A drought is a long period of time when there is not enough rain.
*Many crops died during the **drought**.*
☞ **Say: drowt**

drove
Drove is the past tense of the verb **drive**.

drown
VERB drowns, drowning, drowned
If you drown, you die because you have gone under water and have not been able to breathe.

drug
NOUN drugs
1 A drug is a medicine that doctors use to treat people who are ill or in pain.
2 A drug is an illegal substance that some people take to make them feel differently. Taking this kind of drug is dangerous.

drum
NOUN drums
A drum is a musical instrument that you hit to make a banging sound.

*Molly banged on the **drum**.*

dry
ADJECTIVE drier, driest
Something that is dry is not wet.
*They came in from the rain and changed into **dry** clothes.*
☞ **Opposite:** wet

a
b
c
Dd
e
f
m
n
o
p
q
r
s
t
u
v
w
x
y
z

a
b
c
Dd
e
f
g
h
i
j
k
l
m
n
o
p
q
r
s
t
u
v
w
x
y
z

duck
NOUN ducks
A duck is a water bird that has oily, waterproof feathers and webbed feet for swimming. A male duck is called a **drake** and baby ducks are called **ducklings**.

duck

Ducks go QUACK QUACK QUACK!

drake

duet
NOUN duets
A duet is a piece of music that is played or sung by two people.
☞ **Say:** dew-**et**

dug
Dug is the past tense of the verb **dig**.

dull
ADJECTIVE duller, dullest
1 Something that is dull is not bright or shiny.
2 Something that is dull is not exciting.
☞ **Similar:** boring, dreary, tedious, uninteresting

dump
VERB dumps, dumping, dumped
If you dump something, you put it down or throw it away carelessly.
*They **dumped** the shopping bags on the floor.*

dune
NOUN dunes
Dunes are hills of sand near the sea or in a desert.

dungeon
NOUN dungeons
A dungeon is an underground prison in a castle.

dungeon
Say:
dun-jun

during
PREPOSITION
During means while something is happening.
*I fell asleep **during** the film.*

dusk
NOUN
Dusk is the time of evening when it starts to get dark.
☞ **Opposite:** dawn

dust
NOUN
Dust is tiny pieces of dirt that float in the air and settle on surfaces.
*The table and chairs are covered in **dust**.*

duty
NOUN duties
If something is your duty, it is your job and you must do it.
*It is the guard's **duty** to make sure the doors are locked.*

dye
VERB dyes, dyeing, dyed
If you dye something, you change its color by soaking it in a colored liquid.

dynamite
NOUN
Dynamite is a powerful substance that explodes when it touches fire.

dyslexic
ADJECTIVE
Someone who is dyslexic finds it difficult to learn reading, writing, and spelling.
☞ **Say:** dis-**lek**-sik

What are male **ducks** called?

Look around the page to find the answer.

a
b
c
d
Ee
f
g
h
i
j
k
l
m
n
o
p
q
r
s
t
u
v
w
x
y
z

each

ADJECTIVE
Each means every single one.
***Each** child received a present.*

eager

ADJECTIVE
If you are eager to do
something, you want to
do it very much.
*The riders were **eager**
to start the race.*
☞ **Similar:** enthusiastic

eagle

NOUN eagles
An eagle is a large bird of
prey that lives in
mountainous areas. Eagles
have very good eyesight for
spotting prey far away.

ear

NOUN ears
Ears are the parts of a person's
body on the side of their head
that they hear with.

early

ADVERB earlier, earliest
1 If you are early, you arrive
before the time when you
should arrive.
2 Early means near the
beginning of the day.
*I like getting up **early**.*
☞ **Opposite:** late

earn

VERB earns, earning, earned
When you earn money,
you get it by working for it.
*Tom **earned** some pocket money
by helping to clean the car.*

earring

NOUN earrings
An earring is a piece of
jewelry that you wear
on your ear.

earth

NOUN
1 Earth is the planet
that we live on.
2 The earth is
the ground.

earthquake

NOUN earthquakes
An earthquake is a violent
shaking of the ground,
caused by movement
deep inside the Earth.

east

NOUN
East is one of the four main
compass directions. East is
the direction in which the
Sun first appears in the
morning.

Easter

NOUN
A festival when Christians
celebrate Christ's rising
from the dead after
being crucified.

easy

ADJECTIVE easier, easiest
Something that is easy is
simple and not difficult to do.
☞ **Opposite:** difficult

eat

VERB eats, eating, ate, eaten
When you eat, you take
food into your mouth and
swallow it.
*Have you **eaten** all your
vegetables?*
☞ **Similar:** chew,
devour, gobble,
munch, nibble,
swallow

Earth

*The planet we live on is called **Earth**.*

echo
NOUN echoes
An echo is a sound that you hear when you speak in a cave or an empty room, and your voice bounces back off the walls so that you hear it again.
☛ **Say: ek**-koe

eclipse
NOUN eclipses
1 An eclipse of the Sun happens when the Moon comes between the Earth and the Sun and hides the Sun's light.
2 An eclipse of the Moon happens when the Earth comes between the Sun and the Moon and hides the light reflected off the Moon.

edge
NOUN edges
The edge of something is the part that is not in the middle.
*She sat down on the **edge** of the desk.*

edit
VERB edits, editing, edited
When you edit something you have written, you read it and change some parts of it to make it better.

educate
VERB educates, educating, educated
To educate people means to teach them so that they learn and understand things.

eel

Eels are slippery and wriggly.

eel
NOUN eels
An eel is a long, thin fish that looks like a snake and lives in rivers and the sea.

effort
NOUN efforts
If you make an effort, you try hard.

egg
NOUN eggs
Some animals lay eggs as a way of having babies. An egg laid by a chicken is surrounded by a hard, smooth shell, and inside the egg a young chick grows. When it is ready, it hatches.

elastic
NOUN
Elastic is a stretchy material.

elbow
NOUN elbows
Your elbow is the part in the middle of your arm where you can bend it.

election
NOUN elections
An election is a time when people vote for someone to be in charge.
*They voted for student council in the **election**.*

electricity
NOUN
Electricity is a form of energy that we use for heating and lighting, and for making machines work. Electricity is produced at a power station and carried along cables and wires.

elephant
NOUN elephants
An elephant is a very large animal that lives in southern Asia and Africa. Elephants have long trunks, which they use to pick up or hold their food. Many elephants also have long tusks made of ivory.

elephant

*The **elephant** is the largest land animal.*

a
b
c
d
Ee
f
g
h
i
j
k
l
m
n

a
b
c
d
Ee
f
g
h
i
j
k
l
m
n
o
p
q
r
s
t
u
v
w
x
y
z

email
NOUN emails
1 An email is a message that you send to someone from your computer to their computer.
VERB emails, emailing, emailed
2 When you email someone you send them a message in an email.
*I **emailed** Jessica about the party.*
☛ **Word history:** The word **email** is short for "electronic mail."

emergency
NOUN emergencies
If there is an emergency, something bad suddenly happens, and people are in danger.
☛ **Say:** ee-**mer**-jen-see

empty
ADJECTIVE
Something that is empty has nothing inside.
☛ **Similar:** vacant, bare
Opposite: full

encourage
VERB encourages, encouraging, encouraged
If you encourage someone, you tell them they are doing well and make them feel that they want to continue trying.
*We cheered to **encourage** our team.*
☛ **Say:** en-**kur**-rij

encyclopedia
NOUN encyclopedias
An encyclopedia is a book that contains information about a lot of different things.
☛ **Say:** en-sye-kloh-**pee**-dee-a

end
NOUN ends
1 The end of something is the place where it stops or finishes.
VERB ends, ending, ended
2 When something ends, it stops or finishes.
*The movie **ends** at 8:30 pm.*
☛ **Opposite:** begin

endangered
ADJECTIVE
An endangered animal or plant is one that might soon become extinct.

endangered

*Tigers are **endangered** in the wild.*

enemy
NOUN enemies
An enemy is someone who strongly dislikes you and fights against you.
☛ **Word history:** The word **enemy** comes from the Latin phrase *in amicus*, meaning "not a friend."

energy
NOUN
1 If you have energy, you feel strong and lively.
2 Energy is power that we use to make machines work.

engine
NOUN engines
An engine is a machine that uses fuel to make something move.

enjoy
VERB enjoys, enjoying, enjoyed
If you enjoy something, you like doing it.
☛ **Similar:** adore, like, love
Opposite: dislike

enormous
ADJECTIVE
Something that is enormous is very large.
☛ **Similar:** gigantic, huge, vast
Opposite: tiny

enter
VERB enters, entering, entered
1 When you enter a place you go into it.
*The train **entered** the tunnel.*
2 If you enter a competition, you take part in it.

entertain
VERB entertains, entertaining, entertained
If you entertain people, you amuse them by doing things that they can watch.

entertainment
NOUN
Entertainment is things people enjoy watching or listening to, like movies or shows.

enthusiastic
ADJECTIVE
If you are enthusiastic about something, you like it a lot and are very interested in it.
☛ **Say:** en-thyoo-zee-**ass**-tik

Entertainment

Here are some words to describe
entertainment – from movies to carnivals!

amazing, colorful, **dazzling**, **Fireworks...**

magical, **spectacular**, stunning,

thrilling, **exciting**... fascinating,

...CARNIVAL pop!

...**blaze**, sparkle, fizz

Z-O-o-m...

whistle!

crackle!

bang! explode

You can go to a ... concert, party, carnival...

**entertainers
are...**
street performers,
actors/actresses,
dancers, clowns, comedians,
acrobats, jugglers,
musicians, singers

FIRE-EATER

show, **circus**, play

**ACTION, ADVENTURE
COMEDY, MUSICAL**

F I L M M O V I E

A good show may be... excellent, fabulous, great, marvelous, superb, **wonderful**
A bad show may be... awful, disappointing, **dreadful**, lousy, **terrible**

a
b
c
d
Ee
f
g
h
i
j
k
l
m
n
o
p
q
r
s
t
u
v
w
x
y
z

entrance
NOUN entrances
The entrance is the way into a place.

envelope
NOUN envelopes
An envelope is a paper container that you put a letter or card in when you are sending it to someone.

environment
NOUN
The environment is the land, water, and air around us.
Recycling is good for the environment.
☞ **Say:** en-**vire**-on-ment

equal
ADJECTIVE
1 Things that are equal are the same size, number, or amount.
Choose two pieces of string that are equal in length.
2 If people are equal in a competition, they each have the same number of points.
☞ **Say:** **ee**-kwul

Equator
NOUN
The Equator is an imaginary line around the middle of the Earth that divides the northern half of the world from the southern half. The Equator is drawn onto maps and globes.
☞ **Say:** ee-**kway**-tor

equipment
NOUN
Equipment is the things that you need for a job or a sport.

error
NOUN errors
An error is a mistake.

erupt
VERB erupts, erupting, erupted
To erupt means to explode suddenly.
When a volcano erupts, hot ash and lava come out of it.

escalator
NOUN escalators
An escalator is a moving staircase that carries people between different floors in a building.

escape

The parrot escaped from its cage.

escape
VERB escapes, escaping, escaped
If you escape, you run away when someone is holding you or keeping you as a prisoner.

estimate
VERB estimates, estimating, estimated
If you estimate an amount, you use all the facts to judge how much it is.

even
ADJECTIVE
1 An even surface is flat and level.
☞ **Opposite:** uneven
2 An even number can be divided by two.
☞ **Opposite:** odd

evening
NOUN evenings
The evening is the end of the day when the Sun sets and it grows dark.
☞ **Opposite:** morning

event
NOUN events
An event is something interesting or exciting that happens.
The fireworks display is a big event each year.

eventually
ADVERB
If you do something eventually, you do it finally, after a long time.

evergreen
ADJECTIVE
An evergreen tree is green all year.

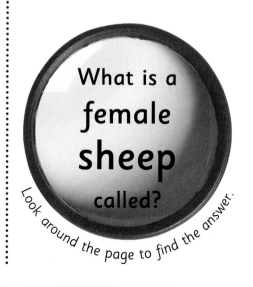

What is a **female sheep** called?

Look around the page to find the answer.

everybody

Everybody or everyone means all people.
Everybody in my family loves chocolate.

everything

Everything means all things.
*He ate **everything** on his plate.*

evidence

NOUN
Evidence is proof that something has happened.

evil

ADJECTIVE
Someone who is evil is very wicked.

evolution

NOUN
Evolution is the way in which animals and plants change gradually over a very long time.

ewe

NOUN ewes
A ewe is a female sheep.
☞ **Say: you**

exaggerate

VERB exaggerates, exaggerating, exaggerated
If you exaggerate, you say that something is bigger, better, or more important than it really is.
*Sally, stop **exaggerating**!*
☞ **Say:** egg-**za**-jur-rate

exam

NOUN exams
An exam is an important test to find out how much you know about something. Exam is short for **examination**.

examine

VERB examines, examining, examined
If you examine something, you look at it very carefully.
☞ **Similar:** inspect, investigate, look at, study

examine Say: egg-za-min

*The police officer **examined** the evidence carefully.*

example

NOUN examples
If you give an example, you talk about one thing that is typical or shows what all the others are like.

excellent

ADJECTIVE
Something that is excellent is extremely good.
*This is an **excellent** painting.*
☞ **Similar:** exceptional, fantastic, great, marvelous, perfect, wonderful
Opposite: awful

except

PREPOSITION
Except means not including one person or thing.
*All the sheep were in the field **except** one.*

exciting

ADJECTIVE
If something is exciting, you enjoy it and it makes you feel happy and interested.
*It was very **exciting** at the fair.*
☞ **Opposite:** boring

excuse

NOUN excuses
An excuse is a reason you give for not doing something that you should have done.
*He had a good **excuse** for not doing his homework.*
☞ **Say:** ex-**kew**-s

exercise

NOUN exercises
1 Exercise is running or playing a sport that you do to make you healthy.
2 An exercise is a set of questions that you answer to help you practice something.

*Tennis is good **exercise**.*

abcdefghijklmnopqrstuvwxyz
a b c d **Ee** f g h i j k l m n o p q r s v w x y z

a
b
c
d
Ee
f
g
h
i
j
l
m
n
o

exhausted
ADJECTIVE
If you are exhausted, you are extremely tired.

exist
VERB exists, existing, existed
Something that exists lives or can be seen in the real world.
*Did Robin Hood really **exist**?*

exit
NOUN exits
An exit is a way out of a building.
*We left by the nearest fire **exit**.*

experiment

*The science **experiment** produced a purple cloud.*

w
x
y
z

expect
VERB expects, expecting, expected
If you expect something to happen, you think that it will happen.
*We are **expecting** her to arrive tomorrow morning.*

expensive
ADJECTIVE
Something that is expensive costs a lot of money.
☞ **Similar:** costly, pricey
Opposite: cheap

experience
NOUN experiences
1 An experience is an important event that you remember for a long time.
*Traveling around the world was a fantastic **experience**.*
2 If you have experience of something, you have done it before and so know about it.
☞ **Say:** ex-**peer**-ree-ents

experiment
NOUN experiments
If you do an experiment, you try doing something to find out what will happen.

explain
VERB explains, explaining, explained
If you explain something, you say how it happens or works.
*Our teacher **explained** how rainbows occur.*

explode
VERB explodes, exploding, exploded
If something explodes, it blows up or bursts apart suddenly and makes a loud noise.

explore
VERB explores, exploring, explored
If you explore a place, you look around it for the first time.

explosion
NOUN explosions
An explosion is a loud noise that happens when a bomb or something else explodes.

extinct
ADJECTIVE
If a type of animal is extinct, there are no more of that type of animal in the world.
*The dodo is an **extinct** bird.*

extra
ADJECTIVE
Extra means more than is usual.

extraordinary
ADJECTIVE
Something that is extraordinary is very unusual and surprising.
☞ **Similar:** amazing, incredible, remarkable, wonderful

extreme
ADJECTIVE
Extreme means very great.
*He was in **extreme** danger.*

extremely
ADVERB
Extremely means very.
*Her clothes were **extremely** dirty.*

eye
NOUN eyes
Your eyes are the parts of your body that you see with.

eyesight
NOUN
Your eyesight is how well you can see.
*I have good **eyesight**.*

F

flowers

fable
NOUN fables
A fable is a story, often with animal characters, that tries to teach us something in an amusing way.
☞ **Similar:** fairy tale, story

face
NOUN faces
Your face is the front of your head, where your eyes, nose, and mouth are.

fact
NOUN facts
A fact is a piece of information that people know is true.
*Mei Ling knows a lot of fascinating **facts**.*

factory
NOUN factories
A factory is a building where people make things using machines.

fade
VERB fades, fading, faded
If something fades, it becomes weaker or less bright.
*The light **fades** in the evening.*

fail
VERB fails, failing, failed
If you fail, you do not manage to do something successfully or well.
*He **failed** the spelling test.*

faint
VERB faints, fainting, fainted
1 When you faint, you become unconscious for a short time.
*He **fainted** in the heat.*
ADJECTIVE fainter, faintest
2 A faint sound, smell, or taste is not very strong.
*She heard a **faint** noise coming from the cupboard.*

fair
NOUN fairs
1 A fair is a place where there are rides, stalls, competitions, and games.
ADJECTIVE fairer, fairest
2 Fair hair is light in color.
3 If something is fair, everyone is treated in the same way or gets the same amount of something.
☞ **Opposite:** unfair
4 Fair weather is dry and sunny.
☞ **Similar:** bright, cloudless, dry, fine, sunny

fairy
NOUN fairies
A fairy is a small, imaginary creature from stories. Fairies often have magical powers.

A fairy waves her wand.

fairy

faith
NOUN
If you have faith in someone, you trust them.
*I have **faith** in my doctor.*

faithful
ADJECTIVE
If someone is faithful to you, they keep helping you and supporting you, and you can trust them.
☞ **Similar:** loyal, reliable, true, trusty

fake
ADJECTIVE
Something that is fake is not real.
*Her coat was made of **fake** fur.*
☞ **Similar:** artificial, false

falcon
NOUN falcons
A falcon is a bird with a sharp beak and claws that is related to the eagle. Falcons are good hunters and can fly very fast.
*The **falcon** flew over the fields.*
☞ **Say:** fal-kun

a b c d e **Ff** g i j k l m n o p q r s t u v w x y z

a b c d e

Ff

g h i j k l m n o p q r s t u v w x y z

fall
NOUN falls
1 Fall is another name for autumn.
2 If you have a fall, you lose your balance and drop to the ground.
VERB falls, falling, fell, fallen
3 To fall means to drop to the ground.
☞ **Similar:** collapse, drop, sink, tumble

false
ADJECTIVE
1 Something that is false is not true.
*He gave the police **false** information.*
☞ **Similar:** incorrect, untrue, wrong
Opposite: true
2 Something that is false is not real.
*He wore a **false** beard.*
☞ **Similar:** artificial, fake, synthetic
Opposite: real

familiar
ADJECTIVE
If something is familiar to you, you know it well.
*I saw a **familiar** face in the crowd.*
☞ **Opposite:** unfamiliar

family
NOUN families
1 Your family is all the people who are related to you.
*I come from a large **family**.*
2 A family of animals or plants is a group of them that are similar to each other and are related to each other.
*Tigers belong to the cat **family**.*

famous
ADJECTIVE
If someone is famous, a lot of people know them and recognize them.
*She is a **famous** movie star.*
☞ **Similar:** celebrated, legendary, well-known

fan
NOUN fans
1 A fan is a person who likes and supports a person, a music group, or a sports team.
2 A fan is something that moves air around to make you feel cooler.

fan

Keep cool with a fan.

fang
NOUN fangs
1 An animal's fangs are the long, pointed teeth that it uses for tearing up its food.
2 A snake's fangs are long, sharp teeth that contain poison.

fantastic
ADJECTIVE
Something that is fantastic is very good.
*We had a **fantastic** vacation.*
☞ **Similar:** excellent, fabulous, great, marvelous, super, terrific, wonderful

fantasy
NOUN fantasies
Fantasy is a story about magical things that are not real and not possible.

far
ADVERB farther or further, farthest or furthest
1 If you go far, you go a long way.
2 If something is far away, it is a long way away.
*They live in a place **far** away from the city.*
☞ **Opposite:** near

farm
NOUN farms
A farm is a place where people grow crops, or keep animals for meat, or milk.

farmer
NOUN farmers
A farmer is someone who lives and works on a farm.

fascinate
VERB fascinates, fascinating, fascinated
If something fascinates you, you find it very interesting.
*Dinosaurs **fascinate** me.*
☞ **Say:** fas-in-ate

fashion

NOUN fashions

Fashion is the type of clothes that people like to wear at a particular time.

fast

VERB fasts, fasting, fasted

1 When you fast, you do not eat food for a time, usually because of your religion.
*Muslims **fast** during the month of Ramadan.*

ADJECTIVE faster, fastest

2 Something that is fast can move very quickly.
*He loves driving **fast** cars.*

☞ **Similar:** quick, rapid, swift
Opposite: slow

ADVERB

3 If you run fast, you run quickly.

fasten

VERB fastens, fastening, fastened

If you fasten things together, you tie or join them together.
*She **fastened** the buttons.*

fat

NOUN fats

1 Fat is a substance that is stored under your skin.

2 Fat is an oily substance that people use in cooking.
*You shouldn't eat too much **fat**.*

ADJECTIVE fatter, fattest

3 Someone who is fat has a lot of fat on their body.

☞ **Similar:** chubby, overweight, plump, stout, tubby
Opposite: thin

father

NOUN fathers

Your father is your male parent.

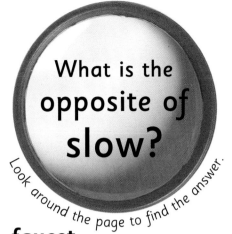

What is the **opposite of slow?**

Look around the page to find the answer.

faucet

NOUN faucets

You turn a faucet on to allow water to flow out.

fault

NOUN faults

1 If there is a fault in a machine, there is something wrong with it and it does not work correctly.
*There was a **fault** in the computer.*

2 If something is your fault, you made it happen.
*It was my **fault** we were late.*

3 A fault is a large split in the Earth's surface.

☞ **Say:** fawlt

favor

NOUN favors

If you do someone a favor, you do something kind that will help them.

favorite

ADJECTIVE

Your favorite thing or person is the one you like the best.
*What is your **favorite** color?*

fawn

NOUN fawns

A fawn is a young deer.

fax

NOUN faxes

1 A fax is a picture or message that is recorded electronically on a fax machine. A fax is sent by telephone lines to another fax machine, where it is printed out.

VERB faxes, faxing, faxed

2 If you fax something to someone, you send it to them using a fax machine.

fear

NOUN fears

Fear is the feeling of being afraid.

☞ **Similar:** anxiety, horror, panic, terror

fearless

ADJECTIVE

Someone who is fearless is not at all afraid.

feast

NOUN feasts

A feast is a large meal that you have to celebrate something.

☞ **Word history:**
The word **feast** comes from the Latin word *festa*, which means "a festival."

feather

NOUN feathers

A bird's feathers are the soft, light things that cover its body.

*As light as a **feather**…*

feathers

a
b
c
d
e
Ff
g
h
i
j
k
l
m
n
o
p
q
r
s
t
u
v
w
x
y
z

77

a
b
c
d
e

Ff

w
x
y
z

feed
VERB feeds, feeding, fed
1 If you feed a person or an animal, you give them food.
2 When animals feed, they eat food.
*Caterpillars **feed** on leaves.*

feel
VERB feels, feeling, felt
1 The way you feel is the mood you are in or the emotions that you have.
*I **feel** happy today.*
2 If you feel something, you touch it with your hands or your body so that you know what it is like.
***Feel** the cat's soft fur.*

feeling
NOUN feelings
A feeling is an emotion, such as happiness, sadness, or anger.

female
ADJECTIVE
Female animals produce eggs or give birth to babies.
☞ **Opposite:** male

fence
NOUN fences
A fence is a barrier that separates one piece of land from another.

ferocious
ADJECTIVE
A ferocious animal is fierce and dangerous.
☞ **Similar:** savage, vicious

ferry
NOUN ferries
A ferry is a boat that carries people and cars across a small stretch of water.

festival
NOUN festivals
A festival is a celebration or special event, often with music and dancing.

fetch
VERB fetches, fetching, fetched
If you fetch something, you go and get it and bring it back.
*The dog **fetched** the stick.*
☞ **Similar:** bring, carry, deliver, obtain, retrieve

fever
NOUN fevers
If you have a fever, your body is very hot because you are ill.
*Sam couldn't go to school because he had a **fever**.*

ferocious

Word history: The word **ferocious** comes from the Latin words *ferox ocis*, which mean "with wild eyes."

few
ADJECTIVE fewer, fewest
A few means a small number of people or things.
*There are a **few** chocolates left in the box.*
☞ **Opposite:** many

fiction
NOUN
Stories that have been made up and are not true are called fiction.
*Do you enjoy reading **fiction** or nonfiction?*
☞ **Opposite:** fact, nonfiction

fidget

VERB fidgets, fidgeting, fidgeted
If you fidget, you keep moving around in an annoying way.

field

NOUN fields
A field is an area of land where grass grows, crops are grown, or animals graze. A field can be used to play sports like football or soccer.

fierce

ADJECTIVE fiercer, fiercest
A fierce person or animal is violent and dangerous.
*A **fierce** dog growled ferociously at the mailman.*
☛ **Similar:** brutal, cruel, dangerous, ferocious, vicious

fight

VERB fights, fighting, fought
1 When people fight, they hit each other or use weapons to try to hurt each other.
☛ **Similar:** attack, scuffle, struggle, tussle, wrestle
2 When people fight, they argue with each other.
☛ **Similar:** bicker, quarrel, squabble

*A shark's **fin** breaks the surface.*

fin

file

NOUN files
1 A file is a folder that you keep important pieces of paper in.
2 A file on a computer is a place where you keep information.
3 If you walk in single file, you walk with one person behind the other.

fill

VERB fills, filling, filled
When you fill a container, you put as much into it as it can hold.

film

NOUN films
1 A film is a roll of special plastic that you put in a camera for taking photographs.
2 A film is a movie, a moving picture that tells a story and is shown on a screen.
VERB films, filming, filmed
3 When you film something, you take moving pictures of it.
*Joe's studio **filmed** a movie on our street.*

fin

NOUN fins
The fins on a fish are the parts that stick out from the sides of its body and help it to swim.

final

NOUN finals
1 A final is the last game in a competition, which decides who the winner is.
ADJECTIVE
2 The final thing is the last one.
*This is the **final** week of classes.*

fine

NOUN fines
1 A fine is an amount of money you have to pay as a punishment for doing something wrong.
ADJECTIVE finer, finest
2 Something that is fine is all right.
*That jacket looks **fine**.*
3 Fine weather is dry and sunny.
☛ **Similar:** bright, clear, cloudless, fair, pleasant, sunny

finger

NOUN fingers
Your fingers are the long, thin parts at the ends of your hands.

fingerprint

NOUN fingerprints
A fingerprint is a mark that your finger leaves when it touches something.
*The detective found the thief's **fingerprints** on the table.*

finish

VERB finishes, finishing, finished
1 If something finishes, it ends.
☛ **Similar:** end, stop
2 When you finish something, you have done all of it.

a
b
c
d
e
Ff
g
h
i
j
k
l

s
t
u
v
w
x
y
z

fire
NOUN fires
A fire is a mass of heat, light, and flames when something is burning.

fire engine
NOUN fire engines
A fire engine is a large vehicle that fire fighters travel in to get to a fire.

Fire!

Call out the fire engine!

fire fighter
NOUN fire fighters
A fire fighter is someone whose job is to put out fires and rescue people in danger.

firework
NOUN fireworks
Fireworks are things that burn or explode in an attractive, colorful way when you light them.
There were beautiful fireworks on the Fourth of July.

firm
ADJECTIVE firmer, firmest
1 Something that is firm is hard and solid.
☛ **Similar:** dense, hard, rigid, solid, stiff
2 If something is firm, it is fixed in place and you cannot move it.
3 If someone is firm, they are strict and will not change their mind.

first
ADJECTIVE
The first person or thing is the one before all the others.

fish
NOUN fish or fishes
1 A fish is an animal that lives underwater and breathes through gills.
VERB fishes, fishing, fished
2 When you fish, you use a net or rod to try to catch fish.

flag
The flags have been

fishhook
NOUN fishhooks
A fishhook is a hook that is used for catching fish.

fish story
NOUN
A fish story is an extravagant or fanciful story which has no basis in truth.
He told a good fish story.

fist
NOUN fists
A fist is a shape that you make with your hand when you curl up your fingers and thumb tightly.

fit
VERB fits, fitting, fitted, or fit
If something fits, it is the right size or shape to go somewhere.
The wardrobe fit the tiny room perfectly.

fitness
NOUN
Fitness is how strong and in shape you are.

fix
VERB fixes, fixing, fixed
When you fix something, you repair it.
A person came to fix the television.
☛ **Similar:** mend, repair

put up for the festival.

flag
NOUN flags
A flag is a piece of cloth that is used as colorful decoration or has a design that represents a country.

flame
NOUN flames
Flames are the bright points of burning gas that you see in a fire.

flap
VERB flaps, flapping, flapped
1 If something flaps around, it moves around in the wind.
2 When birds flap their wings, they move them up and down.

flash
NOUN flashes
1 A flash is a sudden, bright light.
☞ **Similar:** blaze, flicker, spark
2 If something happens in a flash, it happens very fast.
VERB flashes, flashing, flashed
3 If something flashes, it shines brightly for a short time.
☞ **Similar:** gleam, glimmer, glisten, shimmer, shine, sparkle

flat
ADJECTIVE flatter, flattest
1 Something that is flat is level and even.
*You need a **flat** surface for painting.*
2 If a ball or tire is flat, it has no air inside it.

flavor
NOUN flavors
The flavor of food or drink is what it tastes like.

fleece
NOUN fleeces
A fleece is a jacket or top made of a warm, thick material.

flew
Flew is the past tense of the verb **fly**.

flight
NOUN flights
1 Flight is when something flies.
2 A flight is one trip of an airplane that takes passengers from place to place.

fling
VERB flings, flinging, flung
If you fling something, you throw it suddenly and roughly.
☞ **Similar:** hurl, lob, toss

flip
VERB flips, flipping, flipped
When you flip something, you turn it over quickly.

flipper
NOUN flippers
1 Flippers are the flat limbs that some sea creatures, such as dolphins and seals, use for swimming.
2 Divers wear flippers on their feet to help them move through the water.

float
VERB floats, floating, floated
If something floats, it stays on the surface of water and does not sink.

flock
NOUN flocks
A flock of birds or animals is a large group of them.

flood
NOUN floods
1 A flood happens when a large amount of water covers the land.
VERB floods, flooding, flooded
2 When a river floods, it spills out and covers the land around it.

floor
NOUN floors
1 The floor is the surface that you walk on inside a building.
2 A floor of a large building is one level inside it.
*I live on the sixth **floor**.*

flour
NOUN
Flour is a powder that is made by crushing wheat. You use flour to make bread and cakes.
☞ **Say:** flower

flipper

a b c d e **Ff** g h i j k l m n o p q r s t u v w x y z

flow
VERB flows, flowing, flowed
Something that flows moves along steadily.
*The river **flows** by our house.*

flower
NOUN flowers
A flower is a colorful part of a plant that contains the seeds.

flu
NOUN
The flu is an illness caused by a virus that makes you feel ill and gives you a sore throat, cough, and runny nose. Flu is short for **influenza**.

fluorescent
ADJECTIVE
Something that is fluorescent seems to shine and give off light.
☞ **Say: floor-es-ent**

flush
VERB flushes, flushing, flushed
When you flush something, you clean it by making water move through it quickly.

flute
NOUN flutes
A flute is a musical instrument made of wood or metal. You hold it sideways in front of your mouth and play it by covering holes with your fingers and blowing across a hole at one end.
*She played the **flute** beautifully.*

fly
NOUN flies
1 A fly is a very common insect that you often see in houses in the summer.
VERB flies, flying, flew, flown
2 If something flies, it moves through the air.
☞ **Similar:** flutter, glide, hover, soar

foal
NOUN foals
A foal is a baby horse.

focus
VERB focuses, focusing, focused
When you focus a camera or a telescope, you change the controls slightly so that you can see through it more clearly.

*There was a thick **fog** on the day they set off on their journey.* foggy foggy foggy

fog

fog
NOUN
Fog is a thick cloud that hangs in the air close to the ground and makes it difficult to see things. When there is fog in the air, you can say that it is **foggy**.

fold
VERB folds, folding, folded
When you fold something, you bend one part of it neatly over another.
*He **folded** the card in half.*

What is a baby horse called?
Look around the page to find the answer.

follow
VERB follows, following, followed
If you follow someone, you go along behind them.
*The dog **followed** him home.*

food
NOUN
Food is what you eat to help you live and grow.

fool
NOUN fools
A fool is a very silly or stupid person.

foolish
ADJECTIVE
Someone who is foolish is silly and lacks sense.
*A clown is **foolish** and funny.*
☞ **Similar:** crazy, silly

foot
NOUN feet
Your feet are the parts of your body that you stand on.

football
NOUN
Football is a game in which teams of players try to score points at opposing ends of a field. The ball that they use is called a **football**.

Food

Eating a daily mixture of these foods
will help your body to be healthy.

Carbohydrates

Carbohydrates are foods that form the
main part of your diet.

Pasta

Cereal

bake, boil, mash, roast

Rice

light, soft

Potatoes

brown

Bread

Fruit

A fruit is the part of a plant that
contains seeds.

Strawberries

fresh

Grapes

Banana

soft

delicious

Watermelon

fruity

juicy

Orange

Vegetables

A vegetable is a plant or part of
a plant, that we eat
for food.

crunchy

Carrots

healthy

Beans

Cabbage

sweet

Corn on the cob

Meat

Meat is the part of an animal that
we can eat.

salty

Fish

Shellfish

spicy, tasty

Sausages

Chicken

raw steak

Meat

Dairy

Dairy food is food that is produced
in a dairy.

fatty

Butter

Egg

Yogurt

buttery, creamy, milku, smooth, thick

Cheese

cold

Milk

a
b
c
d
e
Ff
g
h
i
j
k
l
m
n
o
p
q
r
s
t
u
v
w
x
y
z

footprint
NOUN footprints
A footprint is a mark that your foot leaves on the ground.

forbid
VERB forbids, forbidding, forbade, forbidden
If you forbid someone to do something, you tell them they must not do it.
*The adults have **forbidden** us to play football on wet grass.*

force
NOUN forces
1 Force is a power that pushes or pulls something.
*The **force** of the wind blew her hat off.*
2 A force is a group of people who fight or do a job together.
*The police **force** makes sure the streets are safe.*
VERB forces, forcing, forced
3 If you force someone to do something, you make them do it.

forehead
NOUN foreheads
Your forehead is the part of your face above your eyes.

foreign
ADJECTIVE
Something that is foreign comes from another country.
*Can you speak any **foreign** languages?*
☞ **Say: for**-in

forest
NOUN forests
A forest is a large area where a lot of trees grow close together.

forget
VERB forgets, forgetting, forgot, forgotten
If you forget something, you do not remember it.
☞ **Opposite:** remember

forgive
VERB forgives, forgiving, forgave, forgiven
If you forgive someone, you stop being angry with them about something bad that they did.

fork
NOUN forks
1 A fork is a tool with sharp spikes. You use a fork to eat your food, and you use a big fork to dig in the garden.
2 A fork in a road is a place where it divides into two roads going in different directions.

fossil
This ancient animal shell has become a fossil.

form
NOUN forms
1 A form is a piece of paper on which you have to answer questions and give information.
*I filled in a **form** to join the library.*
2 One form of something is one type of it.
*Trains are a **form** of transportation.*

fort
NOUN forts
A fort is a building like a castle that has high walls to protect it from attack.
☞ **Word history:**
The word **fort** comes from the Latin word *fortis*, meaning "strong," so a fort is a strong place.

fortune
NOUN
1 If you have good fortune, you are lucky.
☞ **Opposite:** misfortune
2 A fortune is a lot of money.
*He won a **fortune** in the lottery.*

forward
ADVERB
If you move forward, you move in the direction that is in front of you.
*He ran **forward** to meet us.*

fossil
NOUN fossils
A fossil is the remains of a plant or animal that died many years ago and has turned to stone.
☞ **Word history:**
The word **fossil** comes from the Latin word *fossilis*, meaning "dug up," because many fossils are dug up out of the ground.

fought
Fought is the past tense of the verb **fight**.
☞ **Say: fawt**

found
Found is the past tense of the verb **find**.

fountain
A beautiful fountain

fountain
NOUN fountains
A fountain is water that sprays up into the air, sometimes through a statue.

fox
NOUN foxes
A fox is an animal with reddish-brown fur and a long, bushy tail. Foxes belong to the dog family and eat small animals and birds.

fraction
NOUN fractions
A fraction is a part of a whole number.
*One-third is a **fraction**.*

fragile
ADJECTIVE
Something that is fragile is delicate and will break easily.
*The glass vase is **fragile**.*
☞ **Similar:** brittle, delicate, flimsy, weak
Opposite: tough

frame
NOUN frames
The frame on something is the part that goes around the edge and holds it in place.
*Lily bought a **frame** for her favorite vacation photo.*

freckle
NOUN freckles
Freckles are small, light brown spots on some people's skin.

free
ADJECTIVE
1 If something is free, you do not have to pay for it.
*With this magazine, you get a **free** CD.*
2 If you are free, you are not locked up.
*The prisoners were finally **free**.*
3 If you are free, you can do whatever you want.

freeze
VERB freezes, freezing, froze, frozen
1 If something freezes, it becomes solid because it is so cold.
*Water **freezes** and becomes ice.*
2 If you are freezing, you are very cold.

freezer
NOUN freezers
A freezer is a machine that freezes food so that you can store it and keep it fresh for a long time.

frequent
ADJECTIVE
Something that is frequent happens often.
*There will be **frequent** showers during the afternoon.*

fresh
ADJECTIVE fresher, freshest
1 Something that is fresh is new.
*Start each story on a **fresh** page.*
2 Fresh food is not old or rotten, and is not frozen or canned.
*Would you like a **fresh** strawberry?*
3 Fresh water is not salty.

What is the opposite of tough?
Look around the page to find the answer.

fridge
NOUN fridges
A fridge or refrigerator is a machine like a large, cold cupboard, that keeps food cool and fresh.

friend
NOUN friends
A friend is someone that you like and who likes you.

friendly
ADJECTIVE friendlier, friendliest
Someone who is friendly is kind and helpful and shows that they like you.
☞ **Similar:** affectionate, kind, neighborly, warm

frighten
VERB frightens, frightening, frightened
If something frightens you, it makes you feel afraid.
☞ **Similar:** scare, terrify

fresh

Fresh strawberries

frog

frog
NOUN frogs
A frog is a small animal that can swim and jump. Frogs are amphibians and live near water.

Which frog is the prince?

frogs

front
NOUN fronts
The front of something is the part that faces forward.
☞ **Opposite:** back

frost
NOUN frosts
Frost is ice that forms on the ground outside in very cold weather. When there is frost, you can say that the weather is **frosty**.

frown
VERB frowns, frowning, frowned
When you frown, you move your eyebrows together and wrinkle your forehead to show that you are angry or puzzled.

frozen
ADJECTIVE
1 Something that is frozen is solid because it is very cold.
2 If you are frozen, you are very cold.

fruit
NOUN fruits
A fruit is the part of a plant that contains the seeds. A lot of fruits taste sweet, and we can eat them. Apples, pears, bananas, and oranges are all fruits.
☞ **Rhymes:** boot

fry
VERB fries, frying, fried
When you fry food, you cook it in hot oil.
*Isabella **fried** an egg in a frying pan.*

full
ADJECTIVE fuller, fullest
If something is full, it has a lot of things inside and no room for any more.
*I can't eat anymore—I'm **full**!*
☞ **Opposite:** empty

fun
NOUN
If you have fun, you enjoy yourself.
*The treasure hunt was lots of **fun**.*

funeral
NOUN funerals
A funeral is a ceremony that happens when someone has died.

funnel
NOUN funnels
1 A funnel is a tube that is wide at one end and narrow at the other. You use a funnel for pouring liquid through a small opening.
2 The funnel on a ship is a smokestack.

funny
ADJECTIVE funnier, funniest
1 Something that is funny makes you laugh or smile.
☞ **Similar:** amusing, comical, entertaining, hilarious, humorous, witty
2 Something that is funny is strange or odd.
*What's that **funny** noise?*
☞ **Similar:** curious, mysterious, odd, peculiar, puzzling, strange

fur
NOUN
Fur is the soft hair on an animal's body.

furious
ADJECTIVE
If you are furious, you are very angry.
☞ **Say: fyoor**-ree-us
Similar: fuming, irate, livid

furniture
NOUN
Movable objects, such as chairs, beds, and cupboards are called furniture.

furry
ADJECTIVE furrier, furriest
A furry animal has fur on its body.

future
NOUN
The future is the time that is to come.
*In the **future** people might travel to Mars.*
☞ **Opposite:** past

G

Go!

gain
VERB gains, gaining, gained
If you gain something,
you get it.
*She has **gained** an inch in
height in six months.*
☞ **Opposite:** lose

galaxy
NOUN galaxies
A galaxy is a large
group of stars. The
Milky Way is a galaxy.
☞ **Word history:**
The word **galaxy**
comes from the Greek
word *galaxias*, which
means "milky,"
because a galaxy
looks white and
milky in the sky.

gale
NOUN gales
A gale is a strong wind.

gallery
NOUN galleries
A gallery is a large room
where you can look at
pictures on the walls.

gallop
VERB gallops, galloping,
galloped
When a horse gallops,
it runs very fast.
☞ **Similar:** canter,
race, run, rush

game
NOUN games
1 A game is something that
you play for fun.
2 A game is a sports match in
which you try to score points
and beat other players.

gang
NOUN gangs
A gang is a group
of people who do
things together.
☞ **Similar:** band,
crowd, group,
mob, team

garage
NOUN garages
1 A garage is a place where
you keep a car.
2 A garage is a place where
cars are repaired.

garbage
NOUN
Garbage is any matter
that is no longer wanted
or needed.

garbage Say: **gar-bij**

garden
NOUN gardens
A garden is a piece of ground
where you grow fruit,
flowers, and vegetables.

Fabulous flowers grow in the garden.

a
b
c
d
e
f
Gg
h
i
j
k
l
m
n
o

a
b
c
d
e
f
Gg
h
i
j
k
l
m
n
o
p
q
r
s
t
u
v
w
x
y
z

gas
NOUN gases
A gas is a substance like air that is not a liquid or a solid.

gasp
VERB gasps, gasping, gasped
If you are gasping, you are breathing quickly because you are out of breath.
*He rose to the surface of the water, **gasping** for air.*

gate
NOUN gates
A gate is a door in a fence that you can open and shut.

gather
VERB gathers, gathering, gathered
If you gather things, you collect them together.

gave
Gave is the past tense of the verb **give**.

gaze
VERB gazes, gazing, gazed
If you gaze at something, you stare at it for a long time.
☛ **Similar:** gape, stare

gear
NOUN gears
The gears on a bike or in a car are the parts that control how fast it goes or whether it goes forward or backward.

generous
ADJECTIVE
Someone who is generous is kind and shares things with other people or gives people things.
☛ **Opposite:** mean

genius
NOUN geniuses
A genius is someone who is very intelligent.
☛ **Say: jeen**-yus

gentle
ADJECTIVE gentler, gentlest
If you are gentle, you are kind and careful not to hurt or damage things.
☛ **Opposite:** rough

gentleman
NOUN gentlemen
Gentleman is a polite word for a man.

genuine
ADJECTIVE
Something that is genuine is real, and not false.
*The diamond ring is not a fake— it's **genuine**.*

geography
NOUN
Geography is the subject in which you study the Earth and the ways people live in the world.
☛ **Say:** je-**og**-raf-ee
Word history: The word **geography** comes from the Greek words *geo*, meaning "earth," and *graphia*, meaning "describing," so geography is the subject in which you describe the Earth.

germ
NOUN germs
A germ is a tiny plant or animal that lives in the air or on things around us and can make us ill.

get
VERB gets, getting, got
When you get something, you gain it or someone gives it to you.
☛ **Similar:** gain, receive, win

ghost
NOUN ghosts
A ghost is the spirit of a dead person. Some people believe they can see ghosts.
☛ **Say: goest**
Similar: phantom, spirit

giant
NOUN giants
A giant is a huge person in fairy tales or stories.

genuine Say:
jen-yoo-in

gift
NOUN gifts
A gift is a present.
*He wrote to his aunt to thank her for her kind **gift**.*

gigantic
ADJECTIVE
Something that is gigantic is very big.
☛ **Say:** jie-**gan**-tik
Similar: enormous, giant, huge, massive, vast

giggle
VERB giggles, giggling, giggled
When you giggle, you laugh a lot in a nervous or silly way.
*Ruby couldn't stop **giggling**.*
☛ **Similar:** chuckle, laugh, snicker

Ghosts

All kinds of ghostly things haunt
this page of spooky words.

Creepy cobwebs

Bats screech

WHOOOOOOOOO screams

disturbing, echoing, fearful...

appear, disappear, float, frighten, glide, haunt

A... crumbling, dark,
gloomy, lonely, terrifying
... haunted house

shriek

Ghosts... rattling chains

BOO!

Sigh

Skeletons ... crumble, creep, shake, shiver

Ghosts are... awful, dreadful, ghoulish, horrible, invisible, nasty

A spooky...
clock,
library,
mirror,
passage,
portrait,
tower,
trapdoor

groan

creak

HOWL

mysterious cat

whisper

murmur

SCARY

squeaking
rats

slithering

snake

89

a
b
c
d
e
f
Gg
h
i

p
q
r
s
t
u
v
w
x
y
z

giraffe
NOUN giraffes
A giraffe is a very tall animal with a long neck. Giraffes live in Africa.

Giraffes have l - o - n - g necks.

giraffe

girl
NOUN girls
A girl is a young female person.
*It was a **girls**-only pop group.*

give
VERB gives, giving, gave, given
If you give something to someone, you hand it to them and let them have it.
*Please will you **give** me some of your chocolate?*

glad
ADJECTIVE
If you feel glad, you feel happy.
*I am **glad** to be back home.*
☞ **Similar:** cheerful, delighted, happy, joyful, pleased

gladiator
NOUN gladiators
A gladiator was a man who was trained to fight to entertain people in ancient Rome.

glamorous
ADJECTIVE
Someone who is glamorous is beautiful or handsome, and rich.

glance
VERB glances, glancing, glanced
If you glance at something, you look at it quickly.
☞ **Similar:** peek, peep

glare
VERB glares, glaring, glared
If you glare at someone, you look at them in an angry way.
☞ **Similar:** frown, glower, scowl, stare

glass
NOUN glasses
1 Glass is a substance that you can see through. Windows and many bottles are made of glass.
2 A glass is a cup made of glass that you drink out of.
3 People wear glasses over their eyes to help them to see better. Glasses are pieces of special glass or plastic that make things look bigger, smaller, or clearer.

glide
VERB glides, gliding, glided
If something glides along, it moves along smoothly.
*A swan **glided** across the lake.*

globe
NOUN globes
1 The globe is the world.
2 A globe is a model of the world.

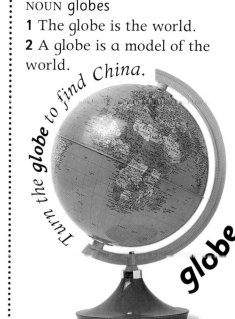

Turn the globe to find China.

globe

gloomy
ADJECTIVE
A gloomy place is dark.
☞ **Similar:** black, dark, dreary

glorious
ADJECTIVE
Something that is glorious is beautiful or wonderful.
☞ **Similar:** fine, gorgeous, magnificent, splendid, superb, wonderful

glove
NOUN gloves
You wear gloves on your hands to keep them warm when the weather is cold.

glow
VERB glows, glowing, glowed
When something glows, it gives off a steady light.
☞ **Similar:** gleam, shine

glue
NOUN glues
Glue is a sticky substance that you use for sticking things together.

goldfish

*Shiny **goldfish** swim around a glass tank.*

gnaw
VERB gnaws, gnawing, gnawed
When an animal gnaws on something, it chews it.
☞ **Similar:** munch, nibble

gnaw Say: naw

*The dog **gnawed** a bone.*

go
VERB goes, going, went, gone
If you go somewhere, you move so that you are there. *Sophie's not here—she's **gone** to her friend's house.*

goal
NOUN goals
1 The goal is the net that you aim the ball at to score points in certain games. *The goalkeeper guarded the **goal**.*
2 When you score a goal, you throw, kick, or strike a ball into a net and get a point. *Bill scored two **goals** in the soccer game.*
3 A goal is something that you want to do. *My **goal** in life is to become a doctor.*

goat
NOUN goats
A goat is a farm animal. Goats are kept for their milk. A baby goat is called a **kid**.

god
NOUN gods
1 God is the name of the being that some people, such as Christians, Jews, and Muslims, worship and believe made the world.
2 A god is any being that people worship.

goggles
NOUN
Goggles are special glasses that you wear to protect your eyes.

gold
NOUN
Gold is a shiny, yellow metal that is very valuable. Something that is made of gold or looks like gold is called **golden**.

goldfish
NOUN
A goldfish is a type of orange fish that some people keep as a pet.

golf
NOUN
Golf is a game that you play by hitting a small ball with a special stick called a **golf club**. The goal is to hit the ball into a series of holes in the ground.

good
ADJECTIVE better, best
1 Something that is good is pleasant and enjoyable. *Did you have a **good** vacation?*
☞ **Similar:** great, nice, pleasant, super, wonderful
2 Something that is good is well made or well done. *That's a **good** painting.*
☞ **Similar:** excellent, fine, skillful, superior, wonderful
3 Someone who is good is nice and well-behaved.
☞ **Opposite:** bad, disobedient
4 If you are good at something, you can do it well. *She's **good** at math.*
☞ **Similar:** skilled, talented

a
b
c
d
e
f
Gg
h
i
j
k
l
m
n
o
p
q
r
s
t
u
v
w
x
y
z

Is **greedy** an **adverb** or an **adjective**?

Look around the page to find the answer.

goose

NOUN geese

A goose is a large bird that lives near water. Farmers sometimes keep geese for their eggs and meat. A male goose is called a **gander**.

gorgeous

ADJECTIVE

1 Something that is gorgeous is very nice to look at.
*What a **gorgeous** view!*
☞ **Similar:** attractive, good-looking, striking
2 Someone who is gorgeous is very good-looking.
☞ **Similar:** beautiful, handsome, pretty, stunning
Say: gor-jus

gorilla

NOUN gorillas

A gorilla is a large animal with dark fur that lives in the jungles of Africa. Gorillas are the largest and strongest apes in the world.

government

NOUN governments

The government is the group of people who run a country.
☞ **Say: guv**-ern-ment

grab

VERB grabs, grabbing, grabbed

If you grab something, you take it or pick it up quickly and roughly.
*He **grabbed** his coat and ran to the station.*
☞ **Similar:** clutch, grip, snatch

graceful

ADJECTIVE

Someone who is graceful moves in a smooth, beautiful way.
*Ballet dancers are **graceful**.*
☞ **Opposite:** clumsy

gradually

ADVERB

If something happens gradually, it happens slowly, little by little.
*The water **gradually** ran out.*

grain

NOUN grains

1 Grain is the seeds of a cereal crop such as wheat or barley.
2 A grain of sand is one small piece of it.

gram

NOUN grams

In the metric system, you measure how much something weighs by saying how many grams it weighs.

grammar

NOUN

The rules that we use when we are writing or speaking a language are called grammar.

grand

ADJECTIVE grander, grandest

Something that is grand is big and impressive.
☞ **Similar:** elegant, impressive, magnificent, majestic

grandchild

NOUN grandchildren

Someone's grandchild is the child of their son or daughter.

grandfather

NOUN grandfathers

Your grandfather is the father of your mother or father. You can also call your grandfather your **grandad** or **grandpa**.

grandmother

NOUN grandmothers

Your grandmother is the mother of your mother or father. You can also call your grandmother your **grandma** or **granny**.

grasshopper

A grasshopper

grape

NOUN grapes

A grape is a small, round fruit with green or black skin and soft, juicy flesh. Grapes can be used to make wine.

grapefruit

NOUN grapefruit or grapefruits

A grapefruit is a large, round, yellow fruit with a thick skin and a sour taste.

graph

NOUN graphs

A graph is a diagram that shows information about something.
☞ **Similar:** chart, diagram

grass

NOUN grasses

Grass is a plant with thin, green leaves that grows on the ground in yards, parks, and fields.

jumps far and high.

grasshopper

NOUN grasshoppers

A grasshopper is an insect with long legs that can jump very high.

grateful

ADJECTIVE

If you are grateful, you are glad that you have something or glad that someone has done something for you.

gravel

NOUN

Gravel is a mixture of tiny pieces of stone.

gravity

NOUN

Gravity is the natural force that pulls things down toward the Earth.

gravy

NOUN

Gravy is a hot sauce that you eat with meat.

gray

ADJECTIVE

Something that is gray is the color of clouds on a rainy day.

graze

VERB grazes, grazing, grazed

1 When animals graze, they eat grass and plants.
2 If you graze your skin, you scrape it and make it bleed.
*I fell and **grazed** my knee.*
☞ **Similar:** cut, scratch

great

ADJECTIVE greater, greatest

1 Great means very big.
☞ **Similar:** enormous, huge, large, massive, vast
2 A great person is important and powerful.
3 Something that is great is very good.
☞ **Similar:** excellent, superb, marvelous, terrific, wonderful

*I love fresh **green** peas.*

green

greedy

ADJECTIVE greedier, greediest

Someone who is greedy eats or wants more of something than they really need.
*George was **greedy** at dinner.*

green

ADJECTIVE

Something that is green is the color of grass.

greenhouse

NOUN greenhouses

A greenhouse is a building made of glass in which you grow plants.

greet

VERB greets, greeting, greeted

When you greet someone, you say hello to that person.

grew

Grew is the past tense of the verb **grow**.

grill

NOUN grills

A grill is a cooking appliance with parallel metal bars.

a
b
c
d
e
f
Gg
h
i
j
k
l
m
n
o
p
q
r
s
t
u
v
w
x
y
z

grin
VERB grins, grinning, grinned
When you grin, you give a big smile.

grind
VERB grinds, grinding, ground
When you grind something, you crush it into a powder.

grip
VERB grips, gripping, gripped
If you grip something, you hold on to it firmly.
☞ **Similar:** clasp, grab, grasp, hold, seize

groan
VERB groans, groaning, groaned
If you groan, you make a loud, deep sound because you are unhappy or in pain.
☞ **Similar:** cry, moan

ground
NOUN
The ground is the surface of the Earth.
*The apple fell to the **ground**.*

group
NOUN groups
A group is a number of people who are doing something together.
☞ **Similar:** band, gang, team

grow
VERB grows, growing, grew, grown
1 When something grows, it gets bigger.
☞ **Opposite:** shrink
2 Grow means become.
*She was beginning to **grow** sleepy.*

growl
VERB growls, growling, growled
When an animal growls, it makes a low, angry sound in its throat.
*The dog **growled** every time I came near.*

growth
NOUN
Growth is the way in which plants and animals change as they become bigger and older.

grunt
VERB grunts, grunting, grunted
When a pig grunts, it makes a short, rough sound.

guard
NOUN guards
1 A guard is someone who watches and looks after a person or protects a place.
VERB guards, guarding, guarded
2 If you guard something, you keep it safe.
*A dog is **guarding** the house.*
☞ **Say:** gard

guess
VERB guesses, guessing, guessed
When you guess the answer to something, you say what you think it might be, although you do not know for sure.
*We had to **guess** what she was holding.*

guest
NOUN guests
A guest is someone who stays at a house or a hotel.
☞ **Rhymes:** best

Growth

All animals grow and change as they get older.

The duck egg cracks.

Hatching

One hour old
The duckling has just hatched.

Two days old
The duckling heads for the water. She's big enough for her first swim.

guide
NOUN guides
1 A guide is someone whose job is to show people around places.
*The **guide** took us around the museum.*
2 A guide to a place is a book with maps and information about the place.
VERB guides, guiding, guided
3 If you guide someone to a place, you show them the way there.
*I **guided** the tourists to the main square in the town.*

guilty
ADJECTIVE
Someone who is guilty has done something wrong.
☛ **Opposite:** innocent

guitar
NOUN guitars
A guitar is a musical instrument with strings. You pull the strings with your fingers to make different sounds.

Pat likes to play his red guitar.

gulp
VERB gulps, gulping, gulped
If you gulp a drink down, you drink it quickly.
☛ **Similar:** guzzle, slurp, swallow, swig

gum
NOUN gums
1 Your gums are the parts inside your mouth around your teeth.
2 Gum is a type of candy that you chew for a long time and do not swallow.

gym
NOUN gyms
A gym is a large room where people can play sports or do exercise using special equipment. Gym is short for **gymnasium**.
☛ **Say: jim**
Word history: The word **gym** comes from the Greek word *gumnásion*, meaning "exercise." The Greek word *gumnós* originally meant "naked," because in ancient Greece athletes trained naked.

gymnast
NOUN gymnasts
A gymnast is a person who does gymnastics.
☛ **Say: jim**-nast

gymnastics
NOUN
Gymnastics is a sport in which people do movements and jumps to show how strong and agile they are.
*Sarah is great at **gymnastics**.*
☛ **Say:** jim-**nass**-ticks

a
b
c
d
e
f
Gg
h
i
j
k
l
m
n
o
p
q
r
s
t
u
v
w

Three weeks old
The duckling has grown into a young duck. She still stays close to her mother.

The yellow feathers are falling out and white feathers are beginning to grow.

Fully grown
The duck is now a fully grown adult, ready to lay eggs and have ducklings of her own.

H

a
b
c
d
e
f
g
Hh
i
j
k
l
m
n
o
p
q
r
s
t
u
v
w
x
y
z

hole

habit
NOUN habits
A habit is something that you do a lot without thinking. *Biting your nails is a bad **habit**.*

habitat
NOUN habitats
A habitat is the natural place where an animal, bird, or plant lives and grows.

hail
NOUN
Hail is drops of frozen rain.

hair
NOUN
Hair grows on your head and body, and on the skin of some animals.

hairbrush
NOUN hairbrushes
A hairbrush is a brush for your hair.

haircut
NOUN haircuts
When you have a haircut, someone cuts your hair into a shape or style.

hairdresser
NOUN hairdressers
A hairdresser is someone whose job is to cut people's hair.

hairy
ADJECTIVE
Something that is hairy is covered in hair.
☞ **Similar:** fleecy, furry, woolly

half
NOUN halves
If you divide something into two halves, you divide it into two equal parts. Each part is called one half.

halfway
ADVERB
If something is halfway between two places, it is in the middle between the two places.

hall
NOUN halls
1 A hall is a corridor or small room just inside the front door of a house.
2 A hall is a large room that people use for meetings and other events.

Halloween Pumpkins scare away spooks on Halloween.

Halloween
NOUN
Halloween is October 31, when some people dress up in costumes and get candy.

ham
NOUN
Ham is meat from a pig that has been salted or smoked to keep it fresh.

hamburger
NOUN hamburgers
A hamburger is a flat, round piece of ground beef that you usually eat in a bun.

hamburger

Word history: The word **hamburger** comes from the name of the German city of Hamburg.

hammer
NOUN hammers
A hammer is a tool with a heavy piece of metal on one end that you use to hit nails into wood.

hamster

NOUN hamsters

A hamster is a small animal that looks like a mouse with no tail. Some people keep hamsters as pets.

hand

NOUN hands

Your hands are the parts of your body at the ends of your arms that you use for gripping and holding.

handle

NOUN handles

1 A handle is the part of something that you hold in your hand.

VERB handles, handling, handled

2 If you handle something, you touch it or hold it in your hand.

*Please do not **handle** the fruit.*

☞ **Similar:** feel, finger, hold, stroke, touch

handlebar

NOUN handlebars

The handlebars on a bicycle are the parts that you hold and turn to steer.

handsome

ADJECTIVE

A handsome man or boy is attractive and pleasant to look at.

☞ **Similar:** attractive, good-looking, gorgeous

handstand

NOUN handstands

If you do a handstand, you put your hands on the ground and kick your legs up into the air.

handwriting

NOUN

Handwriting is writing that you do by hand, using a pen or pencil.

hang

VERB hangs, hanging, hung

If you hang something up, you attach it somewhere by the top so that the bottom part falls loosely down.

*We **hung** our coats on the coatrack.*

Hanukkah

*A menorah (candlestick) used at **Hanukkah***

Hanukkah

NOUN

Hanukkah is the Jewish festival of lights.

happen

VERB happens, happening, happened

When something happens, it takes place.

happy

ADJECTIVE happier, happiest

If you are happy, you feel pleased and cheerful.

☞ **Similar:** cheerful, contented, glad, merry, pleased, satisfied

Opposite: sad, unhappy

harbor

NOUN harbors

A harbor is a sheltered place where ships can come to anchor and unload goods.

*A yacht sailed into the **harbor**.*

hard

ADJECTIVE harder, hardest

1 Something that is hard is solid and firm to touch.

*The ground was dry and **hard**.*

☞ **Similar:** dense, firm, rigid, solid, stiff, tough

Opposite: soft

2 Something that is hard is difficult to do.

*These math problems are **hard**.*

☞ **Similar:** complicated, difficult, tough

Opposite: easy

hare

NOUN hares

A hare is an animal that looks like a big rabbit. Hares can run fast and can hear very well with their long ears.

happy

*Harry is a **happy** baby.*

a
b
c
d
e
f
g
Hh
i
j
k
l
m
n
o
p
q
r
s
t
u
v
w
x
y

a b c d e f g Hh I m n o p q r s t u v w x y z

harm
NOUN
1 If you do harm to something, you damage it or hurt it.
VERB harms, harming, harmed
2 If you harm someone, you hurt them. Something that can harm you is **harmful**. Something that will not harm you is **harmless**.

A hawk hunts other birds in the sky.

hawk

harvest
NOUN harvests
1 The harvest is the time when crops are cut and fruit and vegetables are picked.
VERB harvests, harvesting, harvested
2 When you harvest a crop, you cut it or pick it because it is ready to eat.

hat
NOUN hats
A hat is something that you wear on your head.

hatch
VERB hatches, hatching, hatched
When an animal or bird hatches, it comes out of an egg and is born.
*The chicks **hatched** today.*

hate
VERB hates, hating, hated
If you hate something, you have a strong feeling that you do not like it.
*I never drink coffee because I **hate** it!*
☛ **Opposite:** love

haunted
ADJECTIVE
A place that is haunted has ghosts or spirits in it.

have
VERB has, having, had
If you have something, it is yours or you own it.

hawk
NOUN hawks
A hawk is a bird that has a hooked beak and hunts other creatures for food.

hay
NOUN
Grass that has been cut and dried is called hay. People feed hay to animals.

hay fever
NOUN
If you get hay fever, you sneeze a lot when there is pollen in the air.

Look around the page to find the answer.

What do **hedgehogs** do if they feel frightened?

head
NOUN heads
1 Your head is the part of your body that contains your brain.
2 The head of a group of people is the leader.
*Alex is **head** of the committee.*

headache
NOUN headaches
If you have a headache, you have a pain in your head.

headlight
NOUN headlights
The headlights on a car are the lights at the front.

headline
NOUN headlines
The headlines in a newspaper are printed in large letters. They are the titles of reports that follow.

headphones
You wear headphones on your ears when you want to listen to the radio or to music but do not want anyone else to hear it.

heal
VERB heals, healing, healed
When a cut heals, it gets better.

healthy
ADJECTIVE healthier, healthiest
1 If you are healthy, you are well and not ill.
☛ **Similar:** fit, strong, well
2 Things that are healthy are good for you.
*A **healthy** diet includes lots of fruit and vegetables.*
☛ **Say:** hell-thee

heap
NOUN heaps
A heap is a pile of things lying on top of each other. *She left her clothes in a **heap**.*
☛ **Similar:** mass, mound, mountain, pile, stack

hear
VERB hears, hearing, heard
If you can hear a sound, you notice it using your ears. *Did you **hear** that bird?*

heart
NOUN hearts
1 Your heart is the organ in your chest that pumps blood around your body.
2 A heart is a shape. People often draw hearts to show that they love someone.
☛ **Say:** hart

heat
NOUN
1 When there is heat, something feels hot.
VERB heats, heating, heated
2 When you heat something, you make it warmer. *We **heated** some water.*

heaven
NOUN
Heaven is the happy place where some people believe you go when you die.

heavy
ADJECTIVE heavier, heaviest
Something that is heavy weighs a lot.
☛ **Say:** hev-ee
Opposite: light

hedge
NOUN hedges
A hedge is a line of bushes at the edge of a field or yard.

hedgehog
NOUN hedgehogs
A hedgehog is a small animal that is covered in spines. Hedgehogs roll into a ball when they feel frightened.

heel
NOUN heels
1 Your heel is the back part of your foot. *Someone stepped on her **heel**.*
2 The heel on a shoe is the high part at the back.

*A **helicopter** hovers high in the sky.*

Word history:
The word **helicopter** comes from the Greek words *helix*, meaning "spiral" and *pteron*, meaning "wing." So a helicopter has spiral wings that spin around and around.

height
NOUN heights
1 The height of something is how high it is.
2 Your height is how tall you are.
☛ **Say:** hite

helicopter
NOUN helicopters
A helicopter is a type of aircraft with large blades that spin around on top of it.

helmet
NOUN helmets
A helmet is a strong hat that you wear to protect your head.

help
VERB helps, helping, helped
If you help someone, you do something for that person.
☛ **Similar:** aid, assist

hen
NOUN hens
A hen is a female chicken.

herb
NOUN herbs
An herb is a plant that people use to give flavor to food or to make medicines.

*The truck is **heavier** than the cat.*

a
b
c
d
e
f
g
Hh
i
j
k
l
m
n
o
p
q
r
s
t
u
v
w
x
y
z

hieroglyphics

a
b
c
d
e
f
g
Hh
i
j
k
l
m
n
o
p
q
r
s
t
u
v
w
x
y
z

herd

NOUN herds
A herd of animals is a large group of them.
☞ **Similar:** flock, group, pack, troop

here

ADVERB
Here means in this place.
*Do you live **here**?*

hero

NOUN heroes
1 A hero is a very brave man or boy.
2 The hero in a story is the man or boy that the story is about.

heroine

NOUN heroines
1 A heroine is a very brave woman or girl.
2 The heroine in a story is the woman or girl that the story is about.

hexagon

NOUN hexagons
A hexagon is a shape with six straight sides.

hibernate

VERB hibernates, hibernating, hibernated
When an animal hibernates, it goes to sleep for the winter.
☞ **Say: hie**-ber-nate

hiccup

NOUN hiccups
If you have hiccups, you make sudden sounds in your throat by breathing in quickly.
*You'll get **hiccups** if you drink too quickly.*

hide

VERB hides, hiding, hid, hidden
If you hide something, you put it in a place where people cannot see it.
*She couldn't remember where she had **hidden** her keys.*
☞ **Similar:** conceal, cover

hibernate

Word history:
The word **hibernate** comes from the Latin word *hibernare*, meaning "to spend the winter somewhere."

hieroglyphics

NOUN
Hieroglyphics is a type of writing in which you use pictures instead of words. The ancient Egyptians used hieroglyphics.

high

ADJECTIVE higher, highest
1 Something that is high in the air is a long way away from the ground.
2 Something that is high is very tall.
*We had to climb over a **high** wall.*
☞ **Similar:** big, tall
Opposite: low

hill

NOUN hills
A hill is an area of high ground.

Hindu

NOUN Hindus
A Hindu is a person who follows **Hinduism**, an Indian religion. Hindus worship many gods, and believe that when people die, they are born again.

hip

NOUN hips
Your hips are the joints where your legs join onto your body.

Say: hie-roh-glif-iks

hippopotamus
NOUN hippopotamuses or hippopotami
A hippopotamus is a very large animal that lives in Africa. Hippopotamuses spend most of the time in lakes or rivers, and eat water plants.
☞ **Word history:** The word **hippopotamus** comes from a Greek word meaning "horse of the river."

hiss
VERB hisses, hissing, hissed
When something hisses, it makes a noise like air escaping from a tire.

history
NOUN
History is the subject in which you study things that happened to people in the past.

hit
NOUN hits
1 If something is a hit, people like it and it is successful.
The song was a big **hit**.
VERB hits, hitting, hit
2 If you hit someone, you bang them with your hand.
That boy **hit** *me!*
3 If you hit something, you knock it or bump into it.
The tennis player **hit** *the ball.*
☞ **Similar:** bang, strike, whack

hive
NOUN hives
A hive is a large box that bees live in.

hobby
NOUN hobbies
A hobby is something that you do for enjoyment in your spare time.
Gardening is my **hobby**.

hockey
NOUN
Hockey is a game in which teams of players hit a ball with a curved stick and try to score goals.

The snake **hissed**.

hisssssss

hold
VERB holds, holding, held
1 When you hold something, you keep it in your hands.
Would you like to **hold** *our new puppy?*
☞ **Similar:** carry, clutch, cuddle, grasp, hug
2 If something holds a certain amount, it can have that amount inside it.
This bottle will **hold** *two pints of water.*

hole
NOUN holes
A hole is a gap or opening in something.
☞ **Similar:** break, crack, gap, opening, rip, slit, space, split

holiday
NOUN holidays
A holiday is a time when you do not have to go to school or work.
I'm looking forward to the Thanksgiving **holiday**.
☞ **Word history:** A **holiday** was originally a "holy day," when people took a day off work to celebrate a religious festival.

hollow
ADJECTIVE
Something that is hollow has an empty space inside.
Owls often make their nests in **hollow** *trees.*

holly
NOUN
Holly is a green plant with prickly leaves and red berries. People sometimes decorate their homes with holly.

holy
ADJECTIVE
Something that is holy is special because it is connected with religion.

a
b
c
d
e
f
g

Hh

i
j
k
l
m
n
o
p
q
r
s
t
u
v
w
x
y
z

pony
This is a palomino horse.

forelock
mane
withers
tail
hock
hoof
muzzle
knee
fetlock

Horse
Here are some words about horses and horse equipment.

riding hat
reins
saddle
bridle
bit
stirrup
girth

The equipment a horse wears for riding is called "tack."

home
NOUN homes
Your home is the place where you live.

honest
ADJECTIVE
Someone who is honest tells the truth and does not steal things.
☞ **Say: on**-nist
Similar: decent, good, trustworthy, truthful, virtuous
Opposite: dishonest

honey
NOUN
Honey is a sweet, sticky food that bees make.
☞ **Say: hun**-ee

hood
NOUN hoods
A hood is a part of a jacket or top that covers your head.

hoof
NOUN hoofs or hooves
An animal's hooves are its hard feet. Horses and deer have hooves.

hoop
NOUN hoops
A hoop is a round strip of plastic, wood, or metal.

hoot
VERB hoots, hooting, hooted
When an owl hoots, it makes a loud sound.
*I heard an owl **hooting** for a long time the other night.*

hop
VERB hops, hopping, hopped
When you hop, you jump on one leg.

hope
VERB hopes, hoping, hoped
If you hope that something will happen, you want it to happen.
☞ **Similar:** desire, dream, long, wish, yearn

hopeful
ADJECTIVE
If you are hopeful that something will happen, you think that it might happen.
*I am **hopeful** that I will win.*

horn
NOUN horns
1 An animal's horns are the tough, pointed, bony parts on its head.
*A rhinoceros has one **horn**.*
2 A horn is a musical instrument made of brass that you play by blowing through it.
3 A horn is something that can make a loud noise to warn people of danger.

horrible
ADJECTIVE
Something that is horrible is very unpleasant or frightening.
☞ **Similar:** awful, disgusting, dreadful, ghastly, hideous, horrid, nasty, repulsive, revolting, terrible

horror
NOUN
If something fills you with horror, it makes you feel shocked and frightened.
*They watched in **horror** as the house burned down.*

stallion
An adult male horse. The father is also called the "sire."

mare
An adult female horse. The mother is also called the "dam."

long ears

Donkeys and zebras are members of the horse family.

spiked mane

striped coat

zebra

foal

donkey

horse

NOUN horses
A horse is a large animal that people use for riding and pulling carts.

hose

NOUN hoses
A hose is a long tube that water can go through.
*A **hose** is useful for watering flowers.*

hospital

NOUN hospitals
A hospital is a place where people go when they are sick or injured and need to be treated by a doctor.

hot

ADJECTIVE hotter, hottest
1 Something that is hot has a very high temperature.
*The bars of the heater are very **hot**.*
☞ **Similar:** boiling, burning, fiery, roasting, scalding, scorching
Opposite: cold
2 Hot food is very spicy.

hotel

NOUN hotels
A hotel is a place where people can pay to eat a meal and stay the night.

huddle

*Baby rabbits **huddle** together for warmth.*

hour

NOUN hours
An hour is 60 minutes. There are 24 hours in a day.
☞ **Say:** ow-er

house

NOUN houses
A house is a building that people live in.
*The Simpson family had lived in the same **house** for 40 years.*
☞ **Similar:** dwelling, home, residence

howl

VERB howls, howling, howled
1 If a wolf or dog howls, it makes a loud, whining sound.
2 If someone howls, they cry loudly.

huddle

VERB huddles, huddling, huddled
If people huddle together, they stay close to each other because they are cold or frightened. A team huddles to make a plan secretly.

hug

VERB hugs, hugging, hugged
If you hug someone, you hold them in a loving way.
☞ **Similar:** cuddle, embrace

huge

ADJECTIVE
Something that is huge is very big.
*That cake is **huge**!*
☞ **Similar:** colossal, enormous, giant, gigantic, great, immense, large, massive, vast

hum

VERB hums, humming, hummed

When you hum, you sing with your lips closed.

human

NOUN humans

A human is a man, woman, or child. A human is also called a **human being**.

☞ **Say: hew**-mun

Hh

humid

ADJECTIVE

If the weather is humid, it is warm and damp.

☞ **Similar:** damp, muggy, sticky

humor

NOUN

If you have a sense of humor, you can see when things are funny.

humor

☞ Say:

*Her sense of **humor** made me laugh.*

hump

NOUN humps

A hump is a large, round lump. Camels have humps on their backs.

hundred

NOUN hundreds

A hundred is the number 100.

hung

Hung is the past tense of the verb **hang**.

hungry

ADJECTIVE

If you are hungry, you want to eat something.

☞ **Similar:** famished, ravenous, starving

hunt

VERB hunts, hunting, hunted

1 When animals or people hunt, they kill other animals for food.

*Lions **hunt** in packs.*

2 If you hunt for something, you look everywhere because you are trying to find it.

hurl

VERB hurls, hurling, hurled

If you hurl something, you throw it as hard as you can.

*She **hurled** the cushion across the room.*

☞ **Similar:** chuck, fling, lob, sling, throw, toss

hew-mer

hurricane

NOUN hurricanes

A hurricane is a violent storm with strong winds.

hurry

VERB hurries, hurrying, hurried

When you hurry, you do things quickly because you do not have much time.

*He had to **hurry** to deliver the package on time.*

hurt

VERB hurts, hurting, hurt

1 If you hurt a part of your body, you injure it.

*I **hurt** my leg when I fell.*

☞ **Similar:** bruise, cut, injure, wound

2 If a part of your body hurts, you can feel pain in it.

*My broken arm **hurts**.*

☞ **Similar:** ache, sting, throb

husband

NOUN husbands

A woman's husband is the man she is married to.

hush

NOUN

When there is hush, there is no noise.

*There was a **hush** as the teacher came into the room.*

☞ **Similar:** quiet, silence

hut

NOUN huts

A hut is a small, wooden house.

☞ **Similar:** cabin, shack, shed

hygiene

NOUN

Hygiene is keeping things clean.

*Good **hygiene** is important in the kitchen.*

☞ **Say: hie**-jeen

a
b
c
d
e
f
g
i
j
k
l
m
n
o
p
q
r
s
t
u
v
w
x
y
z

I

ice

NOUN
Ice is frozen water.

iceberg

NOUN icebergs
An iceberg is a huge piece of ice floating in the sea.

ice cream

NOUN ice creams
Ice cream is a sweet, frozen food that is made from cream or milk and flavored with fruit or chocolate.

ice cream

Ice cream is a delicious dessert.

ice rink

NOUN ice rinks
An ice rink is a large area of ice that people can skate on.

ice skate

NOUN ice skates
Ice skates are special boots with metal blades on the bottom that you wear when you are skating on ice.

icicle

NOUN icicles
An icicle is a long, thin piece of ice that is hanging down from a high place.

icing

NOUN
Icing is a sweet substance that you put on the top of cakes.

idea

NOUN ideas
An idea is a thought that you have in your head.

ideal

ADJECTIVE
Something that is ideal is perfect in every way.

identical

ADJECTIVE
If things are identical, they are exactly the same.

identify

VERB identifies, identifying, identified
If you identify something, you can say exactly what it is. If you identify someone, you can say who they are.

ice skate

Ice skates help you to move over ice.

idiot

NOUN idiots
An idiot is someone who is very silly or stupid.

idle

ADJECTIVE
Someone who is idle is lazy.

igloo

NOUN igloos
An igloo is a round building made of snow and ice.
☞ **Word history:** The word **igloo** comes from *iglu*, an Inuit word used by the people who live in Alaska and the far north of Canada. It is their word for "house."

ignorant

ADJECTIVE
Someone who is ignorant does not know very much.

ignore

VERB ignores, ignoring, ignored
If you ignore someone, you take no notice of them.

ill

ADJECTIVE
If you feel ill, you do not feel well.
☞ **Similar:** sick, sickly, unhealthy, unwell

a
b
c
d
e
f
g
h
Ii
j
k
l
m
n
o
p
q
r
s
t
u
v
w
x
y
z

a b c d e f g h **li** j k l m s t u v w x y z

illegal
ADJECTIVE
If something is illegal, you are not allowed to do it because it is against the law.
☞ **Similar:** criminal, outlawed, unlawful, wrongful
Opposite: legal

illness
NOUN illnesses
If you get an illness, you become ill.

illustrate
VERB illustrates, illustrating, illustrated
If you illustrate a story, you draw pictures to go with it.

illustrate

*Jess **illustrated** her story with a toucan.*

illustration
NOUN illustrations
An illustration is a picture in a book. Someone who draws illustrations is called an **illustrator**.

image
NOUN images
An image is a picture of something or someone.
*The lake reflected a perfect mirror **image** of the house.*

imaginary
ADJECTIVE
Something that is imaginary is not real and only exists in stories or in someone's imagination.
*The unicorn is an **imaginary** animal.*
☞ **Say:** i-**maj**-in-air-y
Similar: fictional, invented, mythical

imagination
NOUN
If you use your imagination, you think of new ideas.
*Jack has a good **imagination**.*

imagine
VERB imagines, imagining, imagined
When you imagine something, you think about it and make a picture of it in your mind.
☞ **Say:** i-**ma**-jin

imitate
VERB imitates, imitating, imitated
If you imitate someone, you copy them.
☞ **Similar:** impersonate, mimic

immediately
ADVERB
If you do something immediately, you do it very quickly, without waiting.
*I must mail this birthday card **immediately** or it will be late.*
☞ **Similar:** instantly, promptly

immigrate
VERB immigrates, immigrating, immigrated
When people immigrate, they come into a country in order to live there.

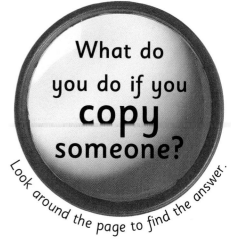

What do you do if you COPY someone?

Look around the page to find the answer.

impatient
ADJECTIVE
1 If you are impatient, you feel angry because you have to wait.
*He was **impatient** to start.*
2 If you are impatient with someone, you quickly become annoyed with them.
*He was **impatient** with his little brother.*
☞ **Similar:** irritable, snappy

important
ADJECTIVE
1 If something is important, it means a lot to you.
*Winning this competition is very **important** to me.*
☞ **Similar:** serious, vital
2 An important person has a lot of power.
☞ **Similar:** famous, well-known

impossible
ADJECTIVE
If something is impossible, you cannot do it.
*It is **impossible** for people to fly like birds.*

improve
VERB improves, improving, improved
If you improve, you get better at doing something.

include

VERB includes, including, included

If you include something, you have it or put it with other things.

*I think we should **include** some pictures in our project.*

inconvenient

ADJECTIVE

If something is inconvenient, you find it difficult or annoying.

*Steep stairs are **inconvenient** for a lot of people.*

☛ **Say:** in-kon-**vee**-nyent
Similar: annoying, awkward, difficult, irritating, tiresome
Opposite: convenient

incorrect

ADJECTIVE

Something that is incorrect is wrong.

*I'm sorry, you are **incorrect**!*

increase

VERB increases, increasing, increased

When a number or an amount increases, it gets bigger.

*My allowance **increases** every year.*

☛ **Opposite:** decrease

incredible

ADJECTIVE

If something is incredible, it is so strange that you find it difficult to believe.

☛ **Similar:** absurd, impossible, surprising, unbelievable

independent

ADJECTIVE

Someone who is independent can do things for themselves and decide things for themselves.

index

NOUN indexes

An index is a list of all the things that are included in a book, with numbers for the pages where you can find each thing.

He **inflated** the balloon with air.

individual

NOUN individuals

1 An individual is a person.

ADJECTIVE

2 Something that is individual is for just one person.

indoors

ADVERB

Indoors means inside a building.

*Let's go **indoors** now.*

☛ **Opposite:** outdoors

industry

NOUN industries

An industry is a business that makes things or sells things.

*A lot of people work in the food **industry**.*

infant

NOUN infants

An infant is a very young child.

☛ **Word history:** The word **infant** comes from the Latin word *infans*, meaning "a young child who cannot speak."

infection

NOUN infections

If you get an infection, a germ gets into your body and makes you ill.

infinity

NOUN

Infinity is a time, number, or place that never ends.

*Looking at the night sky is like looking into **infinity**.*

inflate

VERB inflates, inflating, inflated

When you inflate something, you blow or pump air into it to make it bigger.

☛ **Opposite:** deflate

a
b
c
d
e
f

li

k
l
m
n
o
p
q
r
s
t
u
v
w
x
y
z

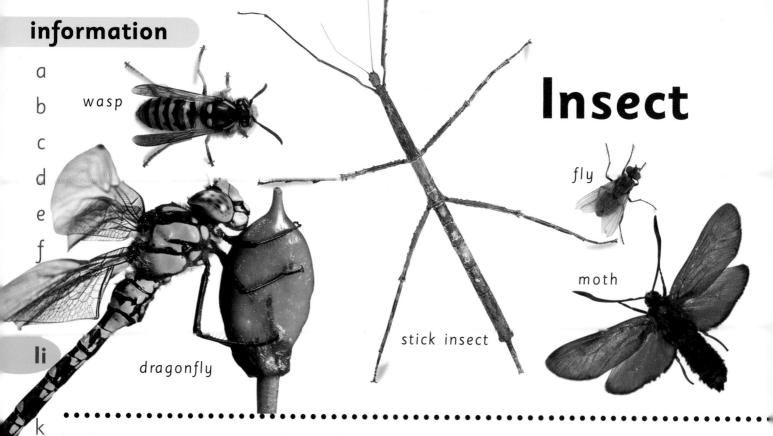

wasp

dragonfly

Insect

fly

moth

stick insect

information

NOUN

Information is facts about something.

*We had to find **information** about wild animals in Africa.*

☞ **Similar:** data, evidence, facts

ingredient

NOUN ingredients

Ingredients are the things that you mix together to make something.

☞ **Say:** in-**gree**-dee-ent

inhabitant

NOUN inhabitants

The inhabitants of a place are the people who live there.

initial

NOUN initials

Your initials are the first letters of your names. For example, if your name is William Grout, your initials are W.G.

☞ **Say:** i-**nish**-ul

injection

NOUN injections

If you have an injection, a doctor puts some medicine into your body using a needle.

injure

VERB injures, injuring, injured

If you injure a part of your body, you hurt it.

☞ **Similar:** break, cut, hurt, wound

injury

NOUN injuries

If you have an injury, you hurt a part of your body.

ink

NOUN inks

Ink is a black or colored liquid that you use for writing or drawing.

innocent

ADJECTIVE

Someone who is innocent has not done anything wrong.

☞ **Opposite:** guilty

insect

NOUN insects

An insect is a small animal with six legs. Insects usually have wings and do not have a backbone. Flies, bees, beetles, and butterflies are all insects.

inside

NOUN insides

The inside of something is the part in the middle.

*The **inside** of the church is really beautiful.*

☞ **Opposite:** outside

inspect

VERB inspects, inspecting, inspected

If you inspect something, you check it carefully.

*We **inspect** all the cars before they leave the factory.*

inspector

NOUN inspectors

An inspector is someone whose job is to check things.

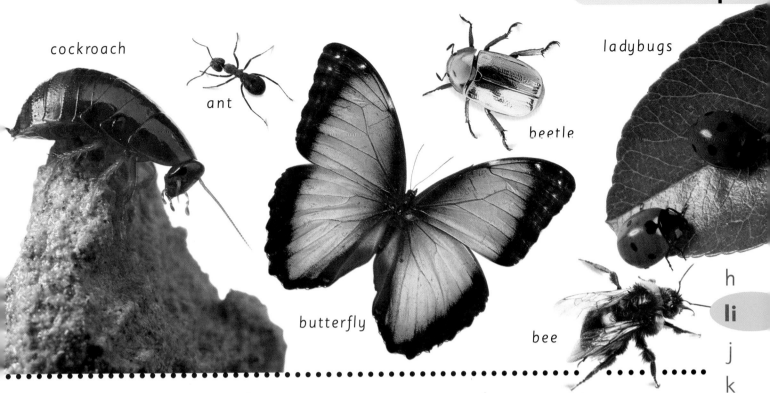

cockroach

ant

beetle

ladybugs

butterfly

bee

h
li
j
k
l
m
n
o
p
q
r
s
t
u
v
w
x
y
z

instant
ADJECTIVE
Something that is instant
happens quickly.
*The show was an **instant**
success.*

instead
ADVERB
Instead of means in the place
of another person or thing.
*I chose the red pen **instead** of
the blue one.*

instruction
NOUN instructions
If someone gives you an
instruction, they tell you
what you should do.
*Read the **instructions** before
you use the machine.*

instrument
NOUN instruments
1 An instrument is something
that you use for making music.
*He plays two musical
instruments.*
2 An instrument is a tool.

insult
VERB insults, insulting, insulted
If you insult someone, you
call them names or say
mean things to them.

intelligent
ADJECTIVE
An intelligent person is smart
and learns things quickly.
☞ **Similar:** brainy, bright,
clever, gifted, quick, sharp, smart
Opposite: stupid

interactive
ADJECTIVE
An interactive game is one
in which you can control
the way in which things
happen.
*I like playing **interactive**
computer games.*

interest
VERB interests, interesting,
interested
If something interests you,
you like it and want to learn
more about it.

interesting
ADJECTIVE
If something is interesting, it
holds your attention and is
not boring.

international
ADJECTIVE
Something that is
international involves
several different countries.

internet
NOUN
The internet is a system for
finding out information from
all over the world using your
computer.

interrupt
VERB interrupts, interrupting,
interrupted
1 If you interrupt someone,
you stop them from talking.
*Please don't **interrupt** while
I'm speaking!*
2 If you interrupt something,
you stop it from happening
for a short time.

109

a
b
c
d
e
f
g
h
Ii
j
k
l
m
n
o
p
q
r
s

interview

NOUN interviews
An interview is a meeting where someone has to answer questions.
*He felt a little nervous before his **interview**.*

intestine

NOUN intestines
Your intestine is the long tube that leads away from your stomach. Food is digested in your intestine as well as in your stomach.
☞ **Say:** in-**tes**-tin

introduce

VERB introduces, introducing, introduced
When you introduce someone, you say their name and explain who they are.
*At my new school I had to **introduce** myself.*

introduction

NOUN introductions
The introduction is the part of a book or story that explains who the characters are or what it is going to be about.

invade

VERB invades, invading, invaded
When people invade a country, they enter it and attack it.
☞ **Similar:** attack, occupy, raid, storm

invent

VERB invents, inventing, invented
If you invent something, you think of it and design it for the first time. Something that you invent is called an **invention**.
*Alexander Graham Bell **invented** the telephone.*

Who **invented** the telephone?

Look around the page to find the answer.

investigate

VERB investigates, investigating, investigated
If you investigate something, you try to find out about it.
*The police are **investigating** yesterday's robbery.*

invisible

ADJECTIVE
If something is invisible, you cannot see it.
☞ **Opposite:** visible

invitation

NOUN invitations
If you get an invitation, you are asked to go to a party.

invite

VERB invites, inviting, invited
If you invite someone to go with you somewhere, you ask them.

involve

VERB involves, involving, involved
If you are involved in something, you take part in it.

iron

NOUN
1 Iron is a strong, heavy metal found in rocks. People use iron to make things such as tools and gates.
2 You use a hot iron to make clothes smooth after they have been washed.

Islam

NOUN
Islam is the Muslim religion. Muslims believe there is one God, Allah, and that Mohammed is His prophet.

island

NOUN islands
An island is a piece of land that is completely surrounded by water.
☞ **Say:** **eye**-land

itch

VERB itches, itching, itched
If your skin itches, it feels uncomfortable and you want to rub or scratch it.

ivy

NOUN ivies
Ivy is a green plant that climbs up walls and trees.

ivy Say: eye-vee

Ivy covered the old brick wall.

J

jab
VERB jabs, jabbing, jabbed
If you jab someone, you poke them with your finger.
*He **jabbed** me in the ribs to get my attention.*
☞ **Similar:** dig, elbow, nudge, poke, prod

jacket
NOUN jackets
A jacket is a type of coat.

jackpot
NOUN jackpots
A jackpot is a very large amount of money that you can win.
*The Jones family won the lottery **jackpot**.*

jagged
ADJECTIVE
Something that is jagged has a lot of sharp points and rough edges.
☞ **Similar:** ragged, rough, spiky, uneven

jail
NOUN jails
A jail is a place where criminals are kept locked up.

jam
NOUN jams
1 Jam is a sweet food made with fruit and sugar. You spread jam on bread.
2 If there is a traffic jam, a lot of cars are stuck and cannot move.

jar
NOUN jars
A jar is a glass container in which you keep food.

*The glass **jar** is filled to the brim.*

jaw
NOUN jaws
Your jaw is the bone in your chin that supports your mouth and allows it to open and close.

jazz
NOUN
Jazz is a type of popular music with strong rhythms.

jealous
ADJECTIVE
If you are jealous of someone, you feel angry because they have something that you would like.
*He was **jealous** of his friend's computer.*
☞ **Say: jel**-lus
Similar: envious, resentful

jeans
NOUN
Jeans are pants made of a thick cotton.

jeep
NOUN jeeps
A jeep is a small truck that people use for driving over rough ground.
☞ **Word history:**
The word **jeep** comes from GP, short for "General Purpose" vehicle.

jelly
NOUN
Jelly is a sweet food made from fruit and sugar.

jellyfish
NOUN
A jellyfish is a sea animal that has a soft, clear body and long tentacles.

jet
NOUN jets
1 A jet of water is a stream of water moving quickly through the air.
2 A jet is a fast aircraft.

a
b
c
d
e
f
g
h
i
Jj
k
l
m
n
o
p
q
r
s
t
u
v
w
x
y
z

a
b
c
d
e
f
g
h
i
Jj
k
l

p
q
r
s
t
u
v
w
x
y
z

Jew
NOUN Jews
A Jew is someone whose religion is Judaism.

jewel
NOUN jewels
1 A jewel is a precious stone that has been cut and polished. Diamonds, rubies, and emeralds are all jewels.
2 A jewel is an ornament made of precious stones and metals that people wear.

jewelry
NOUN
Jewelry is things like necklaces, bracelets, and rings, that people wear on their bodies.

She wore simple jewelry—just a gold heart.

jigsaw puzzle
NOUN jigsaw puzzles
A jigsaw puzzle is a puzzle with a lot of different pieces that you have to fit together to make a picture.

job
NOUN jobs
1 A job is something that you have to do.
*Your **job** is to pick up all the pencils.*
2 Your job is the work that you do to make money.
*What **job** do you want to do when you grow up?*

jockey
NOUN jockeys
A jockey is a person who rides a horse in races.

Look around the page to find the answer.

What are your knees and elbows known as?

jog
VERB jogs, jogging, jogged
When you jog, you run slowly and steadily.
☞ **Similar:** run, trot

join
VERB joins, joining, joined
1 When you join things together, you connect them.
☞ **Similar:** attach, connect, tie
2 When you join a club, you become a member of it.

joint
NOUN joints
A joint is a place in your body where two bones meet. Your knees and your elbows are joints.

joke
NOUN jokes
1 A joke is something that you say or do to make people laugh.
VERB jokes, joking, joked
2 If you are joking, you are not being serious, but are saying or doing something just to make people laugh.
*I was only **joking**.*

jolt
VERB jolts, jolting, jolted
If something jolts, it shakes or bumps.
*The truck **jolted** along the bumpy track.*
☞ **Similar:** bump, jerk, knock, shake

journalist
NOUN journalists
A journalist is someone who gathers news and writes about it in a newspaper or talks about it on the television.
*When I'm older, I want to be a **journalist**.*
☞ **Say:** jer-nal-list

journey
NOUN journeys
If you go on a journey, you travel somewhere.
☞ **Say:** jer-nee
Word history: The word **journey** comes from the old French word *jornée*, which meant the "distance that you could travel in one day."

joyful
ADJECTIVE
If you are joyful, you are very happy.
☞ **Similar:** cheerful, delighted, glad happy, merry

joystick
NOUN joysticks
A joystick is a control that you use to play computer games. It is a short stick that you can move in different directions.

Judaism
NOUN
Judaism is the religion of Jewish people. Jews believe in one God, and in the teachings of the Old Testament and the Talmud, the Jewish holy books.
☞ **Say: joo**-dee-izm

judge
NOUN judges
1 A judge is the person in charge of a court who decides how people should be punished when they have done something wrong.
2 The judge in a competition is the person who decides who the winner is.
VERB judges, judging, judged
3 When you judge something, you decide how good or bad it is.
*She enjoyed **judging** the dog competition.*

juggle
VERB juggles, juggling, juggled
When you juggle, you keep several objects in the air at the same time by throwing and catching them.

*It takes practice to learn how to **juggle**.*

juice
NOUN juices
Juice is the liquid that you can squeeze out of fruit or vegetables.

juicy
ADJECTIVE
Juicy food has a lot of juice in it.
*The fruit was really **juicy**.*

jungle
NOUN jungles
A jungle is a thick, tropical forest.
☞ **Word history:** The word **jungle** comes from the Hindi word *jangal*, which means an "area of land that is overgrown with plants."

junior
ADJECTIVE
Junior means for children.
*We are going to have a **junior** basketball tournament.*

*Frogs can **jump** a long way.*

judo
NOUN
Judo is a sport from Japan. Two people fight with special movements, throwing each other to the ground.
☞ **Word history:** The word **judo** comes from the Japanese words *ju* and *do*, meaning "gentle way."

jump
VERB jumps, jumping, jumped
When you jump, you throw yourself into the air.
☞ **Similar:** bound, hop, leap, prance, spring, vault

junction
NOUN junctions
A junction is a place or point where things meet.

junk
NOUN
You can describe things that are broken or no use as junk.

jury
NOUN juries
A jury is a group of people who sit in a court and decide whether the person on trial is guilty or not guilty.

a
b
c
d
e
f
g
h
i
j
Kk
l
m
n
o
p
q
r
s
t
u
v
w
x
y
z

K

king

kangaroo
NOUN kangaroos
A kangaroo is an Australian animal. Kangaroos can hop fast on their strong back legs. The females carry their young in a pouch on their front.

keep
VERB keeps, keeping, kept
1 If you keep something, you have it and do not give it away.
*Why do you want to **keep** your old bike?*
2 Keep means remain.
*Please **keep** still!*
3 If you keep doing something, you do not stop.
*He **kept** walking.*

kennel
NOUN kennels
A kennel is a shelter for a dog or cat.

kettle
NOUN kettles
A kettle is a special container that you boil water in.

key
NOUN keys
1 A key is a piece of metal that has been cut into a special shape so that it will fit into a lock and open it.
2 The keys on a computer are the parts that you press with your fingers to make it work.

keyboard
NOUN keyboards
1 The keyboard on a computer is the part with all the buttons on it that you press to make it work.
2 A keyboard is a musical instrument like a piano that works with electricity.

kick
VERB kicks, kicking, kicked
When you kick something, you hit it with your foot.
*He **kicked** the football over the goalpost.*

kid
NOUN kids
1 A kid is a child.
2 A kid is a baby goat.

kill
VERB kills, killing, killed
If you kill something, you make it die.
*She **killed** the wasp with a rolled-up newspaper.*
☛ **Similar:** assassinate, execute, murder, slaughter

kilogram
NOUN kilograms
In the metric system, when you measure how much something weighs, you say how many kilograms it weighs.

kilometer
NOUN kilometers
In the metric system, when you say how far away a place is, you say how many kilometers away it is.

kind
NOUN kinds
1 One kind of thing is one type.
*There are lots of different **kinds** of bird.*
ADJECTIVE kinder, kindest
2 Someone who is kind helps other people and gives them things.
*It was **kind** of Aunt Julia to help us move.*
☛ **Similar:** fair, friendly, generous, helpful, nice, sympathetic, warm
Opposite: unkind

king
NOUN kings
A king is a man who rules a country.

kiss
VERB kisses, kissing, kissed
When you kiss someone, you touch them with your lips to show that you like them or love them.

kitchen
NOUN kitchens
A kitchen is a room where people cook food.

kite
NOUN kites
A kite is a very light toy that you fly in the air on the end of a long string.

The kite swooped and dived in the sky.

kitten
NOUN kittens
A kitten is a young cat.

knee
NOUN knees
Your knee is the part that you can bend in the middle of your leg.

kneel
VERB kneels, kneeling, kneeled, or knelt
When you kneel, you stand on your knees.

knickers
NOUN
Knickers are loose-fitting short pants gathered at the knee.

knife
NOUN knives
You use a knife for cutting things. It has a sharp blade and a handle that you hold.
☞ Say: nife

knight
NOUN knights
A knight is a soldier from medieval times who rode a horse and wore armor.
☞ Say: nite

knit
VERB knits, knitting, knitted
When you knit, you make clothes and blankets from wool, using large needles.
☞ Say: nit

knob
NOUN knobs
1 A knob is a round handle on a piece of furniture.
2 A knob is a button that you turn to make something work.
☞ Similar: button, handle, lever, switch
Say: nob

knock
VERB knocks, knocking, knocked
1 When you knock on a door, you bang on it.
2 If you knock something, you bump it by accident.
She knocked over the glass.
☞ Similar: bash, bump, hit
Say: nok

knot
NOUN knots
A knot is a piece of string or rope that has been twisted or tied into a difficult shape.
☞ Say: not

know
VERB knows, knowing, knew, known
1 If you know something, you have it in your mind and understand it.
Do you know what the capital of France is?
2 If you know someone, you have met them before.
☞ Say: no

knuckle
NOUN knuckles
Your knuckles are the parts of your body where your fingers join your hands.
☞ Say: nuk-ul

koala
NOUN koalas
A koala is an Australian animal that lives in eucalyptus trees and eats leaves and bark.

Koalas live in Australia.

a b c d e f g h i j Kk l m n o p q r s

a
b
c
d
e
f
g
h
i
j
k
Ll
m
n
o
p
q
r
s
t
u
v
w
x
y
z

Ha Ha Ha

La gh

Hee Hee Hee

label
NOUN labels
A label is a small piece of paper or cloth that is attached to something and gives you information about it.

lace
NOUN laces
1 Lace is thin material with small holes. It often decorates the edges of clothes.
2 The laces on your shoes are the pieces of string that you tie to fasten them.

ladder
NOUN ladders
A ladder is a tall frame with rungs or steps, which you use for climbing up or down.

lady
NOUN ladies
Lady is a polite word for a woman.

Ladybug, ladybug,

ladybug
NOUN ladybugs
A ladybug is a small, red beetle with black spots.

lake
NOUN lakes
A lake is a large area of water surrounded by land.

lamb
NOUN lambs
A lamb is a young sheep.

lamp
NOUN lamps
A lamp is a small light that works by using electricity, oil, or gas.

land
NOUN lands
1 The land is the part of the world that is not covered by sea.
2 A land is a country.
*He was the best dancer in the **land**.*
VERB lands, landing, landed
3 When something lands, it comes back to the ground after it has been in the air.
*The plane **landed** in a field.*

fly away home.

lane
NOUN lanes
A lane is a narrow road.

language
NOUN languages
A language is all the words that people use to speak or write to each other.
☛ **Say: lang**-gwij

语言

*This means **language** in Chinese.*

lap
NOUN laps
1 Your lap is the top part of your legs when you are sitting down.
*The kitten curled up on her **lap**.*
2 One lap of a racetrack is one time around it.
*The runners were on the last **lap** of the race.*
VERB laps, lapping, lapped
3 When water laps against something, it splashes gently against it.
*The waves **lapped** against the beach.*
4 When an animal laps up water, it drinks using its tongue.

laptop

NOUN laptops

A laptop is a small computer that you can carry around and can use on your lap.

large

ADJECTIVE larger, largest

Something that is large is big.

☞ **Similar:** big, enormous, gigantic, huge, massive, vast

Opposite: small

last

VERB lasts, lasting, lasted

1 How long something lasts is how long it takes before it is finished.

*My riding lesson **lasts** an hour.*

ADJECTIVE

2 The last one is the only one left.

*Who ate the **last** cookie?*

☞ **Opposite:** first

3 Last night or last week means the one that has just finished.

*We went to the movies **last** night.*

late

ADJECTIVE later, latest

If you are late, you do something after the time when you should do it.

*They were **late** for dinner.*

☞ **Similar:** delayed, overdue

Opposite: early

laugh

VERB laughs, laughing, laughed

When you laugh, you make a loud noise because you think that something is funny.

☞ **Say:** laff

Similar: chuckle, giggle, smile, snicker

law

NOUN

The law is the set of rules that all the people who live in a country must obey. The law is usually made by the government of a country.

lawn

NOUN lawns

A lawn is an area of grass in a yard or park.

lay

VERB lays, laying, laid

1 If you lay something somewhere, you put it there carefully.

*We **laid** all of our paintings out on the table.*

☞ **Similar:** leave, place, put, rest

2 When a bird lays an egg, it produces it from its body.

3 Lay is the past tense of the verb **lie**.

layer

NOUN layers

A layer is an amount of something that covers a surface.

*We put a **layer** of newspaper over our desks.*

lazy

ADJECTIVE lazier, laziest

Someone who is lazy does not want to work hard.

*Come and help us—don't be **lazy**.*

☞ **Opposite:** hard-working

lead

NOUN leads

1 If you are in the lead, you are in first place in a race or competition.

*She was in the **lead** all the way around the racetrack.*

VERB leads, leading, led

2 If you lead people to a place, you take them there.

☞ **Similar:** escort, guide, steer

3 If you lead a group of people, you are in charge of them.

*She **leads** by example.*

☞ **Rhymes:** feed

leader

NOUN leaders

The leader of a group of people is the person in charge.

*The **leader** of the group gave us clear instructions.*

☞ **Similar:** boss, captain, chief, commander, head, skipper

*Green **leaves** flutter in the breeze.*

leaf

leaf

NOUN leaves

The leaves on a plant are the thin, flat, green parts that grow on the stem or branches.

leak

NOUN leaks

A leak is a small hole or crack in something that lets liquid come out.

*There is a **leak** in this bottle.*

a
b
c
d
e
f
g
h
i
j
k

Ll

y
z

117

lean

lean
VERB leans, leaning, leaned
1 If you lean on something, you rest against it.
2 If something is leaning to one side, it bends to one side.

leap
VERB leaps, leaping, leaped or leapt
If you leap, you jump high into the air.
☞ **Similar:** bound, hop, jump, skip, spring

learn
VERB learns, learning, learned
When you learn about something, you find out about it and understand it.
*We **learned** how to make a cake at school today.*

least
ADJECTIVE
The least amount is the smallest amount.
*The person who has the **least** points loses the game.*

leather
NOUN
Leather is a material made from the skin of an animal. Shoes and bags are often made of leather.

leave
VERB leaves, leaving, left
1 When you leave a place, you go away from it.
*We'll **leave** after lunch.*
2 If you leave something, you do not take it with you.
*I **left** my swimsuit at school.*
3 If you leave something alone, you do not touch it.

led
Led is the past tense of the verb **lead**.

l e a p

He leapt over the hurdle.

l e m o n
A lemon as yellow

left
1 Left is the past tense of the verb **leave**.
ADJECTIVE
2 Your left side is the side that is opposite your right side.
*She writes with her **left** hand.*
☞ **Opposite:** right

leg
NOUN legs
1 Your legs are the long parts of your body between your hips and your feet.
2 The legs on a piece of furniture are the parts that it stands on.
*A chair has four **legs**.*

legal
ADJECTIVE
If something is legal, you are allowed to do it because it is within the law.
☞ **Say:** lee-gal
Opposite: illegal

legend
NOUN legends
A legend is a very old story.

legend Say: **lej-und**

as the Sun

lemon
NOUN lemons
A lemon is a yellow fruit with a sour taste.

lemonade
NOUN
Lemonade is a sweet and tart drink made from lemons.

lend
VERB lends, lending, lent
If you lend something to someone, you let them have it or use it for a short time.
☛ **Opposite:** borrow

length
NOUN lengths
1 The length of something is how long it is.
*We measured the **length** of the football field.*
2 A length of something is a long piece of it.

leopard
NOUN leopards
A leopard is a large animal that lives in Africa and Asia and belongs to the cat family. Leopards hunt at night and are good at climbing trees.
☛ **Say: lep**-ard

leotard
NOUN leotards
A leotard is a tight piece of clothing that you wear to dance or do gymnastics.
☛ **Say: lee**-o-tard
Word history: A **leotard** is named after a French man called Jules Leotard, who first invented it.

less
ADJECTIVE
If you have less of something, you do not have as much.
*I've got **less** chocolate than you!*
☛ **Opposite:** more

lesson
NOUN lessons
A lesson is a time when someone teaches you something.
*I have a piano **lesson** today.*

let
VERB lets, letting, let
If you let someone do something, you allow them to do it.
*The farmer **let** the children play in his fields.*

letter
NOUN letters
1 A letter is one of the symbols that we use to write words. There are 26 letters in the English alphabet.
2 A letter is a message that you write and send to someone.

lettuce
NOUN lettuces
Lettuce is a vegetable with large green leaves that people eat in salads.

library
NOUN libraries
A library is a place where you can go to borrow books, movies, and CDs.
☛ **Word history:** The word **library** comes from the Latin word *libraria*, meaning "bookshop."

lick
VERB licks, licking, licked
When you lick something, you touch it with your tongue.

lie
VERB lies, lying, lied
1 When you lie, you say something that you know is untrue.
*Michael **lied** when he said that I broke the window.*
VERB lies, lying, lay, lain
2 When you lie down, you rest with all your body flat on a bed or on the ground.
*I'm tired so I'm going to **lie** on my bed.*

Where can you go to borrow books?

Look around the page to find the answer.

life
NOUN lives
1 If there is life in a place, there are living things there.
*Is there **life** on Mars?*
2 Your life is the time that you are alive.
*My grandma had a long, happy **life**.*

a
b
c
d
e
f
g
h
i
j
k
Ll
m
n
o
p
q
r
s
t
u
v
w
x
y
z

lifeboat

NOUN lifeboats

A lifeboat is a boat for rescuing people who are in trouble at sea.

lift

NOUN lifts

1 If someone gives you a lift, they give you a ride in their car.

VERB lifts, lifting, lifted

2 When you lift something up, you pick it up.

light

NOUN lights

1 A light is something that shines to help you see in the dark.

*I had to turn on the **light** so I could see.*

VERB lights, lighting, lit

2 When you light something, you make it catch fire.

*We **lit** a candle.*

ADJECTIVE lighter, lightest

3 Something that is light does not weigh much.

*Your bag is very **light**.*

☞ **Opposite:** heavy

4 A light color is not very dark.

*Her dress was **light** blue.*

☞ **Opposite:** dark

lighthouse

NOUN lighthouses

A lighthouse is a tall tower with a bright, flashing light. The light warns ships that there are dangerous rocks near the coast.

lightning

NOUN

Lightning is a flash of light in the sky during a thunderstorm.

like

VERB likes, liking, liked

1 If you like someone, you get along well with them.

*I **like** our new teacher.*

2 If you like something, you enjoy it or think it is good.

*Do you **like** orange juice?*

☞ **Similar:** admire, adore, enjoy, love

Opposite: dislike

ADJECTIVE

3 If one thing is like another, it is similar to it.

*He looks **like** his brother.*

likely

ADJECTIVE

If something is likely, it will probably happen.

☞ **Opposite:** unlikely

limit

NOUN limits

A limit is a place or level where something ends.

line

NOUN lines

1 A line is a long, thin mark.

*Draw a **line** down the side of the page.*

2 A line of things is a straight row of them.

*There was a long **line** of people waiting to get into the museum.*

*The beam from the **lighthouse** warned ships to keep away.*

lighthouse

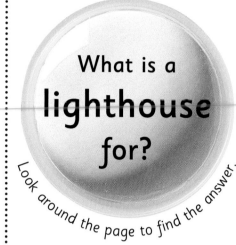

What is a lighthouse for?

Look around the page to find the answer.

lion

NOUN lions

A lion is a large, fierce animal that lives in Africa and India. Lions belong to the cat family and hunt animals such as antelopes and zebras. A female lion is called a **lioness**.

lip

NOUN lips

Your lips are the soft edges where your mouth is.

liquid

NOUN liquids

A liquid is a substance such as water that you can pour.

list

NOUN lists

When you make a list, you write down the names of people or things one after the other.

*We need to make a **list** of everyone on the team.*

listen

VERB listens, listening, listened

When you listen, you pay attention and hear something.

lit
Lit is the past tense of the verb **light**.

liter
NOUN liters
A liter is a unit in the metric system that is used for measuring liquids.

litter
NOUN
1 Litter is garbage that people have left lying around.
2 A litter is a number of baby animals that are born at the same time.

little
ADJECTIVE
1 Something that is little is small.
☞ **Similar:** miniature, minuscule, short, small, tiny,
Opposite: big
2 If you only have a little of something, you do not have much.
*I only have a **little** milk left.*
☞ **Opposite:** lot

live
VERB lives, living, lived
1 When you live, you are alive.
*He **lived** to an old age.*
2 The place where you live is the place that is your home.
☞ **Rhymes:** give

live
ADJECTIVE
1 Something that is live is living.
2 A live television show is not recorded, but is shown while it is actually taking place.
☞ **Rhymes:** dive

lizard
NOUN lizards
A lizard is a reptile, usually with four legs and a long tail. Many lizards live in warm countries and eat insects.

Two **lizards** sunbathing

load
NOUN loads
1 A load is an amount of something that you carry.
2 If you have loads of things, you have a lot of them.
☞ **Similar:** lots, masses, piles, stacks, tons
VERB loads, loading, loaded
3 When you load things into a vehicle, you put them in so that you can take them somewhere.

loaf
NOUN loaves
A loaf of bread is a large piece of bread that you can cut into slices.

lock
NOUN locks
1 A lock keeps a door or box shut. You need a key to open a lock.
☞ **Similar:** bolt, catch, fastening, padlock
2 A lock is a place on a canal that raises or lowers the water level, so that boats can move up and down.
VERB locks, locking, locked
3 When you lock something, you shut it by turning a key in a lock.

log
NOUN logs
A log is a thick piece of a tree's trunk or branch.

logo
NOUN logos
A logo is a small picture or sign that a company uses on its products.

lollipop
NOUN lollipops
A lollipop is a candy on a stick, which you lick. A lollipop is also called a sucker.

Delicious **lollipops** are lovely to lick.

lollipop

a b c d e f g h i j k Ll m n o p q r s t y z

mammal
NOUN mammals
A mammal is an animal that is warm-blooded and has hair or fur on its body. Female mammals feed their babies with milk. Cows, lions, and whales are all mammals. People are also mammals.

man
NOUN men
A man is an adult male person.

manage
VERB manages, managing, managed
1 The person who manages a store or business is in charge of it. This person is the **manager**.
*She **manages** a store, and has two assistants to help her.*
2 If you manage to do something, you do it even though it is difficult.
*She **managed** to swim all the way across the bay.*

manner
NOUN manners
1 The manner in which you do something is the way in which you do it.
*She always greets us in a friendly **manner**.*
2 Your manners are the way you behave when you are with other people.

many
ADJECTIVE
Many means a large number of people or things.
*There were so **many** people that I couldn't find my sister.*
☛ **Similar:** loads, lots, plenty, tons
Opposite: few

map
NOUN maps
A map is a drawing of a place. Maps show where towns, roads, rivers, and mountains are.

marathon
NOUN marathons
A marathon is a very long running race. A marathon is 26 miles 385 yards (42.19 km) long.
☛ **Word history:** When the Greek army defeated its enemies near the town of Marathon in 490 BC, a runner was sent to Athens with the good news. The modern marathon race is the same distance as the distance that ancient messenger ran.

I won lots of multicolored marbles.

marble
NOUN marbles
1 Marble is a hard stone that people sometimes use for building.
2 Marbles are small, glass balls that children play with.

Marine life

Spectacular marine life makes its home in the sea.

clown fish

angel fish

jellyfish

hermit crab

grape coral

brain coral

me

measu

VERB meas
measured
When you
you find o

meat

NOUN
Meat is th
part of an
animal tho
we can ea

medal

NOUN med
A medal is
round piec
metal on a
ribbon tha
given to yo
when you
a competiti
or when yo
have done
something
brave.

media

NOUN
The media
magazines,

medicin

NOUN medic
Medicine is
or a pill tho
make you b
are sick.
☛ **Say: me**

medium

ADJECTIVE
Something t
not very big
small. It is i

march

VERB marches, marching,
marched
When you march, you walk
with quick, regular steps, like
a soldier.
*The band **marched** in time to
the music.*

margarine

NOUN
Margarine is a soft substance
made from vegetable oils.
You spread it on bread like
butter.

marine ~Say:~
mar-een

marine

ADJECTIVE
Marine animals live in the
sea. Marine life is life in
the sea.

mark

NOUN marks
A mark is a scratch or
stain on something.
☛ **Similar:** blot, scratch,
smudge, spot, stain

market

NOUN markets
A market is a place where
you can buy things.
*We bought some fruit at
the **market**.*

marmalade

NOUN marmalades
Marmalade is jam made
from oranges.

married

ADJECTIVE
Someone who is married has
a husband or wife.

marry

VERB marries, marrying, married
When you marry someone,
you become their husband
or wife.

marsh

NOUN marshes
A marsh is an area of low
land near a river or the sea.
It is always wet and muddy.

marsupial

NOUN marsupials
A marsupial is an animal
that carries its babies in a
special pouch. Kangaroos
and koalas are marsupials.
☛ **Say:** mar-**soo**-pee-al

marvelous

ADJECTIVE
Something that is marvelous
is very good.

mash

VERB mashes, mashing, mashed
When you mash food, you
crush it so that it becomes
soft and smooth.

mask

NOUN masks
You wear a mask over your
face to hide it or protect it.

a
b
c
d
e
f
g
h
i
j
k
l
Mm
n
o
p

turtle

sea horse

mullet fish

sea anemone

lobster

sea cucumber

a me
NOU
1 A
2 A
of n
you
on c

mc
NOU
1 A
two
I'm
matc
☞ S
conte
2 A
that
roug
a fla
VERB
match
3 If t
the sc
This j

ma
NOUN
1 Mat
Her d
shiny
2 A m
that y
build
They u
materi
tree-ho

mat
NOUN
Mathe
which
and sh
often c
☞ Wo
mathe
Greek
meanin

mend

VERB mends, mending, mended
If you mend something that is broken, you fix it.
☞ **Similar:** fix, rebuild, repair

mental

ADJECTIVE
When you do mental arithmetic, you work out the problems in your head, without writing them down.

mention

VERB mentions, mentioning, mentioned
If you mention something, you talk about it a little bit but not very much.

menu Say: **men**-yoo

menu

NOUN menus
1 The menu in a restaurant is the list of things you can buy to eat there.
2 A menu on a computer is a list of things you can choose from.

mermaid

NOUN mermaids
In stories, a mermaid is a sea creature that has the body of a woman and the tail of a fish.

merry

ADJECTIVE merrier, merriest
If you are merry, you are happy and cheerful.
Everyone was very merry at the party.
☞ **Similar:** cheerful, happy, jolly, joyful

mess

NOUN messes
If a place is in a mess, it is dirty or untidy.
There was a big mess after they had finished cooking.
☞ **Similar:** chaos, clutter, disorder, untidiness

message

NOUN messages
If you leave a message for someone, you leave some written or recorded words for them to tell them something.

messy

ADJECTIVE messier, messiest
If a place is messy, it is dirty or untidy.
Your bedroom is always messy!
☞ **Opposite:** neat

met

Met is the past tense of the verb **meet**.

metal

NOUN metals
A metal is a hard substance that is found in rocks. Iron, gold, and copper are all metals.

meteorite

NOUN meteorites
A meteorite is a piece of rock that falls to Earth from space without burning up. A piece of rock that burns up as it enters the Earth's atmosphere is called a **meteor**.
☞ **Word history:** The words **meteor** and **meteorite** come from the Greek word *meteoros*, meaning "high up in the air."

meter

NOUN meters
In the metric system, when you say how long something is, you say how many meters it is.

method

NOUN methods
The method you use to do something is the way in which you do it.

mice

Mice is the plural of **mouse**.

Three little field mice scampering along

mice

microphone

NOUN microphones

You speak or sing into a microphone to make your voice sound louder.

microwave

NOUN microwaves

A microwave is an oven that cooks food quickly by passing electrical signals through it.

midday

NOUN

Midday is in the middle of the day.

☞ **Opposite:** midnight

middle

NOUN middles

The middle of something is the part near the center. *His house is in the **middle** of a forest.*

midnight

NOUN

Midnight is 12 o'clock at night.

☞ **Opposite:** noon

might

VERB

If something might happen, it is possible that it will happen. *It **might** snow later.*

☞ **Say:** mite

mild

ADJECTIVE milder, mildest

1 A mild soap or shampoo is not very strong and will not hurt your skin.
2 Mild weather is warm.

mile

NOUN miles

When you say how far away a place is, you say how many miles away it is.

milk

NOUN

Milk is the white liquid that mammals produce to feed their babies. People drink cow's milk, and also use it to make butter, cream, yogurt, and cheese.

milkshake

NOUN milkshakes

A milkshake is a sweet drink that is made with milk.

milkshake

A delicious strawberry milkshake

millennium

NOUN millenniums or millennia

A millennium is one thousand years.

millimeter

NOUN millimeters

In the metric system, you can measure how long something is by saying how many millimeters it is. You use millimeters for measuring short lengths.

million

NOUN millions

A million is a thousand thousands (1,000,000).

millionaire

NOUN millionaires

A millionaire is a very rich person who has money and property worth more than a million dollars.

mind

NOUN minds

1 Your mind is the way that you think and remember things.
☞ **Similar:** brain, intelligence
2 If you change your mind, you change something that you had already decided. *I've changed my **mind**—I don't want to go shopping now.*

mine

NOUN mines

A mine is a deep hole in the ground where coal or metals are dug out of rock.

miniature

ADJECTIVE

Miniature means very small.
☞ **Say:** min-ee-a-cher

a b c d e f g h i j k l **Mm** n o p q r s t u v w x y z

a
b
c
d
e
f
g
h
i
j
k
l
m
Nn
o
p
q
r
s
t
u
v
w
x
y

new

ADJECTIVE newer, newest
1 If something is new, it has only just been made or you have only just bought it.
*Do you like my **new** shirt?*
2 If you go to a new place, you go to a place where you have not been before.
*We're moving, so I'll be going to a **new** school.*
☞ **Opposite:** old

news

NOUN
The news is information about things that are happening in the world.
*Do you watch the **news** on television?*

next

ADJECTIVE
1 The next person or thing is the one that comes immediately after this one.
*Who is the **next** person in line?*
2 The next room or house is the one nearest to you.
*My brother sleeps in the **next** room.*

nibble

VERB nibbles, nibbling, nibbled
When you nibble food, you eat it by taking very small bites.

*Chipmunks love **nibbling** nuts.*

nibble

Where does the word nightmare come from?

Look around the page to find the answer.

nice

ADJECTIVE nicer, nicest
1 Something that is nice is pleasant.
*We had a **nice** day at the beach.*
☞ **Similar:** enjoyable, fun, interesting, lovely, pleasant
Opposite: horrible
2 A nice person is kind to other people.
☞ **Similar:** charming, friendly, generous, likable, pleasant, polite
Opposite: mean, unkind

niche

NOUN niches
A niche is a hollow in a wall used as a place for statues or vases.

nickname

NOUN nicknames
A nickname is a short, friendly name that you call someone instead of their real name.
*William's **nickname** is Bill.*

niece

NOUN nieces
Your niece is the daughter of your brother or sister.
☞ **Say:** neess

night

NOUN nights
Night is the time between sunset and sunrise when the sky is dark.
☞ **Opposite:** day

nightgown

NOUN nightgowns
A nightgown is a dress that girls and women wear to sleep in. A nightgown is also called a **nightie**.

nightmare

NOUN nightmares
A nightmare is a bad, frightening dream.
☞ **Word history:** The word **nightmare** comes from the words "night" and "mare." A mare was the name of an evil spirit that was believed to sit on your chest at night and give you horrible dreams.

nocturnal

ADJECTIVE
Nocturnal animals are active at night.
*Bats are **nocturnal**.*

nod

VERB nods, nodding, nodded
When you nod your head, you move it up and down.
*She **nodded** in my direction.*

noise

NOUN noises
A noise is a sound that you can hear, especially a loud, unpleasant one. Something that makes a loud noise is **noisy**.
*He was making a lot of **noise**.*
☞ **Similar:** racket, uproar
Opposite: quiet

Nightlife

Many animals are active at night.
Here are some words to describe
nightlife.

whooooo!

owl

moths

bright, brilliant, full, shining

MOON

nocturnal monkey

diving

Swooping

glowing

fireflies

bat

squeak!

bush baby

big eyes

chase, creep, follow, hunt, prowl

tiger

dark, dim, gloomy, shadowy, shady

thick undergrowth

ROAR!

Growl!

opossum

a
b
c
d
e

octopus

NOUN octopuses or octopi
An octopus is a sea animal that has eight arms called tentacles. It uses its tentacles for catching crabs and fish to eat.
☞ **Word history:** The word **octopus** comes from the Greek words *octo* and *pous*, which mean "eight feet."

Why are you wearing odd socks?

odd

m
n

Oo

odd

p
q
r
s
t
u
v
w
x
y
z

ADJECTIVE odder, oddest
1 Something that is odd is strange and not normal.
He was wearing some very **odd** *clothes!*
☞ **Similar:** bizarre, extraordinary, peculiar, strange, weird
Opposite: normal
2 Odd socks or shoes do not go together as a pair.
3 An odd number cannot be divided by two.
☞ **Opposite:** even

offer

VERB offers, offering, offered
If you offer something to someone, you ask them if they would like it.
He **offered** *her some grapes.*

140

office

NOUN offices
An office is a place where people work at desks.

officer

NOUN officers
1 An officer is a member of the police.
2 In the army, navy, or airforce, an officer is someone who gives orders to other people.

oil

NOUN
1 Oil is a thick, black liquid that is found underground. We use oil to make gasoline and plastics.
2 Oil is a thick, clear, smooth liquid that you use in cooking. This type of oil comes from the seeds of plants.

ointment

NOUN ointments
An ointment is a substance that you put on your skin when it is sore to make it better.
☞ **Similar:** cream, lotion

old

ADJECTIVE older, oldest
1 Something that is old has been used for a long time.
We found some **old** *toys in the attic.*
☞ **Similar:** ancient, old-fashioned, worn-out
Opposite: new
2 Someone who is old has lived for a long time.
☞ **Similar:** aged, elderly, mature
Opposite: young

onion

NOUN onions
An onion is a round, white vegetable with a strong taste and smell. The smell of onions sometimes makes your eyes water.

online

ADJECTIVE
When you are online, you are working on a computer that is connected to the internet.

open

VERB opens, opening, opened
1 When you open a door, you move it so that people can go through it.
☞ **Similar:** unbolt, unfasten, unlock
2 When you open something, you take the lid or wrapping off of it.
May I **open** *my presents now?*
ADJECTIVE
3 Something that is open is not closed or shut.
Come in, the door is **open**.

old

My favorite teddy is very old.

quality

NOUN qualities
The quality of something is how good or bad it is.
*Use a good **quality** tape to record the movie.*
☞ **Say: kwol**-i-tee

quantity

NOUN quantities
A quantity is an amount.

*I can't believe we ate such a large **quantity** of food in one weekend!*

quantity

Say:

kwon-ti-tee

quarrel

VERB quarrels, quarreling, quarreled
When people quarrel, they shout at each other because they are angry with each other.
☞ **Say: kwor**-rul
Similar: argue, squabble

quarry

NOUN quarries
A quarry is a place where stone is dug out of the ground.
☞ **Say: kwor**-ee

quarter

NOUN quarters
1 If you divide something into four quarters, you divide it into four equal parts. Each part is called one quarter.
2 A quarter is a coin worth 25 cents.
☞ **Say: kwor**-ter
Word history: The word **quarter** comes from the Latin word *quartus*, which means "fourth."

queen

NOUN queens
A queen is a woman who rules a country.

query

VERB queries, querying, queried
When you query something, you ask questions about it.

question

NOUN questions
When you ask a question, you ask someone something because you want to know the answer.
☞ **Opposite:** answer

quick

ADJECTIVE quicker, quickest
Something that is quick does not take long. You can also say that you do something **quickly**.
*It was a **quick** journey.*
☞ **Similar:** fast, speedy, swift
Opposite: slow

quiet

ADJECTIVE quieter, quietest
If it is quiet in a place, there is no noise. If you are quiet, you do not make any noise. You can also say that you do something **quietly**.
☞ **Similar:** calm, peaceful, silent, still
Opposite: noisy

quilt

NOUN quilts
A quilt is a thick cover that you put on a bed. It usually has many shapes sewn on and has many designs.

quite

ADVERB
Quite means fairly.
*I am **quite** good at running.*
☞ **Similar:** moderately, pretty, rather

quiz

NOUN quizzes
A quiz is a short oral or written test.
*We had a **quiz** at school today.*

161

a
b
c
d
e
f
g
h
i
j
k
l
m
n
o
p
q
Rr
s
t

R

ring ring ring ring ring ring ring ring ring ring ring ring ring

rabbit

NOUN rabbits

A rabbit is a small, furry animal. Rabbits live underground in burrows and eat grass and roots.

*Two furry **rabbits** twitch their noses.*

race

NOUN races

A race is a competition to see who can go the fastest. *Joshua won the **race**.*

rack

NOUN racks

A rack is a special shelf for putting things on.

racket

NOUN rackets

1 A racket is a bat that you use to play tennis and badminton.
2 A racket is a very loud, annoying noise.
*He was making a terrible **racket** with his drums.*
☛ **Similar:** uproar

radiator

NOUN radiators

A radiator is a heater attached to a wall. A radiator contains steam from hot water.
☛ **Say: ray**-dee-ay-tor

radio

NOUN radios

A radio is a machine that you use to listen to programs that are broadcast.

raffle

NOUN raffles

When there is a raffle, people buy tickets with numbers printed on them, and if their number is chosen, they win a prize. *He won a teddy bear in the **raffle**.*

raft

NOUN rafts

A raft is a small, flat boat that is made from logs, which are tied together.

rag

NOUN rags

A rag is a small, torn piece of cloth.

rage

NOUN

Rage is very great anger. *She left in a **rage**.*
☛ **Similar:** anger, fury

rail

NOUN rails

1 A rail is a long metal or wooden bar.
*Hold onto the **rail** as you climb.*
2 If you travel by rail, you travel on a train.

railroad

NOUN railroads

1 A railroad line is the two metal bars that trains travel along.
2 If you travel on the railroads, you travel on a train.

rain

NOUN

1 Rain is water that falls from the clouds in drops.
VERB rains, raining, rained
2 When it rains, water falls from the clouds.
☛ **Similar:** drizzle, pour, spit

rainbow

NOUN rainbows

A rainbow is an arc of colors that appears in the sky when the sun shines during rain.

*A **rainbow** shines between the clouds.*

rainbow

raindrop

NOUN raindrops

A raindrop is one drop of rain.

rain forest

NOUN rain forests

A rain forest is a hot, wet jungle that grows in tropical countries.

raise

VERB raises, raising, raised

If you raise something, you lift it up.

rake

NOUN rakes

A rake is a tool that you use to gather up leaves into a pile or to smooth over soil.

Ramadan

NOUN

Ramadan is a time each year when Muslims do not eat between the time the sun comes up in the morning and the time it sets at night.

ramp

NOUN ramps

A ramp is a slope that you go up or down.
*We drove up a **ramp** to the boat.*

rang

Rang is the past tense of the verb **ring**.

range

NOUN ranges

A range of things is a lot of different things.
*There is a **range** of activities for children at the camp.*

rapid

ADJECTIVE

Rapid means quick.
*The **rapid** horse beat the others to the finish.*
☞ **Similar:** fast, quick, speedy, swift

rare

ADJECTIVE rarer, rarest

If something is rare, you do not see it very often.
*Wild tigers are now **rare**.*
☞ **Similar:** scarce, unusual
Opposite: common

rash

NOUN rashes

If you have a rash, you have red, itchy spots on your skin.

raspberry

NOUN raspberries

A raspberry is a juicy, red fruit that grows on a bush.

rat

NOUN rats

A rat is an animal that looks like a big mouse. Rats have strong front teeth, which they use to gnaw food.

rather

ADVERB

1 Rather means somewhat.
*He looked **rather** sad.*
☞ **Similar:** fairly, slightly, somewhat
2 If you would rather have or do something, you would prefer to have or do that thing.
*I don't want to go to the movies—I would **rather** stay at home.*

Look around the page to find the answer.

What is the opposite of rare?

raspberry Say: raz-bair-ee

ran

Ran is the past tense of the verb **run**.

ranch

NOUN ranches

A ranch is a large farm where animals are kept.

*We picked some **raspberries** for lunch.*

a b c d e f g h i j k l m n o p q **Rr** s t u v w x y z

a
b
c
d
e
f
g
h
i
j
k
l
m
n
o
p
q
Rr
s
t
u
v
w
x
y
z

rattle

NOUN rattles

1 A rattle is a baby's toy that makes a noise when you shake it.

VERB rattles, rattling, rattled

2 When something rattles, it makes a loud noise.

☞ **Similar:** bang, clang, clank, clatter, jangle

raw

ADJECTIVE

Raw food has not been cooked.

Some raw vegetables are very good for you.

ray

NOUN rays

A ray of light is a beam of light.

razor

NOUN razors

A razor is a sharp tool that people use to shave.

reach

VERB reaches, reaching, reached

1 If you reach toward something, you stretch out your hand to touch it.

2 If you reach a place, you arrive there.

react

VERB reacts, reacting, reacted

When you react to something that has happened, you say or do something because it has happened.

*When his bike was stolen, he **reacted** by bursting into tears.*

☞ **Say:** ree-**akt**

read

VERB reads, reading, read

When you read, you look at words that are written down and understand them.

ready

ADJECTIVE

If you are ready, you are prepared and so you can do something.

*Are you **ready** to leave?*

☞ **Say:** red-ee

Similar: all set, organized, prepared

We finally **reached** the top of the hill. reach

real

ADJECTIVE

Something that is real is true, and is not false.

*Is that **real** gold?*

☞ **Similar:** genuine, true

Opposite: fake

realize

VERB realizes, realizing, realized

When you realize that something is true, you begin to understand it.

*She **realized** she was going to be late for school.*

Look around the page to find the answer.

What is the word for making something smaller?

really

ADVERB

1 Really means very.

*The film was **really** funny.*

2 Really means in real life.

*Is it **really** true that you're leaving?*

reason

NOUN reasons

1 The reason why you do something is the thing that makes you do it.

*Can you explain the **reason** why you hit your brother?*

2 The reason why something happens is the thing that causes it to happen.

receipt

NOUN receipts

A receipt is a piece of paper that shows you have received something or paid for it.

☞ **Say:** ri-**seet**

receive

VERB receives, receiving, received

When you receive something, someone gives it or sends it to you.

☞ **Say:** ri-**seeve**

Similar: gain, get, obtain

recipe

NOUN recipes

A recipe tells you how to cook something.

☞ **Say: res**-i-pee

recite

VERB recites, reciting, recited

When you recite a poem, you say it out loud without reading it.

*He **recited** the poem that he'd learned by heart.*

recognize

VERB recognizes, recognizing, recognized

If you recognize someone, you know who they are. If you recognize something, you know what it is.

*He **recognized** his friend's bike.*

record

NOUN records

1 The record for doing something is the fastest, best, or most that it has ever been done.

*He holds the world **record** for the 100-meter race.*

2 A record is a piece of information that is written down.

*She kept a **record** of the day's events in her diary.*

☞ **Say: rek**-ord

record

VERB records, recording, recorded

1 When you record sound or pictures, you store them on tape, film, or disk.

*I **recorded** the film last night.*

2 If you record information, you write it down.

☞ **Say:** ri-**kord**

recorder

NOUN recorders

A recorder is a small musical instrument that you blow into. You make different notes by covering different holes with your fingers.

recover

VERB recovers, recovering, recovered

When you recover, you get better after you have been ill.

rectangle

NOUN rectangles

A rectangle is a shape that has four straight sides. A rectangle is not square, but has two long sides and two short sides. Something that is the shape of a rectangle is **rectangular**.

recycle

Say: **ree-sie-kul**

*It helps the environment to **recycle**.*

recycle

VERB recycles, recycling, recycled

To recycle things means to use them again, often by turning them into new things. Glass, plastics, paper, and metal can all be recycled.

red

ADJECTIVE

Something that is red is the color of blood.

☞ **Similar:** crimson, rosy, ruby, scarlet

reduce

VERB reduces, reducing, reduced

If you reduce something, you make it smaller.

*The store **reduced** its price on all apples.*

☞ **Say:** ri-**doos**

refer

VERB refers, referring, referred

If you refer to something, you mention it.

referee

NOUN referees

The referee in a game is the person who watches the game and makes sure that people follow all the rules.

reference

ADJECTIVE

Reference books give you information.

reflection

NOUN reflections

A reflection is the image that you see when you look in a mirror.

reflection *A cat stares at its reflection.*

a
b
c
d
e
f
g
h
i
j
k
l
m
n
o
p
q
Rr
s

a
b
c
d
e
f
g
h
i
j
k
l
m
n
o
p
q
Rr
s
t
u
v
w
x
y
z

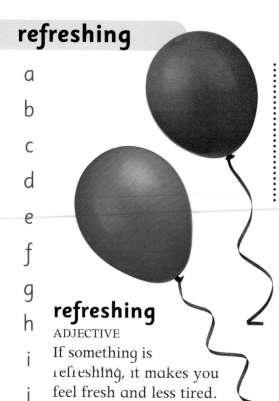

refreshing

ADJECTIVE

If something is refreshing, it makes you feel fresh and less tired.

refreshments

NOUN

Refreshments are things to eat and drink.
We had some refreshments after the game.

refrigerator

NOUN refrigerators

A refrigerator is a machine that keeps food and beverages cool and fresh. A refrigerator is also called a **fridge**.

refuse

VERB refuses, refusing, refused

If you refuse to do something, you say that you will not do it.
He refused to give her the ball.
☞ **Say:** ri-**fyooz**

register

NOUN registers

A register is a book in which you keep a list of names.
☞ **Word history:** The word **register** comes from the Latin word *regestum*, which means "list."

regret

VERB regrets, regretting, regretted

If you regret doing something, you are sorry that you did it.
He regretted being angry with his sister.

Look around the page to find the answer.

What is the past tense of reply?

rehearse

VERB rehearses, rehearsing, rehearsed

When you rehearse something, you practice it before you do it in front of people.
We need to rehearse the play before we perform it.
☞ **Say:** ri-**herss**

reign

VERB reigns, reigning, reigned

When someone reigns, they are the king or queen of a country.
☞ **Say: rain**

rein

NOUN reins

Reins are leather straps that you use to control a horse when you are riding it.
☞ **Say: rain**

reindeer

NOUN reindeer or reindeers

A reindeer is a deer with large antlers that lives in cold, Arctic regions.

relative

NOUN relatives

Your relatives are the people who are in your family.

relax

VERB relaxes, relaxing, relaxed

When you relax, you rest and feel comfortable.
She relaxed in front of the fire and read her book.
☞ **Similar:** calm down, unwind

release

VERB releases, releasing, released

To release someone means to let them go free. To release something means to let go of it.
They released the prisoner.

release

Marcus released the balloons.

relief
NOUN
If something is a relief, you are glad that it has happened because it means you can stop worrying.
*It was a **relief** when the exam was over.*
☞ **Say:** ri-**leef**

religion
NOUN religions
A religion is a set of beliefs and ideas about God or gods.

reluctant
ADJECTIVE
If you are reluctant to do something, you do not want to do it.
*He was **reluctant** to cross the old bridge.*
☞ **Similar:** hesitant, unwilling
Opposite: eager

rely
VERB relies, relying, relied
If you rely on someone, you need them and depend on them.
*Young birds **rely** on their parents for food.*
☞ **Say:** ri-**lie**

remain
VERB remains, remaining, remained
1 If you remain in a place, you stay there.
*He **remained** there alone.*
2 To remain means to stay.
*She **remained** calm while everyone else panicked.*

remark
NOUN remarks
A remark is something that you say.

remember
VERB remembers, remembering, remembered
If you remember something, you think about it again.
*She suddenly **remembered** she had left her bag on the bus.*

remind
VERB reminds, reminding, reminded
To remind someone of something means to make them think about it again.

remove
VERB removes, removing, removed
If you remove something, you take it off or take it away.
*She **removed** her shoe to get a stone out.*

repair
VERB repairs, repairing, repaired
When you repair something, you mend it.
☞ **Similar:** fix, mend

repeat
VERB repeats, repeating, repeated
If you repeat something, you say it again.

reply
VERB replies, replying, replied
If you reply, you say something when someone has spoken to you or asked you a question. The thing that you say is your reply.
*He **replied** to the invitation immediately.*
☞ **Similar:** answer, respond

report
NOUN reports
A report is a piece of writing that gives information about things that have happened.

lizard

reptile
NOUN reptiles
A reptile is a cold-blooded animal that has dry, scaly skin and lays eggs. Crocodiles, snakes, lizards, and tortoises are all reptiles.

tortoise

crocodile

Word history:
The word **reptile** comes from the Latin word *repere*, which means "to crawl," because many reptiles crawl along the ground.

reptile

snake

a
b
c
d
h
i
j
k
m

Rr

s
t
u

rescue

air-rescue helicopter

fire fighter

fire engine

police car

police officer

rescue

VERB rescues, rescuing, rescued
If you rescue someone, you save them from danger.

research

NOUN
When you do research, you find out information about something.

resource

NOUN resources
A resource is something that people can use.
*Oil is a natural **resource**.*
☛ **Say:** ree-**sorss**

respect

NOUN
If you have respect for someone, you admire them.
*I have **respect** for my teacher.*

responsible

ADJECTIVE
1 If someone is responsible, they are sensible and you can trust them.
2 If you are responsible for doing something, it is your job.

rest

NOUN
1 A rest is a time when you are relaxing and not working.
☛ **Similar:** break, interval, pause
2 The rest is all the people and things that are left over.
*Taylor ate most of the cake, and I ate the **rest**.*

restaurant

NOUN restaurants
A restaurant is a place where you can go to buy and eat a meal.
☛ **Say:** **rest**-er-ront
Word history: The word **restaurant** comes from the French word *restaurer*, which means "to restore," because a restaurant is a place that "restores" you, or makes you feel stronger.

result

NOUN results
1 The result in a game is the score at the end of the game.
2 The result of something is what happens because of it.

return

VERB returns, returning, returned
1 To return to a place means to go back there.
*We **returned** home after school.*
2 If you return something to someone, you give it back to them.
*Juanita **returned** my book to me.*

reveal

VERB reveals, revealing, revealed
If you reveal something, you uncover it so that people can see it.

revenge

NOUN
Revenge is when you hurt someone or do something unpleasant to them because they have hurt or upset you.

168

To the rescue

If you are in danger, one of these will come to the rescue.

ambulance

paramedic

coast guard rescuer

lifeboat

reward
NOUN rewards
If you give someone a reward, you give them money or something nice because they have done something good.
They offered a reward to anyone who found their cat.
☛ **Similar:** award, prize

rhinoceros
NOUN rhinoceroses
A rhinoceros is a large animal that lives in hot countries. Rhinoceroses have thick skin and one or two horns on their noses.
☛ **Word history:** The word **rhinoceros** comes from the Greek words *rhino* and *keras*, which mean "nose horn."

rhyme
NOUN rhymes
1 A rhyme is a poem in which the last words of some lines have the same sound.
☛ **Similar:** poem, song, verse
VERB rhymes, rhyming, rhymed
2 Two or more words rhyme when they end in the same sound.
☛ **Say: rime**

rhythm
NOUN rhythms
A rhythm is a regular beat in music, dancing, or poetry.
☛ **Say: rith-um**

ribbon
NOUN ribbons
A ribbon is a piece of colored material that you use for tying up a package or tying in your hair.

rice
NOUN
Rice is a plant that grows in warm, wet climates. You can cook and eat the white or brown seeds of the rice plant.

rich
ADJECTIVE richer, richest
Someone who is rich has a lot of money.
☛ **Similar:** affluent, wealthy, well-off
Opposite: poor

riddle
NOUN riddles
A riddle is a difficult puzzle that has a clever or funny answer.

ride
VERB rides, riding, rode, ridden
1 When you ride a horse or bicycle, you sit on it and move along.
I ride my bike to school.
2 When you ride on a bus, train, or other vehicle, you sit on it while it moves.

rhinoceros
Say:
ry-noss-er-us

a b c d e i j k l m n o p q **Rr** s t u v w x y z

a b c d e f g h i j k l m n o p q **Rr** s t u v w x y z

ridiculous

ADJECTIVE

Something that is ridiculous is very silly or strange.

She looked **ridiculous** *in her brother's clothes.*

☞ **Similar:** crazy, foolish, funny

ridiculous Say: ri-dik-yoo-lus

right

ADJECTIVE

1 Your right side is the side that is opposite your left side.

He kicks with his **right** *foot.*

☞ **Opposite:** left

2 Something that is right is correct.

That is the **right** *answer.*

☞ **Similar:** accurate, correct, exact, precise

Opposite: wrong

3 Something that is right is fair and good.

It's not **right** *that she should have all the candy.*

ring

NOUN rings

1 A ring is a piece of jewelry that you wear on your finger.

She was upset at losing her wedding **ring**.

VERB rings, ringing, rang, rung

2 When a bell rings, it makes a pleasant sound because you have hit it or shaken it.

The school bell **rings** *at the end of class.*

☞ **Similar:** chime, clang, jangle, jingle

rinse

VERB rinses, rinsing, rinsed

When you rinse something, you wash it in clean water.

rip

VERB rips, ripping, ripped

If you rip a piece of paper or cloth, you tear it.

He **ripped** *the piece of paper in half.*

☞ **Similar:** rend, shred, split, tear

ripe

ADJECTIVE riper, ripest

Fruit that is ripe is soft and ready to eat.

rise

VERB rises, rising, rose, risen

To rise means to go upward.

☞ **Similar:** ascend, climb

Look around the page to find the answer.

What color is a robin's chest?

river

NOUN rivers

A river is a large stream of water that flows into another river, a lake, or an ocean.

road

NOUN roads

A road is a wide, smooth path that cars and other vehicles can drive along.

☞ **Similar:** highway, lane, street

roar

VERB roars, roaring, roared

1 When an animal roars, it makes a loud, deep, rumbling noise.

The angry lion **roared**.

2 If someone roars, they shout loudly.

☞ **Similar:** bellow, shout, thunder, yell

roast

VERB roasts, roasting, roasted

When you roast meat or vegetables, you cook them in a hot oven or over a fire.

rob

VERB robs, robbing, robbed

To rob someone means to steal things from them.

They **robbed** *the bank.*

robin

NOUN robins

A robin is a small bird with a red chest.

robot

NOUN robots

A robot is a machine that can do jobs that a person usually does.

rocket

NOUN rockets

1 A rocket is a long, thin spacecraft.

2 A rocket is a type of firework that shoots into the sky and explodes.

rod

NOUN rods

A rod is a thin piece of wood or metal.

Jacob got a fishing **rod** *for his birthday.*

Robot

Robots can now perform many different jobs. Here are some words to describe robots.

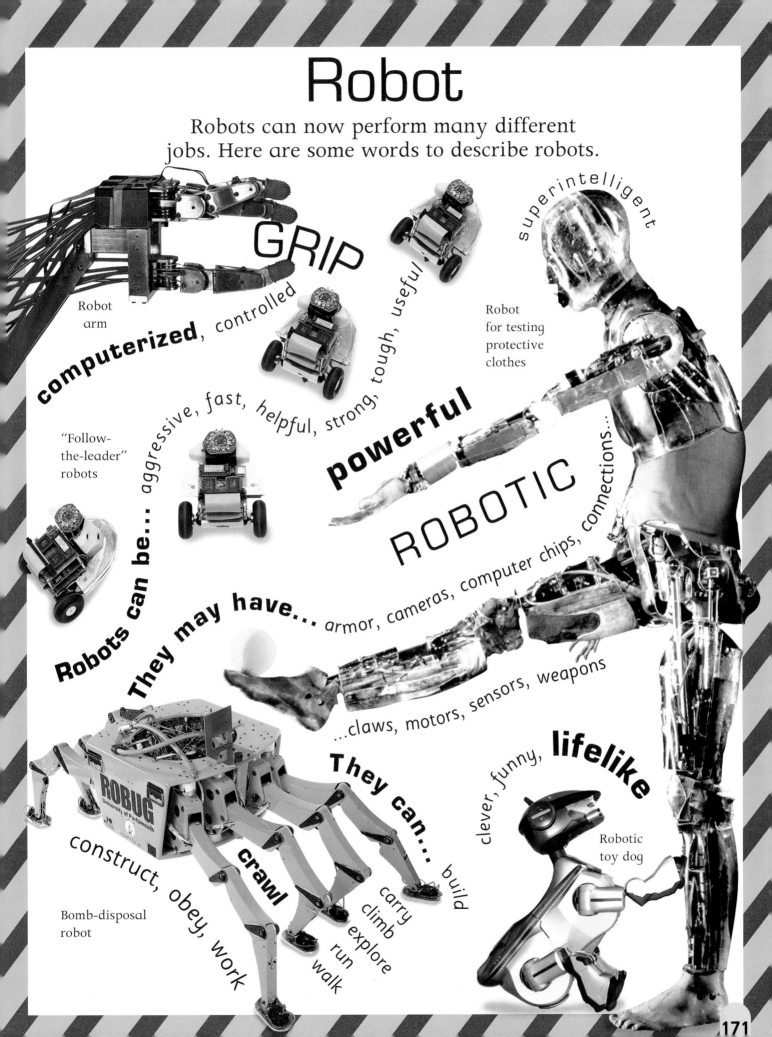

GRIP

superintelligent

Robot arm

computerized, controlled

Robot for testing protective clothes

"Follow-the-leader" robots

aggressive, fast, helpful, strong, tough, useful

powerful

Robots can be...

ROBOTIC

connections...

They may have... armor, cameras, computer chips,

...claws, motors, sensors, weapons

They can... build

clever, funny, lifelike

construct, obey, work

crawl

Bomb-disposal robot

carry climb explore run walk

Robotic toy dog

a
b
c
d
e
f
g
h
i
j
k
l
m
n
o
p
q
Rr
s
t
u
v
w
x
y
z

rodent

NOUN rodents

A rodent is an animal with long front teeth for gnawing food. Rats, mice, and squirrels are rodents.

☞ **Say: roh-dent**

Word history: The word **rodent** comes from the Latin word *rodere*, which means "to gnaw."

roll

NOUN rolls

1 A roll of paper is an amount of it that has been wound onto a tube.
*We bought a **roll** of wrapping paper.*
2 A roll is a small, round piece of bread.
VERB rolls, rolling, rolled
3 When something rolls, it moves along by turning over and over.
*The logs **rolled** down the hill.*
4 When something rolls, it moves along on wheels.
*I let go of the buggy, and it **rolled** down the street.*

roller skate

NOUN roller skates

Roller skates are a type of boots with two rows of wheels attached to the bottom. When you wear them, you go **roller-skating**.
*I got some new **roller skates** for my birthday.*

roof

NOUN roofs

1 The roof on a building is the sloping part on top of it.
2 The roof of your mouth or a cave is the top part inside it.

room

NOUN rooms

1 The rooms in a building are the separate parts inside the building.
*Which **room** will I be sleeping in?*
2 If there is room for something, there is enough space for it.
*Is there any **room** in the car for me?*

root

NOUN roots

The roots on a plant are the parts that grow underground.

rope

*Jack tugged on the **rope**.*

rope

NOUN ropes

A rope is a piece of thick, strong string or wire.
☞ **Similar:** cable, cord

rose

NOUN roses

1 A rose is a flower that grows on a prickly bush.
2 Rose is the past tense of the verb **rise**.

rot

VERB rots, rotting, rotted
When something rots, it is no longer fresh and it goes bad and starts to break down.
☞ **Similar:** crumble, decay

rotten

ADJECTIVE

Something that is rotten is no longer fresh, but has gone bad.

rough

ADJECTIVE rougher, roughest
1 Something that is rough is not smooth or even.
*The sea is very **rough**.*
2 A rough amount is not exact.
☞ **Say: ruff**

roughly

ADVERB

Roughly means more or less, but not exactly.
*There are **roughly** 30 children in each class.*

round

ADJECTIVE

Something that is round is shaped like a circle.

route

NOUN routes

Your route is the way that you go to get from one place to another.
*We drew our **route** on the map.*
☞ **Say: root**

row

NOUN rows

1 A row of things is a line of them.
VERB rows, rowing, rowed
2 When you row a boat, you make it move with oars.
☞ **Rhymes:** toe

royal

ADJECTIVE

Royal means to do with a king or queen.

rub

VERB rubs, rubbing, rubbed

When you rub something, you move your hand backward and forward over it.

*She **rubbed** her wet hair with a towel.*

rubber

rubber

NOUN

Rubber is a soft, stretchy material. Car tires are made of rubber.

rude

ADJECTIVE

Someone who is rude talks or behaves in a way that is not polite.

☛ **Similar:** bad-mannered, impolite

Opposite: polite

rug

NOUN rugs

A rug is a small carpet.

ruin

NOUN ruins

1 The ruins of a building are the broken parts that remain after it has been destroyed.

*The town was in **ruins** after the war.*

VERB ruins, ruining, ruined

2 To ruin something means to spoil it.

*She **ruined** her dress by spilling ink on it.*

rule

NOUN rules

1 A rule is an instruction that tells you what you must and must not do.

*Do you know the **rules** of basketball?*

VERB rules, ruling, ruled

2 To rule a country means to be in charge of it.

*She **ruled** the country for 20 years.*

*All the toys have **rubber** tires.*

ruler

NOUN rulers

1 A ruler is a straight piece of wood, metal, or plastic that you use for measuring and drawing straight lines.

2 A ruler is a person who rules a country.

ruling

NOUN

A ruling is a decision made by someone in authority that people have to obey.

*The **ruling** meant that the students had to arrive on time.*

rumble

VERB rumbles, rumbling, rumbled

When something rumbles, it makes a long, low sound, like the noise thunder makes.

rumor

NOUN rumors

A rumor is a story that is passed from person to person that may or may not be true.

*The **rumors** spread quickly.*

run

VERB runs, running, ran, run

1 When you run, you go forward by moving your legs quickly.

☛ **Similar:** gallop, jog, sprint

2 If you run something, you organize it.

*He **runs** the school cafeteria.*

runway

NOUN runways

A runway is a long, flat strip of ground, from which an airplane can take off and land.

rush

VERB rushes, rushing, rushed

1 If you rush, you run quickly.

*She **rushed** out of the room.*

☛ **Similar:** charge, dash, race, run, sprint

2 If you rush, you hurry to do something quickly.

*Marie **rushed** to finish her work.*

rust

NOUN

Rust forms on some metals when they get wet, and makes them turn brown.

rustle

VERB rustles, rustling, rustled

When leaves rustle, they make a soft sound.

*The leaves on the tree **rustled** in the wind.*

a
b
c
d
e
f

k
l
m
n
o
p
q
Rr
s
t
u
v
w
x
y
z

173

a
b
c
d
e
f
g
h
i
j
k
l
m
n
o
p
q
r
Ss
t
u
v
w
x
y
z

S

Shade

sack
NOUN sacks
A sack is a large, strong bag.

sad
ADJECTIVE sadder, saddest
If you are sad, you are not happy.
*He was **sad** when his best friend moved to Canada.*
☛ **Similar:** depressed, miserable, unhappy, upset
Opposite: happy

saddle
NOUN saddles
The saddle on a horse is the seat that you sit on.
*The **saddle** was made of leather.*

safari
NOUN safaris
A safari is a trip to hunt or watch wild animals, usually in Africa.
☛ **Say:** sa-**far**-ree
Word history: The word **safari** comes from the Arabic word *safara*, meaning "to travel."

safe
NOUN safes
1 A safe is a metal container that you can lock, in which you keep money and valuable things.
ADJECTIVE safer, safest
2 If you are safe, you are not hurt and not in danger.
*Tom phoned home to say that he was **safe** and well.*
☛ **Similar:** unharmed, unhurt, uninjured
3 Something that is safe is not dangerous.
*All the amusement park rides are perfectly **safe**.*

said
Said is the past tense of the verb **say**.

sail
NOUN sails
1 A sail is a large piece of material on a boat that catches the wind and helps to move the boat along.
VERB sails, sailing, sailed
2 When you sail, you travel across water in a ship or boat.
*He **sailed** his boat a long way down the river.*

sailor
NOUN sailors
A sailor is someone who sails on a boat.

salad
NOUN salads
A salad is a mixture of raw vegetables or fruit.

salary
NOUN salaries
Someone's salary is the money that they earn for doing their job.
☛ **Similar:** earnings, pay, wage

sale
NOUN sales
1 If something is for sale, you can buy it.
*Are these toys for **sale**?*
2 When there is a sale, things are sold for less money than usual.
*I always buy clothes that are on **sale**.*

sail

*Sailboats have colorful **sails**.*

salmon

NOUN

A salmon is a large fish that you can eat.
☞ **Say: sam**-un

salt

NOUN

Salt is a white powder that people add to meat and vegetables to improve the flavor. Salt is found in the sea and in rocks. Something that tastes of salt tastes **salty**.

salute

VERB salutes, saluting, saluted
When you salute, you put the side of your hand next to your head as a sign of respect to someone.
*The soldiers **saluted** as they marched past.*

same

ADJECTIVE

If two things are the same, they look or sound like each other.
*She was wearing the **same** dress I was wearing.*
☞ **Similar:** identical, matching, similar
Opposite: different

sand

NOUN

Sand is very small grains of broken rock that you find on beaches or in deserts.

sandal

NOUN sandals
Sandals are open shoes with straps that fasten around your feet.

sandwich

NOUN sandwiches
A sandwich is slices of bread with a filling placed between them.

sandwich

Word history:
The word **sandwich** comes from the name of the Earl of Sandwich, who first made sandwiches popular.

sang

Sang is the past tense of the verb **sing**.

sank

Sank is the past tense of the verb **sink**.

sari

NOUN saris
A sari is a type of dress that women in India and other parts of Asia traditionally wear. It is made from a long piece of cloth that a woman wraps around her body.

sat

Sat is the past tense of the verb **sit**.

satellite

NOUN satellites
1 A satellite is an object that is in orbit around a larger object in space. Planet satellites are called **moons**.
2 A satellite is a machine in orbit around the Earth, which receives and transmits radio and television signals.
☞ **Say: sat**-a-lite

satellite dish

NOUN satellite dishes
A satellite dish is a round, metal dish attached to a building, which can receive television signals sent by satellite.

satsuma

NOUN satsumas
A satsuma is a fruit that looks and tastes like a small, sweet orange.
☞ **Say:** sat-**soo**-ma

sauce Say: SOS

*Would you like some mushroom **sauce** on your chicken?*

sauce

NOUN sauces
A sauce is a liquid that you eat with food.
☞ **Word history:** The word **sauce** comes from the Latin word *salsus*, meaning "flavored with salt."

a
b
c
d
e
f
g
h
i
j
k
l
m
n
o
p
q
r
Ss
t
u
v
w
x
y
z

a
b
c
d
e
f
g
h
i
j
k
l
m
n
o
p
q
r

Ss

t
u
v
w
x
y
z

saucepan
NOUN saucepans
A saucepan is a metal container that you cook food in.
☞ **Say: sos**-pan
Similar: pan, pot

saucer
NOUN saucers
A saucer is a small, shallow plate that you put a cup on.
☞ **Say: saw**-ser

sausage
NOUN sausages
A sausage is a mixture of chopped meat inside a long tube of thin skin.
☞ **Say: sos**-ij

save
VERB saves, saving, saved
1 If you save someone, you take them away from danger. *The firefighter* **saved** *him from the burning house.*
☞ **Similar:** protect, rescue
2 If you save something, you do not waste it.
Save *energy—turn off the light!*
3 If you save money, you keep it so that you can use it later.
He **saved** *up for a year to buy his bicycle.*

saw
1 Saw is the past tense of the verb **see**.
NOUN saws
2 A saw is a tool that you use for cutting wood. It has a blade with sharp teeth.
VERB saws, sawing, sawed
3 When you saw wood, you cut it using a saw.

A scarecrow scares away birds.

scarecrow

say
VERB says, saying, said
1 When you say something, you speak words.
"Hurry up!" I **said.**
☞ **Similar:** comment, declare, exclaim, remark, shout, whisper
2 If a piece of writing says something, it has those words in it.
The sign **says** *"No entry."*

scale
NOUN scales
1 The scales on a fish are hard pieces of skin on its body.
2 You use scales to measure how much things weigh.

scanner
NOUN scanners
A scanner is a machine that copies pictures or writing from a page onto a computer.

scar
NOUN scars
A scar is a mark that stays on your skin after a wound has healed.

scare
VERB scares, scaring, scared
If something scares you, it makes you feel afraid.
My friend jumped out and **scared** *me.*
☞ **Similar:** alarm, frighten, petrify, startle

scarecrow
NOUN scarecrows
A scarecrow is a figure made from sticks and old clothes, used to scare birds away from crops.

scared
ADJECTIVE
If you are scared, you feel afraid.
☞ **Similar:** alarmed, frightened, petrified, startled, terrified, upset

scarf
NOUN scarves
You wear a scarf around your neck to keep you warm, or to look nice.

scarf

Teddy wears a scarf.

scatter

VERB scatters, scattering, scattered

To scatter things means to spread them in many different directions.
The wind scattered the seeds.

scene

NOUN scenes

1 The scene of something is the place where it happens, for example a crime.
Several clues were found at the scene of the crime.
2 A scene in a play or film is one part of it.
3 A scene is a picture of something.
The card showed a winter scene.
☛ **Say: seen**

scent

NOUN scents

1 The scent of a person or animal is the smell that they leave behind them.
The dog followed the scent.
2 Scent is perfume.
☛ **Say: sent**

school

NOUN schools

A school is a place where children go to learn.
☛ **Say: skool**

science

NOUN sciences

Science is the subject in which you study things in the world around you, such as water, electricity, light, metals, plants, and animals.
☛ **Word history:** The word **science** comes from the Latin word *scientia*, which means "knowledge."

scientist

NOUN scientists

A scientist is someone who studies science.

I want to be a scientist.

scientist Say: **sy-en-tist**

scissors

NOUN

You use scissors for cutting things such as paper, cloth, and hair. Scissors have two blades that move apart and then together again.

scold

NOUN scolds, scolding, scolded

To scold someone means to speak to them in an angry way because they have done something wrong.
My father scolded me for being late.
☛ **Similar:** blame, nag, reprimand

scooter

NOUN scooters

A scooter is a toy that you use to ride around on. It has two wheels, and a flat board that you stand on. You put one foot onto the ground and push yourself along.

score

VERB scores, scoring, scored

When you score a point in a game, you win a point.
The teams score three points for a win and one for a tie.

scowl

VERB scowls, scowling, scowled

When you scowl, you make your face look angry.
She scowled when she was given extra homework.

scrap

NOUN scraps

1 A scrap is a small piece of something.
2 Scrap is anything that is broken, worn out, or not useful any more.
The cars were sold as scrap.
☛ **Similar:** garbage, junk

scrape

VERB scrapes, scraping, scraped

To scrape something means to scratch it or pull something sharp across it.

I whizz along on my scooter.

Scooter

scratch

VERB scratches, scratching, scratched

1 If you scratch something, you make a small cut on it.
2 When you scratch, you rub your skin with your nails.

a b c d e f g h i j k l m n o p q r **Ss** t u v w x y z

a b c d e f g h i j k l m n o p q r **Ss** t u v w x y z

scream
VERB screams, screaming, screamed
When you scream, you shout or cry in a loud voice because you are frightened or in pain.
☞ **Similar:** cry, howl, screech, shriek, wail, yell

screech
VERB screeches, screeching, screeched
When you screech, you shout or cry loudly.

screen
NOUN screens
1 A screen is a flat surface on which pictures or films can be shown.
2 The screen on a computer or television is the part where the picture or writing appears.

screw
NOUN screws
A screw is a pointed piece of metal, like a nail. You drive a screw into wood or metal by turning it around and around with a **screwdriver**.

scribble
VERB scribbles, scribbling, scribbled
When you scribble, you write or draw something in a very messy way.

sea
NOUN seas
The sea is the saltwater that covers a large amount of the Earth's surface.

seal
NOUN seals
1 A seal is a sea animal with black fur and flippers that lives in cold seas. Seals eat fish and are excellent swimmers.
VERB seals, sealing, sealed
2 When you seal something, you close it tightly.

Seals dive deep in the sea to catch fish.

s e a l

search
VERB searches, searching, searched
If you search for something, you look for it carefully.
He searched for his ball in the long grass.

seaside
NOUN
The seaside is the land next to the sea.

season
NOUN seasons
1 Seasons are the different parts that a year is divided into. Our four seasons are **spring**, **summer**, **fall**, and **winter**.
2 A sport's season is the time of year when people play that sport.
The football season starts next week.

seat
NOUN seats
A seat is something that you sit on.
☞ **Similar:** bench, chair, stool

seat belt
NOUN seat belts
A seat belt is a strap that you fasten around your body when you are in a car.

second
NOUN seconds
1 A second is a very short period of time. There are 60 seconds in one minute.
ADJECTIVE
2 The second person or thing is the one that comes after the first one.

secret
NOUN secrets
If something is a secret, only a few people know about it.
Don't tell anyone—it's a secret.

secretary
NOUN secretaries
A secretary is a person who works in an office and helps someone else by making business appointments, writing letters, and keeping records.

see

VERB sees, seeing, saw, seen
When you see something, you notice it with your eyes.
I saw a fox in our yard.
☛ **Similar:** glimpse, notice, observe, spot, watch

seed

NOUN seeds
A seed is a small, hard object that is made by a plant. You can put a seed in the ground and it will grow into a new plant.

seek

VERB seeks, seeking, sought
When you seek something, you try to find it.

seem

VERB seems, seeming, seemed
To seem means to appear.

seen

Seen is a past tense of the verb **see**.

seesaw

NOUN seesaws
A seesaw is a balancing toy. Children play on a seesaw by sitting at either end of a board and rocking up and down. It is also known as a **teeter-totter**.

seize

VERB seizes, seizing, seized
If you seize something, you take hold of it suddenly.
The thief seized her bag.
☛ **Say: seez**
Similar: grab, snatch

seeds — *Seeds from the sycamore tree fall to the ground, spinning around and around and around.*

selfish

ADJECTIVE
If you are selfish, you only care about yourself and not about other people.
He was selfish and never shared his toys.
☛ **Opposite:** generous

sell

VERB sells, selling, sold
When you sell something, you give it to someone and they give you money in return.
I sold my old bike to my friend.

semicircle

NOUN semicircles
A semicircle is half a circle.
☛ **Say: sem**-ee-sir-kul

send

VERB sends, sending, sent
When you send something to someone, you arrange for someone to deliver it to them.
Remember to send me a postcard!

sense

NOUN senses
1 The five senses are the five ways in which we can receive information about the world around us. The five senses are **sight**, **hearing**, **touch**, **smell**, and **taste**.
2 If someone has sense, they are able to make good, sensible decisions.
3 If something makes sense, it seems sensible or right.

sensible

ADJECTIVE
Someone who is sensible does the right thing, and does not do silly or stupid things.
☛ **Opposite:** silly

sensitive

ADJECTIVE
1 Something that is sensitive reacts very quickly to things around it.
If you have sensitive skin, you have to be careful which soap you use.
2 Someone who is sensitive becomes upset easily.

sent

Sent is the past tense of the verb **send**.

sentence

NOUN sentences
1 A sentence is a group of words that make sense together. Sentences start with a capital letter and end with a period.
2 A sentence is a punishment that is given to someone by a judge in a law court.
He received a four-year prison sentence.

The red buttons are separate from the other buttons.

separate

separate

VERB separates, separating, separated
1 When you separate things, you take them apart from each other.
ADJECTIVE
2 Things that are separate are not joined to each other or not with each other.

a b c d e f g h i j k l m n o p q r **Ss** t u v w x y z

179

sequence

sequence
NOUN sequences
A sequence is a number of things that follow each other in order.

series
NOUN
1 A series of things is a number of them that follow one another in order.
2 A television series is a television program that is shown in regular episodes.

serious
ADJECTIVE
1 If something is serious, people need to think and talk about it carefully.
Missing so much school is a very serious matter.
☛ **Similar:** important
2 Someone who is serious is not smiling or laughing.
The teacher came in looking serious.
☛ **Similar:** earnest, pensive, severe, stern
3 If something is serious, it is worrying and could be dangerous.

It is Paul's turn to serve.

serve

servant
NOUN servants
A servant is a person who works for another person in their home.

serve
VERB serves, serving, served
1 When you serve someone, you help them by giving them something that they want or need.
The waiter will serve you at your table.
2 When you serve in a game like tennis, you start the game by hitting the ball to your opponent.

service
NOUN services
1 The service in a store or restaurant is how quick and helpful the staff are.
2 A service is something that is provided for people to use if they want to.

set
NOUN sets
1 A set of things is a group of things that belong together.
She has a blue china tea set.
VERB sets, setting, set
2 When you set something somewhere, you put it there carefully.
Lionel set the vase on the table.
☛ **Similar:** place, put, rest
3 When the Sun sets, it goes down in the evening.
The Sun sets in the west.
4 When something sets, it becomes hard.
The cement took a long time to set.

settle
VERB settles, settling, settled
1 If you settle down, you stop moving around and sit or lie quietly.
The teacher told the children to settle down.
2 When you settle an argument, you stop arguing and agree on who is right.
Dad settled the argument for us.

several
ADJECTIVE
Several means a lot of people or things.

Shape up!

Here are some common shapes and their names.

square

rectangle

circle

triangle

semicircle

180

severe

ADJECTIVE
Severe means very bad.
The flight was canceled because of severe weather.
☞ **Similar:** bad, extreme, serious, terrible

sew

VERB sews, sewing, sewed, sewn
When you sew, you join pieces of cloth together using a needle and thread.
☞ **Say: so**

sex

NOUN sexes
Male and female are the two sexes that people and animals are divided into.

shade

NOUN shades
1 If you are in the shade, you are in a cool place where the sun's light and heat cannot reach.
She sat in the shade to read.
☞ **Similar:** dark, darkness, gloom, shadow
2 Different shades of a color are all the same color, but are different because some are darker or lighter than others.

What **liquid** do you use to **wash** your **hair?**

Look around the page to find the answer.

shadow

NOUN shadows
A shadow is a dark shape that is made when something blocks the light.

shake

VERB shakes, shaking, shook, shaken
1 When something shakes, it moves roughly up and down or from side to side.
The bus was shaking and rattling as it drove along.
☞ **Similar:** bump, rock, shudder, wobble
2 When you shake something, you move it roughly up and down.
Shake the jar before opening it.
3 If you are shaking, you cannot stop your body from moving because you are cold or frightened.

shall

VERB
I shall do something means that I will do it.
I shall go shopping later.

shallow

ADJECTIVE
Something that is shallow is not very deep.
He swam in the shallow water.

shame

NOUN
1 If something is a shame, it is sad.
It's a shame you can't come.
2 Shame is the feeling you have when you know that you have done something wrong and feel bad about it.

shampoo

NOUN shampoos
Shampoo is a soapy liquid that you use for washing your hair.

shape

NOUN shapes
You can say what shape something is by saying whether it is a circle, a square, or a triangle.

a
b
c
d
e
f
g
h
i
j
k
l
m
n
o
p
q
r
Ss
t
u
v
w
x
y
z

pentagon hexagon octagon star diamond

181

a
b
c
d
e
f
g
h
i
j
k
l
m
n
o
p
q
r
Ss
t
u
v
w
x
y
z

share

VERB shares, sharing, shared
1 When people share something, they take turns using it.
We don't have enough cups so we'll have to share.
2 When people share something, they divide it up and give some to each person.
I hope you're going to share your chocolate with everyone.

shark

NOUN sharks
A shark is a large fish with rows of sharp teeth. Sharks live in both cold and warm seas and eat fish or small water animals.

sharp

ADJECTIVE sharper, sharpest
Something that is sharp has a thin edge or pointed end that can cut things.
Careful—that knife is sharp!
☞ **Similar:** jagged, pointed
Opposite: blunt

shave

VERB shaves, shaving, shaved
When you shave, you remove hair from your body with a razor.

shed

NOUN sheds
1 A shed is a small building that you keep things in.
VERB sheds, shedding, shed
2 To shed something means to lose it because it drops off.
Some trees shed all their leaves in the fall.

sheep

NOUN
A sheep is an animal with a thick, woolly coat, which is kept on farms to produce meat and wool.

sheer

ADJECTIVE
1 A sheer drop does not slope but goes straight down.
2 Sheer means complete.
He collapsed with sheer exhaustion.

shark

Sharks have very sharp teeth.

sheet

NOUN sheets
1 A sheet is a large piece of cloth that you put on a bed.
2 A sheet of something is a large, flat piece of it.

shelf

NOUN shelves
A shelf is a piece of wood attached to a wall. You put things on shelves.

shells

We collected some shells.

shell

NOUN shells
A shell is a hard part that covers and protects something. Eggs, nuts, and animals such as snails, crabs, and tortoises have shells.

shelter

NOUN shelters
1 A shelter is a place that protects you from the weather or from danger.
The doorway provided a shelter from the rain.
VERB shelters, sheltering, sheltered
2 When you take shelter somewhere, you stay there so that you are safe from the weather or danger.

shepherd

NOUN shepherds
A shepherd is someone who looks after a flock of sheep.

sheriff

NOUN sheriffs

A sheriff is a person who is elected to make sure that people do not break the law in their county.

shield

NOUN shields

1 A shield is a strong piece of metal or leather that soldiers used to carry in battle to protect their bodies.

VERB shields, shielding, shielded

2 To shield something means to protect it.

*She **shielded** her eyes from the sun.*

*The **sheriff** wears a shiny badge.*

ship

NOUN ships

A ship is a large boat.

☞ **Similar:** boat, ferry, vessel, yacht

shipwreck Say: ship-rek

*The whole of the ship's cargo was lost in the **shipwreck**.*

shin

NOUN shins

Your shins are the front parts of your legs below your knees.

shine

VERB shines, shining, shone

When something shines, it gives out light and looks bright.

*The car headlights **shone** on the road ahead.*

☞ **Similar:** blaze, flash, gleam, glow, sparkle, twinkle

shiny

ADJECTIVE shinier, shiniest

Something that is shiny looks bright.

*The old coins looked **shiny** after Sam polished them.*

☞ **Opposite:** dull

shipwreck

NOUN shipwrecks

When there is a shipwreck, a ship is destroyed at sea.

shirt

NOUN shirts

A shirt is a piece of clothing that you wear on the top half of your body. Shirts have sleeves and usually have a collar and buttons down the front.

shiver

VERB shivers, shivering, shivered

When you shiver, your body keeps moving because you are cold or frightened or sick.

*He **shivered** in the cold wind.*

☞ **Similar:** quake, quiver, shake

shock

NOUN shocks

1 If something is a shock, it happens suddenly and surprises you a lot.

2 If you get an electric shock, electricity goes through your body and hurts you.

VERB shocks, shocking, shocked

3 If something shocks you, it surprises you and upsets you.

☞ **Similar:** astonish, astound, horrify

shocked

ADJECTIVE

If you are shocked by something, you are surprised and upset by it.

☞ **Similar:** horrified, shaken, staggered, stunned

shoe

NOUN shoes

You wear shoes on your feet to protect them and keep them warm.

shoe

*Jenny's **shoe** has laces.*

shone

Shone is the past tense of the verb **shine**.

shook

Shook is the past tense of the verb **shake**.

shoot

VERB shoots, shooting, shot

To shoot someone means to fire at them with a gun or other weapon.

a b c d e f g h i j k l m n o p q r **Ss** t u v w x y z

183

a
b
c
d
e
f
g
h
i
j
k
l
m
n
o
p
q
r
Ss
t
u
v
w
x
y
z

shop

NOUN shops

1 A shop is a place where people go to buy things.
☞ **Similar:** store, supermarket
VERB shops, shopping, shopped
2 When you shop, you go to the store to buy things.
*We went **shopping** in the afternoon.*

shore

NOUN shores

The shore is the land at the edge of the sea or a lake.
☞ **Similar:** beach, coast, seashore

short

ADJECTIVE shorter, shortest

1 Something that is short is not very long.
Short hair is fashionable now.
2 Something that is short does not last long.
*The film was **short**.*
☞ **Opposite:** long

shortage

NOUN shortages

When there is a shortage of something, there is not enough of it.

shorts

NOUN

Shorts are short pants that usually end just above your knees.
*We wear **shorts** in the summer.*

shot

1 Shot is the past tense of the verb **shoot**.
NOUN shots
2 A shot is a try.
*The ballplayer took a **shot** at the goal.*

should

VERB

If you should do something, you ought to do it.
*You **should** do your homework before you go out to play.*

shoulder

NOUN shoulders

Your shoulder is the place below your neck where your arms join your body.

shout

NOUN shout

1 A shout is a loud call.
*We heard a **shout** from outside.*
VERB shouts, shouting, shouted
2 When you shout, you speak or call out loudly.
☞ **Similar:** bellow, call, cry, scream, yell

show

NOUN shows

1 A show is something that people perform for others to watch.
☞ **Similar:** concert, performance, play
VERB shows, showing, showed
2 If you show something to someone, you let them see it.
*He **showed** the class his vacation photos.*

shower

NOUN showers

1 If you have a shower, you wash your body by standing under a fine spray of water.
2 If there is a shower, it rains for a short time.
Showers are expected in the afternoon.
☞ **Rhymes:** our

shred

NOUN shreds

A shred of something is a small, narrow strip of it.

shriek

VERB shrieks, shrieking, shrieked

If you shriek, you shout or cry out in a high-pitched voice because you are excited or afraid.
*She **shrieked** when she saw the mouse.*
☞ **Say: shreek**
Similar: howl, scream, screech, squeal, wail, yell

show

Lucy introduced the performers at the start of the show.

184

shrill
ADJECTIVE shriller, shrillest
A shrill sound is sharp and high.

shrink
VERB shrinks, shrinking, shrank, shrunk
When something shrinks, it becomes smaller.
*Her sweater **shrank** in the wash.*

shrug
VERB shrugs, shrugging, shrugged
When you shrug, you raise your shoulders to show that you do not care or do not know.

shuffle
VERB shuffles, shuffling, shuffled
1 When you shuffle cards, you mix them around to change the order they are in.
2 If you shuffle along, you walk slowly, dragging your feet along the ground.

shut
VERB shuts, shutting, shut
1 If you shut something, you close it.
☞ **Similar:** bolt, close, lock
Opposite: open
2 When you shut down your computer, you close the programs you have been using and switch it off.

shy
ADJECTIVE shyer, shyest
Someone who is shy is nervous and frightened when they meet and talk to new people.
☞ **Similar:** bashful, hesitant, nervous, timid

sick
ADJECTIVE sicker, sickest
1 If you are sick, you do not feel well.
2 If you are sick, food comes up out of your stomach and out of your mouth.
☞ **Similar:** ill, unwell

sight
site
Say:

side
NOUN sides
1 The sides of something are the parts at the edges.
*Triangles have three **sides**.*
2 The side of something is the part on the left or right of it.
*We put the chairs at the **side** of the hall.*
3 A side is a team of people who are competing against another group.
*Which **side** are you on?*

sideways
ADVERB
If you move sideways, you move to the side, not forward or backward.
*Crabs walk **sideways**.*

sieve
NOUN sieves
A sieve is a container with a lot of tiny holes in it. You pour things into a sieve to separate solids from liquids, or fine grains from larger pieces.
☞ **Say:** siv

sigh
VERB sighs, sighing, sighed
When you sigh, you let out a long, deep breath slowly because you are tired or sad.

sight
NOUN
1 Your sight is your ability to see things.
*Birds of prey have an excellent sense of **sight**.*
2 A sight is something that you can see.
*The ship was a fine **sight** as it sailed up the river.*

sign
NOUN signs
1 A sign is a picture or symbol that represents something.
*The **sign** for dollars is $.*
2 If you give someone a sign, you move your body in order to tell them something.
*He nodded his head as a **sign** that he wanted to leave.*
3 A sign is a public notice that gives people information.
VERB signs, signing, signed
4 When you sign something, you write your name on it.
*The author **signed** copies of her book.*

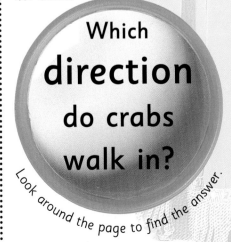

Which **direction** do crabs walk in?

Look around the page to find the answer.

a b c d e f g h i j k l m n o p q r **Ss** t u v w x y z

185

a
b
c
d
e
f
g
h
i
j
k
l
m
n
o
p
q
r
Ss
u
v
w
x
y
z

signal

NOUN signals
If you give someone a signal, you move a part of your body or use an object in order to tell the person something.
*The cyclist put out his right arm as a **signal** that he wanted to turn right.*

signature

NOUN signatures
Your signature is your special way of writing your own name.
☞ **Say: sig**-na-chur

sign language

NOUN
Sign language is a way of talking to people by moving your hands in special ways.
*People who cannot hear often use **sign language**.*

silly

A silly clown shows off on a unicycle.

Sikh

NOUN Sikhs
A Sikh is someone whose religion is Sikhism.
☞ **Say: seek**

silence

NOUN
When there is silence, there is no noise.

silent

ADJECTIVE
Something that is silent does not make any noise. A place that is silent has no noise in it.
☞ **Similar:** calm, hushed, peaceful, quiet, still
Opposite: noisy

silk

NOUN silks
Silk is a type of thin, soft cloth that is made from threads spun by silkworms.

silly

ADJECTIVE sillier, silliest
Something that is silly is not very sensible.
*What a **silly** idea!*
☞ **Similar:** absurd, crazy, foolish, ridiculous

silver

NOUN
Silver is a shiny, white-colored metal that is very valuable. Silver is used for making coins and jewelry.

similar

ADJECTIVE
Things that are similar are almost the same, but not exactly the same.

What **cloth** is made by special **worms?**

Look around the page to find the answer.

simple

ADJECTIVE simpler, simplest
1 Something that is simple is easy to understand or solve.
*The teacher gave us some **simple** math problems.*
☞ **Opposite:** complicated
2 Something that is simple is plain, and not decorated.
*She always wears very **simple** clothes.*
☞ **Opposite:** fancy

sincere

ADJECTIVE
Someone who is sincere is honest and tells the truth.
*She was **sincere** when she said she was sorry.*
☞ **Say: sin-seer**
Similar: genuine, honest, truthful

sincerely

ADVERB
You write "sincerely" at the end of a polite letter, before you finish it by signing your name.

sing

VERB sings, singing, sang, sung
When you sing, you make a musical sound with your voice.
*She has never **sung** in front of other people before.*

single

ADJECTIVE

Single means for only one person.

*They booked two **single** rooms and one double at the hotel.*

singular

NOUN

The singular of a word is the form that you use for only one thing or person.

☛ **Opposite:** plural

sink

NOUN sinks

1 A sink is a basin with faucets, that you can wash things in.

VERB sinks, sinking, sank, sunk

2 When something sinks, it goes down below the surface of water.

*The stone **sank** to the bottom of the pond.*

sip

VERB sips, sipping, sipped

When you sip a drink, you drink it slowly, with small mouthfuls.

siren

NOUN sirens

A siren is a small machine that makes a loud noise to warn people about something.

*We heard a police car's **siren**.*

☛ **Say:** sye-ren

sister

NOUN sisters

Your sister is a girl who has the same mother and father as you.

*I've got two brothers and four **sisters**!*

sit

VERB sits, sitting, sat

1 When you sit, you rest your body by supporting your weight on your behind, rather than on your feet.

2 If something is sitting somewhere, it is there.

*I left my book **sitting** on the kitchen table.*

situation

NOUN situations

A situation is everything that is happening in a particular place at a particular time.

*The people whose houses have flooded are in a desperate **situation**.*

☛ **Say:** sit-yoo-**ay**-shun

size

NOUN sizes

The size of something is how big it is.

*These shoes are the wrong **size**.*

skate

VERB skates, skating, skated

When you skate, you slide along on a hard surface, wearing special shoes with blades or wheels.

*Shall we go **skating** this afternoon?*

skateboard

NOUN skateboards

A skateboard is a small board on wheels that people stand on to ride along. When you are riding on one, you are **skateboarding**.

skeleton

NOUN skeletons

Your skeleton is all the bones in your body. There are 206 bones in a human skeleton.

☛ **Word history:** The word **skeleton** comes from the Greek word *skeletos*, meaning "dried up," because your bones remain after you have died and your body has dried up.

ski

*I enjoy whizzing downhill on **skis**.*

ski

VERB skis, skiing, skied

When you ski, you move over snow on two long, thin sticks called skis.

☛ **Say:** skee

skill

NOUN skills

If you have skill, you can do something very well. Someone who has a lot of skill is **skillful**.

*You need a lot of **skill** to be a professional tennis player.*

☛ **Similar:** ability, flair, talent, technique

skin

NOUN skins

1 Your skin is the part of you that covers all your body.

2 The skin on a vegetable or fruit is the part on the outside.

a b c d e f g h i j k l m n o p q r **Ss** t u v w x y z

187

skinny

ADJECTIVE skinnier, skinniest
Someone who is skinny is very thin and has very little fat on their body.

skip

VERB skips, skipping, skipped
When you skip along, you run along and hop lightly from one foot to another.
*She **skipped** down the road.*
☞ **Similar:** bound, dance, hop, leap, prance

skirt

NOUN skirts
A skirt is a piece of clothing that a woman or girl wears. It fastens around her waist, and can be short or long.

skull

NOUN skulls
Your skull is the bony case that protects your brain.

sky

NOUN skies
The sky is the air above us.
*The **sky** usually looks blue.*

skydiving

NOUN
Skydiving is a sport in which people jump out of an airplane wearing a parachute that opens after they have been falling for a short while.

skyscraper

NOUN skyscrapers
A skyscraper is a very tall building.

slang

NOUN
Slang is the words and phrases that people use when they are laughing and joking together, but not when they are writing or speaking politely.

slant

VERB slants, slanting, slanted
If something slants, it slopes and is not flat or straight.

slap

VERB slaps, slapping, slapped
If you slap someone, you hit that person with the palm of your hand.
☞ **Similar:** hit, smack, strike

skydiving

Skydiving is a daring and exciting sport.

slave

NOUN slaves
A slave is someone who is owned by another person, and has to work for them.

sled

NOUN sleds
A sled has a smooth bottom, and you sit on it to move across snow or ice.

sleep

VERB sleeps, sleeping, slept
When you sleep, you rest with your eyes closed, and your body and mind are not active.
☞ **Similar:** doze, nap, rest, slumber, snooze

sleepy

ADJECTIVE sleepier, sleepiest
If you are sleepy, you feel as if you want to sleep.
☞ **Similar:** drowsy, weary

sleeve

NOUN sleeves
The sleeves on a piece of clothing are the parts that cover your arms.

sleigh

NOUN sleighs
A sleigh is a large sled that is pulled by animals.
☞ **Say: slay**

slept

Slept is the past tense of the verb **sleep**.

slice

NOUN slices
A slice of something is a thin piece of it.
*Would you like a **slice** of cake?*

slide

NOUN slides
1 A slide is a large toy for children to play on. You climb up some steps and then slide down it.
VERB slides, sliding, slid
2 To slide means to move smoothly along.
*She **slid** across the ice.*
☛ **Similar:** glide, skate, skid

slight

ADJECTIVE slighter, slightest
Slight means very small.
*There's a **slight** chance that we might go to England this year.*
☛ **Say:** slite

slightly

ADVERB
Slightly means a little bit.
*She was **slightly** upset.*

slim

ADJECTIVE slimmer, slimmest
Someone who is slim is thin.
☛ **Similar:** lean, slender, trim
Opposite: fat

slimy

ADJECTIVE
Something that is slimy feels wet and sticky.
☛ **Similar:** greasy, oily, slippery

sling

NOUN slings
A sling is a piece of material that you put around an injured arm to support it.
*They learned how to make a **sling** in the first-aid class.*

slip

VERB slips, slipping, slipped
1 If you slip, your foot slides on the floor and you lose your balance.
*I **slipped** on the ice.*
2 If you slip something into a place, you put it there gently.
*He **slipped** some money into my hand.*

slipper

NOUN slippers
Slippers are soft, comfortable shoes that you wear indoors.

slippery

ADJECTIVE
Something that is slippery is smooth or wet, and difficult to grip.
☛ **Similar:** greasy, oily, slimy, smooth

slippery

*Two **slippery** newts*

slit

NOUN slits
A slit is a long, narrow hole or cut in something.
☛ **Similar:** crack, slot, split, tear

slither

VERB slithers, slithering, slithered
When a snake slithers, it slides along the ground.

slogan

NOUN slogans
A slogan is a phrase that is used to advertise something.
☛ **Word history:** The word **slogan** comes from a Gaelic word meaning a "war cry."

slope

NOUN slopes
1 A slope is a piece of land that is not flat, but goes up or down.
*They rolled the ball down the **slope**.*
VERB slopes, sloping, sloped
2 If something slopes, it is not flat but goes up or down at one end.

slot

NOUN slots
A slot is a small, narrow opening for putting something in.
*She put a coin in the **slot**.*

slow

ADJECTIVE slower, slowest
Something that is slow takes a long time to do something or get somewhere.
*The school bus is always **slow**.*
☛ **Opposite:** fast

slowly

ADVERB
If you move or do something slowly, you do not hurry and do not do it quickly.
☛ **Opposite:** quickly

slug

NOUN slugs
A slug is a small, soft, and slimy animal with no legs.

a
b
c
d
e
f
g
h
i
j
k
l
m
n
o
p
q
r
Ss
t
u
v
w
x
y
z

a
b
c
d
e
f
g
h
i
j
k
l
m
n
o
p
q
r
Ss
t
u
v
w
x
y
z

sly

ADJECTIVE slyer, slyest
Someone who is sly
does things in a secretive,
sneaky way.
☞ **Similar:** crafty, cunning,
deceitful, wily

smack

VERB smacks, smacking,
smacked
To smack someone means
to hit them.
☞ **Similar:** hit, slap, strike

small

ADJECTIVE smaller, smallest
Something that is small is
not very big.
☞ **Similar:** little,
minute, tiny
Opposite: big

smart

ADJECTIVE smarter, smartest
Someone who is smart
is intelligent.
☞ **Similar:** bright, clever,
intelligent, quick, sharp
Opposite: stupid

smash

VERB smashes, smashing,
smashed
To smash something means
to break it into lots of pieces.
A baseball hit the window and
***smashed** it.*
☞ **Similar:** break, crack,
shatter

smear

VERB smears, smearing,
smeared
If you smear a surface, you
make it dirty by spreading
something sticky or greasy.

smell

NOUN smells
1 Your sense of smell is your
ability to smell things.
2 The smell that something
has is what it is like when
you sniff it.
The flower had a wonderful
***smell**.*
☞ **Similar:** aroma, fragrance,
odor, perfume, scent
3 If something smells, you
can notice it by sniffing with
your nose.
*Your feet **smell**!*
VERB smells, smelling, smelled
4 When you smell something,
you use your nose to find out
what it is like.
*I **smelled** the cheese to check*
if it was fresh.

Snails leave a trail of slime behind them.

snail

smelly

ADJECTIVE smellier, smelliest
Something that is smelly has
an unpleasant smell.

smile

VERB smiles, smiling, smiled
When you smile, you show
that you are happy by
moving your mouth so that
it turns upward at the sides.
☞ **Similar:** beam, grin,
laugh

smoke

NOUN
Smoke is the black or white
gas that comes from a fire.
☞ **Similar:** fumes, smog,
steam

smooth

ADJECTIVE smoother, smoothest
Something that is smooth is
flat and even, with no sharp
bumps or lumps.
*Her skin was **smooth**.*
☞ **Opposite:** rough

snack

NOUN snacks
A snack is a small amount
of food that you eat between
meals or have instead of a
meal.

snail

NOUN snails
A snail is a small, slimy
animal with no legs and
a hard shell.

snake

NOUN snakes
A snake is a long, thin
animal with no legs. Some
snakes are poisonous,
while others kill
by squeezing their
prey tightly.

What is the opposite of smooth?

Look around the page to find the answer.

snap

VERB snaps, snapping, snapped
1 If you snap your fingers, you move them together so that they make a noise.
2 If something snaps, it breaks suddenly.
*He was worried the rope might **snap**.*
3 If you snap at someone, you shout at them in an angry way.
*Don't **snap** at me! I'm trying to help!*

snarl

VERB snarls, snarling, snarled
When an animal snarls, it growls fiercely and shows its teeth.
*The guard dog **snarled** at the burglar.*

snatch

VERB snatches, snatching, snatched
If you snatch something, you take hold of it quickly.
*I **snatched** my coat and ran out of the house.*
☛ **Similar:** grab, seize

sneak

VERB sneaks, sneaking, sneaked
If you sneak somewhere, you go there in a quiet or secretive way.
*He **sneaked** out of the room when no one was looking.*
☛ **Similar:** creep, sidle, slink

sneeze

VERB sneezes, sneezing, sneezed
When you sneeze, air comes out of your nose suddenly.
*The pepper made her **sneeze**.*

sniff

VERB sniffs, sniffing, sniffed
1 When you sniff, you breathe in noisily through your nose.
*That dog is **sniffing** for her food.*
2 If you sniff something, you smell it.
*Dogs find out about things by **sniffing** them.*

snore

VERB snores, snoring, snored
If you snore, you breathe noisily as you sleep.

snow

NOUN
1 Snow is soft, white flakes of ice that fall from the clouds in cold weather.
VERB snows, snowing, snowed
2 When it snows, snow falls from the clouds.
*It's been **snowing** for days.*

snowball

NOUN snowballs
A snowball is a ball of snow that you make with your hands and throw at people for fun.

snowboarding

NOUN
Snowboarding is a sport in which you slide over snow or ice on a large, flat board called a **snowboard**.

snowdrift

NOUN snowdrifts
A snowdrift is snow that has been blown into a pile by the wind.
*The car is stuck in a **snowdrift**.*

snowflake

NOUN snowflakes
A snowflake is one piece of snow that falls from the clouds.

snowflakes

snowman

*The children made a **snowman**.*

snowman

NOUN snowmen
A snowman is a figure of a person that you make out of snow.

snug

ADJECTIVE
If you are snug, you are warm and comfortable.
*The cat looked very **snug** curled up inside the basket.*

a
b
c
d
e
f
g
h
i
j
k
l
m
n
o
p
q
r
Ss
t
u
v
w
x
y
z

a
b
c
d
e
f
g
h
i
j
k
l
m
n
o
p
q
r
Ss
t
u
v
w
x
y
z

soak

VERB soaks, soaking, soaked
To soak something means to make it very wet.
*James **soaked** me with his water pistol.*
☞ **Similar:** drench, saturate, wet

soaking

ADJECTIVE
Soaking means very wet.

soap

NOUN soaps
You use soap for cleaning your body.

soap opera

NOUN soap operas
A soap opera is a television series that tells the story of the everyday lives of a group of people.

sob

VERB sobs, sobbing, sobbed
If you sob, you cry noisily.
*Charlie is **sobbing** because he lost his teddy bear.*
☞ **Similar:** bawl, cry, howl, weep

soccer

NOUN
Soccer is a team sport. Players can kick or hit the ball with any part of the body except the hands.

sock

NOUN socks
A sock is a piece of clothing that you wear on your foot.

sofa

NOUN sofas
A sofa is a long, comfortable chair for two or three people.

soft

ADJECTIVE softer, softest
1 Something that is soft is not hard or firm.
☞ **Opposite:** hard
2 Something that feels soft feels smooth.
☞ **Opposite:** rough
3 A soft sound is not very loud.

software

NOUN
Software is the programs that you put into a computer to make it work.

soil

NOUN
Soil is earth in which plants can grow.

solar

ADJECTIVE
Solar means to do with the sun.
☞ **Word history:**
The word **solar** comes from the Latin word *solaris*, meaning "sun."

solar system

NOUN
Our solar system is the sun and all the planets that move around it. The nine planets in our solar system are Earth, Jupiter, Mars, Mercury, Neptune, Pluto, Saturn, Uranus, and Venus.

soldier Say:
sole-jer

*A row of toy **soldiers***

soldier

NOUN soldiers
A soldier is someone who fights as part of an army.

sole

NOUN soles
1 The sole of your foot is the bottom part of your foot.
2 The sole of a shoe is the bottom part of it.

solid

NOUN solids
1 A solid is a substance that is hard, and is not a liquid or gas. Ice and rock are solids.
ADJECTIVE
2 Something that is solid is made of the same thing all the way through, and is not hollow.
*This cat is carved from a **solid** block of wood.*
3 Something that is solid is strong and well made.
*They built a **solid** wall around the castle.*
☞ **Similar:** strong, sturdy

solve

VERB solves, solving, solved
When you solve a problem or mystery, you understand it and find the answer to it.

son

NOUN sons
Someone's son is their male child.
☞ **Say:** sun

song

NOUN songs
A song is a piece of music with words that you sing.
☞ **Similar:** anthem, ballad, hymn, lullaby, tune

soon

ADVERB
Soon means after a short time.
*It will be lunchtime **soon**.*

sore

ADJECTIVE
If a part of your body is sore, it hurts.
*My arm was **sore** after I fell.*
☞ **Similar:** aching, painful, tender, throbbing

sorry

ADJECTIVE sorrier, sorriest
If you are sorry, you feel unhappy because of something that you have done.
*I am **sorry** that I broke your window.*
☞ **Similar:** apologetic, ashamed, remorseful, shamefaced
Opposite: pleased

sort

NOUN sorts
1 One sort of thing is one type.
*What **sort** of vacation will you have this year?*
VERB sorts, sorting, sorted
2 To sort things means to arrange them into different types or groups.
*He **sorted** the socks and put them in pairs.*

sought

Sought is the past tense of the verb **seek**.
☞ **Say:** sawt

sound

NOUN sounds
A sound is something that you can hear.
☞ **Similar:** noise, racket

S o u n d
*Cymbals make a loud **sound**.*

soup

NOUN soups
Soup is a liquid food that is made with meat or vegetables.
*We had vegetable **soup** for dinner.*

sour

ADJECTIVE
Something that is sour has a sharp taste, like a lemon.
☞ **Rhymes:** power
Similar: bitter, sharp, tart
Opposite: sweet

south

NOUN
South is one of the directions on a compass. If you keep going south, you will come to the **South Pole**, which is the part of Earth in the far south.

souvenir

NOUN souvenirs
A souvenir is something that you keep to remind you of a person or place.
☞ **Say:** soo-ven-**neer**
Word history: The word **souvenir** comes from the French word *souvenir*, meaning "to remember."

sow

VERB sows, sowing, sowed, sown
When you sow seeds, you put them in the soil so that they will grow into plants.
☞ **Say:** so

a
b
c
d
e
f
g
h
i
j
k
l
m
n
o
p
q
r
Ss
t
u
v
w
x
y
z

a
b
c
d
e
f
g
h
i
j
k
l
m
n
o
p
q
r

Ss

t
u
v
w
x
y
z

space

NOUN

1 Space is the area around Earth, where all the stars and planets are found.

2 A space is a place that is empty.

*We left a **space** for your chair.*

spacecraft

NOUN

A spacecraft is a vehicle that can travel in space.

spaceship

NOUN spaceships

A spaceship is a vehicle in which people can travel in space.

spade

NOUN spades

A spade is a tool that you use for digging.

spaghetti

NOUN

Spaghetti is a type of long, thin pasta.

☞ **Word history: Spaghetti** is an Italian word that means "little pieces of string."

spare

ADJECTIVE

Something that is spare is extra, and you can use it if you need to.

sparkle

VERB sparkles, sparkling, sparkled

If something sparkles, it shines in the light.

*The water **sparkled** in the moonlight.*

☞ **Similar:** flash, gleam, glisten, glow, shine, twinkle

speak

VERB speaks, speaking, spoke, spoken

When you speak, you say words.

spear

NOUN spears

A spear is a long weapon with a sharp point that you throw by hand.

special

ADJECTIVE

Something that is special is different and better than other things.

☞ **Say:** spesh-ul

Similar: exceptional, extraordinary, unusual

Opposite: ordinary

spectacular

ADJECTIVE

Something that is spectacular is very exciting.

*The mountain scenery is **spectacular**.*

speech

NOUN speeches

1 Speech is the ability to speak.

*Animals do not have the power of **speech**.*

2 A speech is a talk that someone gives to an audience.

*The principal made a **speech** at the end of Sports Day.*

speed

NOUN speeds

The speed of something is how fast it is moving.

*The train was traveling at a **speed** of 80 miles per hour.*

spell

NOUN spells

1 A spell is a set of words that are supposed to have a magic power.

*The witch cast a **spell** on her.*

VERB spells, spelling, spelled

2 The way you spell a word is the letters you use to write it.

*How do you **spell** "special?"*

spend

VERB spends, spending, spent

1 When you spend money, you use it to buy things.

*I've **spent** all my allowance.*

2 When you spend time doing something, you use the time to do it.

*We **spent** two weeks camping in the forest.*

star anise

red chilli

spice

NOUN spices

A spice is something that you add to food to make it taste good. Spices are made from the dried parts of plants.

green chilli

*Star anise, chillies, and nutmeg are **spices**.*

spices

nutmeg

spicy

ADJECTIVE

Spicy food has a strong flavor because it has spices in it.

Space

Lost in space? Here are some words to help you find your way around.

sun

sparkle

twinkle

star

burning

boiling

turning

twisting

galaxy

spinning

spacesuit

3-2-1 blast off!

zooming

spacewalking

space shuttle

astronaut

dry

empty

rocky

orbit

satellite

moon

Earth

comet

planets may be... dusty, frozen, humid, icy, volcanic

planets in the Solar System

Mercury Venus Earth Mars Jupiter Saturn Uranus Neptune Pluto

a
b
c
d
e
f
g
h
i
j
k
l
m
n
o
p
q
r

t

spider

NOUN spiders

A spider is a small animal with eight legs. Spiders spin nets of thin, sticky threads called webs, which they use to trap insects for food.

*She watched the **spider** run across the floor.*

spider

spill

VERB spills, spilling, spilled

If you spill something, you let it fall out of the container it is in.

*I nearly **spilled** my drink.*

spin

VERB spins, spinning, spun

1 To spin means to turn around quickly.

*The dancers were **spinning** around and around.*

☞ **Similar:** turn, twirl, twist

2 To spin a thread means to make it.

spine

NOUN spines

1 Your spine is the row of small bones in your back.

2 Spines are stiff, sharp points on an animal or a plant.

spit

VERB spits, spitting, spat

If you spit, you force something out of your mouth.

*She **spat** out the rotten apple.*

splteful

ADJECTIVE

Someone who is spiteful is deliberately nasty to other people.

☞ **Similar:** cruel, hateful, malicious, vicious

splash

VERB splashes, splashing, splashed

When you splash water, you hit it so that it flies up into the air.

*The children **splashed** around in the pool.*

splinter

NOUN splinters

A splinter is a thin, sharp piece of wood or glass.

split

VERB splits, splitting, split

1 If you split something, you divide it into parts.

*He **split** the logs with an ax.*

☞ **Similar:** break, chop, cut, slice

2 If something splits, it tears or breaks.

*The bag **split** open.*

☞ **Similar:** burst, crack, rip

spoil

VERB spoils, spoiling, spoiled

1 If you spoil something, you damage it or destroy it so that you cannot use it any more.

*Don't draw on that photograph —you'll **spoil** it.*

2 To spoil a child means to give them too much, so that they always expect to have their own way.

*You are **spoiling** her.*

Sports

Here are some sports and the equipment you need to play them.

Cycling

Rugby ball

Tennis racket and balls

Gymnastics

Baseball bat, glove, and ball

sponge

NOUN sponges

A sponge is a soft material that soaks up a lot of water. You use sponges for cleaning or washing things.

☞ **Say: spunj**

spooky

ADJECTIVE spookier, spookiest

A spooky place is frightening because it makes you think about ghosts.

spoon

NOUN spoons

A spoon is a tool with a small bowl at one end. You use a spoon for eating or stirring food.

sports

NOUN

Sports are something that you do to have fun and keep your body in shape. Football, running, and golf are all sports.

spot

NOUN spots

1 A spot is a small, round mark.

*There were a few **spots** of paint on the floor.*

☞ **Similar:** blob, blotch, dot, mark, stain

2 A spot is a place.

*It was a perfect picnic **spot**.*

VERB spots, spotting, spotted

3 If you spot something, you see it.

*It was hard to **spot** George in the crowd.*

☞ **Similar:** glimpse, notice, recognize, see

spotlight

NOUN spotlights

A spotlight is a strong light that is used to light up a stage.

spout

NOUN spouts

The spout on a pitcher or teapot is the part that you pour liquid out of.

sprain

VERB sprains, spraining, sprained

If you sprain a part of your body, you hurt it.

*I **sprained** my wrist when I fell off the pony.*

spray

VERB sprays, spraying, sprayed

If you spray water onto something, you cover it with fine drops of water.

*Jim **sprayed** Anne with water while she was sunbathing.*

spread

VERB spreads, spreading, spread

1 If you spread something out, you open it up.

*He **spread** the blanket out on the ground.*

2 When you spread butter on bread, you put it all over the bread.

☞ **Say: spred**

Soccer

Table-tennis paddle and ball

Ice hockey

Swimming

Football helmet

Football

Golf club and balls

a
b
c
d
e
f
g
h
i
j
k
l
m
n
o
p
q
r
Ss
t
u
v
w
x
y
z

spring
NOUN springs
1 Spring is one of the four seasons. Spring follows winter and comes before summer. It is the time when the weather becomes warmer and many plants start to grow.
2 A spring is a coil of thin metal that jumps back into shape after it has been pressed together.
VERB springs, springing, sprang, sprung
3 When you spring, you jump upward in a lively way.
She sprang out of bed.
☛ **Similar:** bound, jump, leap, pounce

sprint
VERB sprints, sprinting, sprinted
When you sprint, you run very fast.
He sprinted toward the bus stop.
☛ **Similar:** dash, race, run, rush, tear

spun
Spun is the past tense of the verb **spin**.

spy
NOUN spies
A spy is a person who gathers information in secret.
Lucy and Amy liked to pretend they were spies.
☛ **Similar:** agent, informer, secret agent

squabble
VERB squabbles, squabbling, squabbled
When people squabble, they argue with each other.

square
NOUN squares
A square is a shape with four equal sides and four right angles.

squirrel

squash
VERB squashes, squashing, squashed
If you squash something, you crush it so that it becomes flat.
☛ **Similar:** crush, flatten, mash, press, squeeze

squash Say: skwosh

squeak
VERB squeaks, squeaking, squeaked
To squeak means to make a short, high sound, like the sound a mouse makes.
☛ **Similar:** cheep, peep, squeal

squeal
VERB squeals, squealing, squealed
To squeal means to make a long, high sound.
The children squealed with laughter.
☛ **Similar:** screech, shriek

squeeze
VERB squeezes, squeezing, squeezed
If you squeeze something, you press it hard.
She squeezed the tube of toothpaste.

squirrel
NOUN squirrels
A squirrel is a small, furry animal with a large, bushy tail. Squirrels eat nuts and berries.
☛ **Word history:** The word **squirrel** comes from the Greek word *skiouros*, meaning "shadow tail."

squirt
VERB squirts, squirting, squirted
When you squirt liquid, you make it shoot out in a thin jet.
He squirted the dishwashing liquid into the sink.
☛ **Rhymes:** dirt

stab
VERB stabs, stabbing, stabbed
To stab something means to push something sharp into it.
She stabbed the potato with a fork to see if it was cooked.

stable
NOUN stables
A stable is a building where horses are kept.

stack

NOUN stacks

A stack is a pile of things, one on top of another.
*There was a **stack** of books on the teacher's desk.*

☞ **Similar:** heap, mound, mountain, pile

stadium

NOUN stadiums or stadia

A stadium is a sports arena with seats all around for spectators.

stag

NOUN stags

A stag is an adult male deer.

stage

NOUN stages

1 A stage is a platform that people stand on to perform plays and shows.
2 One stage of something is one part of it.
*They made the long journey in several **stages**.*

stagger

VERB staggers, staggering, staggered

If you stagger along, you walk in an unsteady way, nearly falling over.

☞ **Similar:** lurch, reel, totter

stain

NOUN stains

A stain is a dirty mark on something.

☞ **Similar:** blotch, mark, spot

stair

NOUN stairs

Stairs are steps.

stale

ADJECTIVE

Food that is stale is not fresh.
*The bread was **stale**.*

stalk

NOUN stalks

The stalk of a flower or leaf is the part that joins it to the plant.

☞ **Say: stawk**

stall

NOUN stalls

A stall is a compartment in a stable or barn where an animal is kept.

☞ **Rhymes:** call

stammer

VERB stammers, stammering, stammered

If you stammer, you find it difficult to speak and you repeat the sounds at the beginning of words.

stamp

NOUN stamps

1 A stamp is a sticker that you put on an envelope or package to show that you have paid for it to be delivered.
VERB stamps, stamping, stamped
2 If you stamp your foot, you bang it down on the ground.

stand

VERB stands, standing, stood

When you are standing, your feet are on the ground and your body is upright.

Stairs

star

NOUN stars

1 Stars are the tiny lights we see in the sky at night. The nearest star to Earth is the sun.
2 A star is a shape with five or more points.
3 A star is a famous person.

stare

VERB stares, staring, stared

If you stare at something, you look at it for a long time.
*It's rude to **stare** at people.*

☞ **Similar:** gape, gawp, gaze, glare, peer

start

NOUN starts

1 The start of something is when it begins.
VERB starts, starting, started
2 To start means to begin.
*The runners lined up, ready to **start** the race.*

☞ **Similar:** begin, commence

startle

VERB startles, startling, startled

If something startles you, it gives you a surprise or a shock.
*The sudden movement **startled** him.*

☞ **Similar:** alarm, frighten, shock, surprise

starve

VERB starves, starving, starved

If someone is starving, they do not have enough food to live.

a
b
c
d
e
f
g
h
i
j
k
l
m
n
o
p
q
r
Ss
t
u
v
w
x
y
z

a
b
c
d
e
f
g
h
i
j

station
NOUN stations
1 A station is a place where buses and trains stop so that people can get on and off.
2 A station is a building used by the police or fire brigade.
*You can report the crime at the police **station**.*
☞ **Say:** stay-shun
Word history: The word **station** comes from the Latin word *statio,* meaning "standing," as a station is a place where you stand and wait.

statue
NOUN statues
A statue is a model of a person or animal made from stone, wood, or metal.

*The **Statue** of Liberty welcomes travelers to New York.*

Ss

p
q
r
t
u
v
w
x
y
z

stay
VERB stays, staying, stayed
1 If you stay in a place, you remain there and do not go away.
*Dad **stayed** at home while we went to the movies.*
☞ **Similar:** linger, remain
2 If you stay in a place, you live there for a short time.
*I went to **stay** with my cousin during the summer vacation.*
3 To stay means to remain.
*It **stayed** sunny all week.*

steady
ADJECTIVE steadier, steadiest
1 If something is steady, it is firm and does not move.
*He held the ladder **steady**.*
☞ **Similar:** balanced, firm, safe, secure, stable
2 Something that is steady continues without getting faster or slower.
☞ **Say:** sted-ee

steak
NOUN steaks
A steak is a thick slice of fish or meat, usually beef.
☞ **Say:** stake

steal
VERB steals, stealing, stole, stolen
To steal something means to take something that does not belong to you.
*Thieves have **stolen** some paintings from the museum.*
☞ **Similar:** pilfer, rob, shoplift, snatch, take

steam
NOUN
Steam is the gas that water turns into when it boils.

steel
NOUN
Steel is a hard, strong metal.

steep
ADJECTIVE steeper, steepest
A steep hill or slope goes up or down sharply.

steer
VERB steers, steering, steered
When you steer something, you control the direction it goes in.
*She **steered** her bicycle into the driveway.*

stem
NOUN stems
The stem of a plant is the main stalk that grows up out of the soil.

step
NOUN steps
1 When you take a step, you put one foot in front of the other and move forward.
2 A step is one of the parts of a staircase or a ladder on which you put your feet.

stepfather
NOUN stepfathers
Your stepfather is a man who is married to your mother but is not your real father.

stepmother
NOUN stepmothers
Your stepmother is a woman who is married to your father but is not your real mother.

s t e m

stereo

NOUN stereos

A stereo is a machine that you use for playing tapes or CDs.

☞ **Say: stair**-ree-oh

stick

NOUN sticks

1 A stick is a long, thin piece of wood.

VERB sticks, sticking, stuck

2 If you stick things together, you glue or fasten them together.

*She **stuck** the model airplane together with glue.*

☞ **Similar:** attach, fasten, glue, join, paste

3 If something sticks out, part of it hangs out from a place.

sticky

ADJECTIVE stickier, stickiest

If something is sticky, it stays on your fingers when you touch it.

stiff

ADJECTIVE stiffer, stiffest

Something that is stiff does not bend or move easily.

*This folder is made of **stiff** cardboard.*

☞ **Similar:** firm, hard, rigid

still

ADJECTIVE

1 Something that is still is not moving or making any sound.

☞ **Similar:** calm, peaceful, quiet, silent

ADVERB

2 Still means even now.

*He is **still** there.*

3 Still means even so.

*I don't like toothpaste, but I **still** have to use it.*

sting

VERB stings, stinging, stung

If an insect stings you, it pricks your skin and hurts you.

Sting

A wasp sting is very painful.

stink

VERB stinks, stinking, stank, stunk

If something stinks, it smells bad.

*This garbage can **stinks**!*

☞ **Similar:** reek

stir

VERB stirs, stirring, stirred

When you stir something, you mix it around with a spoon.

stole

Stole is the past tense of the verb **steal**.

stolen

Stolen is a past tense of the verb **steal**.

stomach

NOUN stomachs

1 Your stomach is the part inside your body where food goes after you have eaten it.

2 Your stomach is the outside part of your body below your chest.

stomach Say: stum-uk

stone

NOUN stones

1 Stone is the hard material that rocks are made of.

*They made a statue out of **stone**.*

2 A stone is a small, loose piece of rock.

stood

Stood is the past tense of the verb **stand**.

stool

NOUN stools

A stool is a chair with no back or arms.

stop

VERB stops, stopping, stopped

1 When something stops, it ends.

☞ **Similar:** cease, end, finish, pause

2 If you stop someone from doing something, you do not allow them to do it.

*The man **stopped** the boy from running into the road.*

stopwatch

NOUN stopwatches

A stopwatch is a watch that you can start and stop to measure how much time something takes.

*Donna used a **stopwatch** to time Brady's run.*

a b c d e f g h i j k l m n o p q r **Ss** t u v w x y z

a b c d e f g h i j k l m n o p q r **Ss** t u v w x y z

store

NOUN stores

1 A store is a large shop.

VERB stores, storing, stored

2 When you store things, you put them away and keep them until you need them.
They stored the sports equipment in the closet.

storm

NOUN storms

When there is a storm, there is a strong wind and heavy rain, hail, or snow.

☞ **Similar:** cyclone, gale, hurricane, tempest

story

NOUN stories

A story tells you about things that have happened to someone. Some stories are about real people and are true, and some are about imaginary people and are not true.

☞ **Similar:** fable, legend, myth, parable, tale

straight

ADJECTIVE straighter, straightest

Something that is straight is not bent or curved.
She drew a straight line.

☞ **Say:** strate

stranded

ADJECTIVE

If you are stranded in a place, you are stuck there and are unable to leave.
He was left stranded on the island.

strange

ADJECTIVE stranger, strangest

Something that is strange is not normal, or not how you expect it to be.

☞ **Similar:** bizarre, funny, odd, peculiar, weird

stranger

NOUN strangers

A stranger is a person you do not know.

strap

NOUN straps

A strap is a strip of leather or cloth that you use for fastening or holding things.

straw

NOUN straws

1 Straw is stalks of dried wheat that you put on the ground for animals to lie on.
2 A straw is a small hollow tube that you use for drinking through.

strawberry

NOUN strawberries

A strawberry is a small, red fruit that is soft and sweet.

stream

NOUN streams

A stream is a small river.

street

NOUN streets

A street is a road in a city or town.
What is the name of the street you live on?

☞ **Similar:** avenue, drive, lane, road

strength

NOUN

The strength of something is how strong it is.
The weight lifter had incredible strength in his arms.

stress

NOUN

If you are under stress, you have a lot of things that you are worried about.

☞ **Similar:** anxiety, pressure, worry

stretch

VERB stretches, stretching, stretched

1 When you stretch something, you pull it so that it becomes longer or bigger.
2 When you stretch out a part of your body, you reach out with it as much as you can.

s t r e t c h

It's good to stretch before exercising.

strict

ADJECTIVE stricter, strictest
Someone who is strict makes people behave well and do the things they are told to do.
*The teacher was **strict**.*
☞ **Similar:** firm, harsh, stern
Opposite: soft

strike

NOUN strikes
1 When there is a strike, people refuse to work because they are unhappy or angry about something, or because they want more money for doing their job.
VERB strikes, striking, struck
2 To strike something means to hit it.
*The tree was **struck** by lightning.*

string

NOUN strings
1 String is thin cord or rope.
2 The strings on a guitar or violin are the parts that you touch to make a sound.

strip

NOUN strips
A strip is a long, narrow piece of something.
*They cut **strips** of colored paper to make the decorations.*

stripe

NOUN stripes
Stripes are narrow bands of color. Something that has stripes is **striped**.

stroke

VERB strokes, stroking, stroked
When you stroke an animal, you rub it gently with your hand.
*He **stroked** the rabbit.*

stroll

VERB strolls, strolling, strolled
When you stroll along, you walk slowly in a relaxed way.
*They **strolled** through the woods.*
☞ **Similar:** dawdle, wander

stroller

NOUN strollers
A stroller is a small chair on wheels, in which you can push a small child.

strong

ADJECTIVE stronger, strongest
1 Something that is strong is tough and will not break easily.
☞ **Similar:** heavy, solid, tough
Opposite: weak
2 Someone who is strong has a powerful body.
*Elephants are very **strong**.*
☞ **Similar:** mighty, muscular
Opposite: weak

struggle

VERB struggles, struggling, struggled
If you struggle to do something, you try very hard to do it.
*He **struggled** with the math problem for a long time.*

What is the plural of story?

Look around the page to find the answer.

stubborn

ADJECTIVE
Someone who is stubborn is determined to have their own way and will not change their mind.
☞ **Say: stub**-ern
Similar: defiant, headstrong, obstinate, willful

stuck

Stuck is the past tense of the verb **stick**.

student

NOUN students
A student is someone who is studying at school, college, or university.
☞ **Say: stew**-dent

studio

NOUN studios
1 A studio is a room where an artist or photographer works.
2 A studio is a room where television programs or music recordings are made.
☞ **Say: stoo**-dee-oh

a b c d e f g h i j k l m n o p q r **Ss** t u v w x y z

striped

*The house is decorated with **striped** wallpaper.*

a
b
c
d
e
f
g
h
i
j
k
l
m
n
o
p
q
r

Ss

t
u
v
w
x
y
z

study
VERB studies, studying, studied
1 If you study something, you look at it carefully.
*She **studied** the flower through a magnifying glass.*
2 When you study a subject, you learn about it.
*We're **studying** the Romans this semester.*
☞ **Similar:** investigate, research

stumble
VERB stumbles, stumbling, stumbled
If you stumble, you trip and almost fall.
☞ **Similar:** slip, stagger, trip

stump
NOUN stumps
A stump is a short part of something that is left behind after the rest has been cut off.
*We sat down on an old tree **stump**.*

stung
Stung is the past tense of the verb **sting.**

stunt
NOUN stunts
A stunt is something clever and dangerous that someone does in a film or performance.
*The **stunt** involved jumping over 15 cars on a motorcycle.*

stupid
ADJECTIVE stupider, stupidest
Someone who is stupid is not very intelligent.
☞ **Say:** stoo-pid
Similar: brainless, dim, foolish, silly, simple, thick
Opposite: intelligent

stutter
VERB stutters, stuttering, stuttered
If you stutter, you find it difficult to speak and you repeat the sounds at the beginning of words.

style
NOUN styles
A style is a shape or design of something.
*Which **style** of tennis racket do you prefer?*
☞ **Say:** stile

subject
NOUN subjects
A subject is one thing that you are talking, writing, or learning about.
*History is my favorite **subject** in school.*
☞ **Similar:** theme, topic

submarine
NOUN submarines
A submarine is a boat that can travel underwater.
☞ **Say:** sub-ma-reen

substance
NOUN substances
A substance is a material.
*There was a sticky **substance** on the table.*

substitute
NOUN substitutes
A substitute is a player who joins in a game if someone else is hurt or tired.
☞ **Say:** sub-sti-toot

subtract
VERB subtracts, subtracting, subtracted
When you subtract numbers, you take one away from the other. Subtracting numbers is called **subtraction.**
*Can you **subtract** five from eight?*
☞ **Word history:** The word **subtract** comes from the Latin word *subtractus*, meaning "pulled away," so when you subtract numbers you pull one away from the other.

submarine
*A **submarine** dives to the depths of the sea.*

subway
NOUN
A subway is an underground railway system.

succeed
VERB succeeds, succeeding, succeeded
If you succeed, you have achieved something.
☞ **Say:** suk-seed
Similar: triumph
Opposite: fail

What is the opposite of **success?**

Look around the page to find the answer.

success

NOUN successes
If something is a success,
it works well.
*His magic act was a **success**.*
☛ **Opposite:** failure

success
Say: **suk-sess**

successful

ADJECTIVE
Something that is successful
works well.

suck

VERB sucks, sucking, sucked
When you suck something,
you hold it in your mouth
and pull on it with your
mouth.

sudden

ADJECTIVE
Something that is sudden
happens quickly, when you
are not expecting it.

suddenly

ADVERB
If something happens
suddenly, it happens quickly,
when you are not expecting it.
*He **suddenly** fell over.*

suffer

VERB suffers, suffering, suffered
1 If you are suffering, you
are in pain.
2 When you have an illness,
you are suffering from it.
*He is **suffering** from the measles.*

sufficient

ADJECTIVE
Sufficient means enough.
*We didn't have **sufficient** money
to buy an ice-cream cone.*

sugar

NOUN
Sugar is a substance that you
add to food and drinks to
make them taste sweet.

suggest

VERB suggests, suggesting,
suggested
If you suggest something, you
mention it and say that you
think it is a good idea.
*I **suggested** going to the park
to ride our bikes.*
☛ **Say:** sug-**jest**
Similar: advise, recommend

suggestion

NOUN suggestions
A suggestion is an idea
that you propose.

suit

NOUN suits
1 A suit is a jacket and skirt
or a jacket and pants that
go together.
*He wore a **suit** to work.*
VERB suits, suiting, suited
2 If something suits you,
it looks nice when you
wear it.
*That dress really **suits** you.*
☛ **Rhymes:** boot

suitable

ADJECTIVE
If something is suitable,
it is right for a particular
purpose.
*These boots are **suitable** for
walking over rough ground.*
☛ **Opposite:** unsuitable

suitcase

NOUN suitcases
A suitcase is a large bag
that you use for carrying
clothing and other things
when you travel.
*She packed her **suitcase** for
the vacation.*

sulk

VERB sulks, sulking, sulked
When you sulk, you are
quiet because you are in
a bad mood.
*Please stop **sulking**.*

sulky

ADJECTIVE
If you are sulky, you are
quiet because you are in
a bad mood.
☛ **Similar:** grumpy, moody

a
b
c
d
e
f
g
h
i
j
k
l
m
n
o
p
q
r
Ss
t
u
v
w
x
y
z

sulky

*Benjamin looks **sulky**.*

a
b
c
d
e
f
g
h
i
j
k
l
m
n
o
p
q
r

Ss

t
u
v
w
x
y
z

sum
NOUN sums
The sum of two numbers is the total that they add up to. *The **sum** of three and seven is ten.*

summer
NOUN summers
Summer is one of the four seasons. Summer follows spring and comes before fall. It is the warmest season of the year.

summit
NOUN summits
The summit is the highest point of a hill or mountain.

sun
NOUN
1 You can see the sun shining in the sky during the day. The sun is the star that is at the center of the **solar system**.
2 If you are in the sun, you are in the light and heat that we get from the sun. *The cat was sleeping in the **sun**.*

sunbathe
VERB sunbathes, sunbathing, sunbathed
When you sunbathe, you sit in the sun so that your skin will turn brown.

sunflower
NOUN sunflowers
A sunflower is a tall plant with large, yellow flowers. The seeds can be eaten or used to make cooking oil.

sung
Sung is a past tense of the verb **sing**.

sunglasses
NOUN
Sunglasses are glasses with dark lenses that you wear to protect your eyes from bright sunlight.

sunk
Sunk is a past tense of the verb **sink**.

sunlight
NOUN
Sunlight is the light from the sun.

sunny
ADJECTIVE sunnier, sunniest
If the weather is sunny, the sun is shining and there are no clouds in the sky.
☞ **Similar:** bright, clear, cloudless, fine, glorious

Sunflowers always face the sun.

sunflower

sunrise
NOUN sunrises
Sunrise is the time when the sun comes up in the morning.

sunscreen
NOUN
Sunscreen is a special cream that you put on your skin to protect it from the sun and to stop it from burning.

sunset
NOUN sunsets
Sunset is the time when the sun goes down in the evening.

sunshine
NOUN
Sunshine is bright light and heat from the sun.

super
ADJECTIVE
Super means wonderful. *We had a **super** time.*
☞ **Similar:** fantastic, great, wonderful
Opposite: awful

superb
ADJECTIVE
Superb means extremely good.
*The food in the hotel restaurant is **superb**.*
☞ **Say:** soo-**purb**
Similar: excellent, fantastic, magnificent, splendid, wonderful
Opposite: awful

supermarket
NOUN supermarkets
A supermarket is a large store that sells food and other things.

supersonic

ADJECTIVE

A supersonic plane travels faster than the speed of sound.

☞ **Say:** soo-per-**son**-ic

supersonic

Supersonic planes go faster than the speed of sound.

superstar

NOUN superstars

A superstar is someone who is very famous.

supper

NOUN suppers

Supper is a meal that you eat in the evening.

support

VERB supports, supporting, supported

1 To support someone or something means to hold them up and stop them from falling.

2 To support someone means to help them.

suppose

VERB supposes, supposing, supposed

If you suppose that something is true, you think that it is true, but you do not know for certain.

*I **suppose** this must be his car.*

☞ **Similar:** assume, guess, presume, think

sure

ADJECTIVE

If you are sure about something, you are certain about it.

*I am **sure** you will enjoy your stay here.*

☞ **Say: shur**

Similar: confident, positive

Opposite: uncertain

surf

VERB surfs, surfing, surfed

1 When you go surfing, you balance on a special board and ride on waves as they begin to break near the seashore.

2 When you surf the Internet, you search it to find information.

surface

NOUN surfaces

The surface of something is the top or outside of it.

*The table has a shiny **surface**.*

☞ **Say: sur**-fis

surfboard

NOUN surfboards

A surfboard is a board that you use for surfing on waves.

*A surfer rides his **surfboard**.*

surfboard

surgery

NOUN surgeries

If you have surgery, you have an operation that involves cutting open part of your body.

surprise

NOUN surprises

1 If something is a surprise, it happens when you do not expect it.

*The bunch of flowers was a wonderful **surprise**.*

VERB surprises, surprising, surprised

2 If something surprises you, it happens when you do not expect it.

☞ **Similar:** amaze, astonish, shock, startle

surprised

ADJECTIVE

If you are surprised by something, you were not expecting it.

*I was **surprised** when I won the competition.*

☞ **Similar:** amazed, astonished, astounded, shocked

surrender

VERB surrenders, surrendering, surrendered

If you surrender, you give yourself up.

*The kidnappers finally **surrendered** to the police.*

surround

VERB surrounds, surrounding, surrounded

To surround a place means to be all around it.

*The police **surrounded** the building.*

a b c d e f g h i j k l m n o p q r **Ss** t u v w x y z

a b c d e f g h i j k l m n o p q r **Ss** t u v w x y z

survive

VERB survives, surviving survived
If you survive, you do not die.
*They all **survived** the crash.*

suspicious

ADJECTIVE
1 If you are suspicious of someone, you think that they might have done something bad.
2 A suspicious person behaves in a strange way and makes you think they might be doing something wrong.
*We saw a **suspicious** character climbing into the house.*
☞ **Say:** sus-**pish**-us

swallow

NOUN swallows
1 A swallow is a small black and white bird with a forked tail.
VERB swallows, swallowing, swallowed
2 When you swallow food, you make it go down your throat and into your stomach.

swan

NOUN swans
A swan is a large bird with a long neck that lives in and around water.

How many syllables are there in "computer?"
Look around the page to find the answer.

swap

VERB swaps, swapping, swapped
To swap something means to give it to someone in return for something else.
*He **swapped** his computer game for her tennis racket.*
☞ **Similar:** change, exchange, trade

swallow

swarm

NOUN swarms
A swarm of insects is a large number of them flying together.
*A **swarm** of bees can be dangerous.*
☞ **Say:** sworm

swear

VERB swears, swearing, swore, sworn
If you swear, you say obscene and unpleasant words.
*She told us never to **swear**.*

sweat

NOUN
1 Sweat is the salty liquid that comes out of your skin when you are hot.
*She was covered in **sweat** after running in the race.*
VERB sweats, sweating, sweated
2 When you sweat, liquid comes out of your skin to cool you down when you are hot.

sweater

NOUN sweaters
A sweater is a thick knitted top that keeps you warm.
*It was so cold he had to wear two **sweaters**.*

sweep

VERB sweeps, sweeping, swept
When you sweep a floor, you clean it using a brush.
*They **swept** the floor after the party.*

sweet

ADJECTIVE sweeter, sweetest
1 Something that is sweet tastes of sugar.
*Grapes and oranges are **sweet** fruit.*
2 Someone who is sweet is very kind.
*It was **sweet** of you to bring me flowers.*

swim

VERB swims, swimming, swam, swum
When you swim, you use your arms and legs to move through water.
*She **swam** from the boat to the shore.*

swimming pool

NOUN swimming pools

A swimming pool is a large area of water where people can go to swim.

swing

NOUN swings

A swing is a seat hung from ropes or chains. You sit on it and move backward and forward.

VERB swings, swinging, swung

2 To swing means to move backward and forward in the air.

switch

NOUN switches

A switch is a button or lever that you use to turn a machine on and off.

swollen

ADJECTIVE

If a part of your body is swollen, it is bigger than usual.

syllable

NOUN syllables

A syllable is a part of a word made up of a single sound. The word "computer" has three syllables.
☞ **Say: sil**-a-bul

*Abby **swings** to and fro.*

swing

symbol

NOUN symbols

A symbol is a picture or sign that represents something.
☞ **Say: sim**-bul
*The dove is a **symbol** of peace.*

symmetrical

ADJECTIVE

If something is symmetrical, it has two halves that match each other.

symmetrical

Say:

simm-met-trik-al

swoop

VERB swoops, swooping, swooped

To swoop means to move suddenly downward through the air.
☞ **Similar:** dive, drop, plunge

sword

NOUN swords

A sword is a weapon with a long, sharp blade and a handle.
☞ **Say: sord**

sympathy

NOUN

If you give someone sympathy, you show that you care about them and feel sorry for them.
*Everyone showed me a lot of **sympathy** when I broke my arm.*
☞ **Say: sim**-pa-thee
Similar: compassion, concern, kindness, support, understanding

synagogue

NOUN synagogues

A synagogue is a building where Jews go to pray.
☞ **Say: sin**-a-gog

synonym

NOUN synonyms

A synonym is a word that means the same as another word. "Large" is a synonym of "big."
☞ **Say: sin**-o-nim

syrup

NOUN syrups

Syrup is a sweet, sticky liquid that you can eat.
☞ **Say: si**-rup
Word history: The word **syrup** comes from the Arabic word *sharab*, meaning "drink."

system

NOUN systems

If things work together in a system, they work together in an organized way.
☞ **Say: sis**-tum

a
b
c
d
e
f
g
h
i
j
k
l
m
n
o
p
q
r
Ss
t
u
v
w
x
y
z

209

a
b
c
d
e
f
g
h
i
j
k
l
m
n
o
p
q
r
s
Tt
u
v
w
x
y
z

T

target

table
NOUN tables
1 A table is a piece of furniture with a flat surface and legs underneath to support it.
2 A table is a way of showing information in lists and columns.
☞ **Word history:** The word **table** comes from the Latin word *tabula*, meaning a flat piece of wood, either for putting food on or for writing on.

tablet
NOUN tablets
A tablet is a small piece of medicine that you swallow whole.

table tennis
NOUN
Table tennis is a game in which you hit a small ball across a large table that has a net across the middle.

tadpole
NOUN tadpoles
A tadpole is a young frog or toad that has no legs and lives in water.

tail
NOUN tails
An animal's tail is the part of it that sticks out at the end of its body.

tailor
NOUN tailors
A tailor is a person who makes suits and other clothes for people.
☞ **Word history:** The word **tailor** comes from the old French word *tailleur*, meaning "cutter," because a tailor is someone who cuts cloth.

take
VERB takes, taking, took, taken
1 When you take something, you remove it from a place.
*Someone has **taken** my pen.*
2 When you take something somewhere, you move it to that place.
*She **took** some toys to school.*
3 When you take someone somewhere, you go with them to that place.
*My father **took** me to the zoo.*
4 When you take one number away from another, you subtract it.

tale
NOUN tales
A tale is a story that is not true.
*"Cinderella" is a fairy **tale**.*
☞ **Similar:** fable, legend, myth, story

tail

A lizard has a long *tail*.

talented
ADJECTIVE
Someone who is talented is good at doing something.
*William is a **talented** musician.*
☞ **Similar:** skillful

talk
VERB talks, talking, talked
When you talk, you say words to someone.
*He **talked** to his sister on the telephone for an hour.*
☞ **Say:** tawk
Similar: chat, discuss, speak

talkative
ADJECTIVE
Someone who is talkative talks a lot.
*Try not to be so **talkative** in class.*

talkative Say:
tawk-at-iv

tall

ADJECTIVE taller, tallest
1 Something that is tall is very high.
*There are some **tall** buildings in Hong Kong.*
☞ **Opposite:** low
2 Someone who is tall has a long body.
*Ravi is the **tallest** in our class.*

tambourine

NOUN tambourines
A tambourine is a musical instrument that you hold in your hand and shake or tap to make a rhythm.
☞ **Say:** tam-bor-**een**

Word history: The word **tambourine** comes from the Persian word *tabira*, meaning "drum."

tambourine

tame

ADJECTIVE tamer, tamest
A tame animal is used to being with people and so is not fierce, and is not afraid of people.
☞ **Opposite:** wild

tan

NOUN tans
1 When you get a tan, your skin turns brown because it has been in the sun.
VERB tans, tanning, tanned
2 When you tan, your skin turns brown in the sun.

tangle

VERB tangles, tangling, tangled
If something gets tangled, it gets twisted and tied into messy knots.

tank

NOUN tanks
1 A tank is a large container for holding liquid.
2 A tank is a heavy vehicle with guns that moves on metal belts instead of wheels.

tap

VERB taps, tapping, tapped
If you tap something, you hit it gently.
☞ **Similar:** hit, knock, pat

tape

NOUN tapes
1 A tape is a long, narrow strip of cloth or plastic. *We held a **tape** across the finishing line.*
2 Tape is a special strip of plastic coated with magnetic powder that you use for recording sounds or movies.
3 Tape is a thin strip of plastic with a sticky film for attaching one thing to another.

tape measure

NOUN tape measures
A tape measure is a tape with inches or centimeters marked on it, that you use for measuring things.

target

NOUN targets
A target is something that you try to hit when you are shooting or throwing something.

tart

NOUN tarts
A tart is a pie that has pastry on the bottom and fruit on top.

taste

NOUN
1 Taste is one of your body's five senses, which you use to find out the flavor of something.
2 The taste of something is what it is like when you put it in your mouth.
*Do you like the **taste** of liquorice?*
VERB tastes, tasting, tasted
3 When you taste something, you put it in your mouth to see what it is like.

tasty

ADJECTIVE tastier, tastiest
Something that is tasty has a nice taste.
☞ **Similar:** delicious, scrumptious

taught

Taught is the past tense of the verb **teach**.
☞ **Say:** tawt

I used a tape measure to measure my height.

a
b
c
d
e
f
g
h
i
j
k
l
m
n
o
p
q
r
s
Tt
u
v
z

211

a
b
c
d
e

taxi
NOUN taxis
A taxi is a car that you can travel in by paying the driver money.
☞ **Say: tak**-see

I hailed a taxi to take me home.

j
k

tea
NOUN
Tea is a drink that you make by pouring boiling water onto the dried leaves of the tea plant.

teach
VERB teaches, teaching, taught
When you teach someone something, you tell them about it or show them how to do it.
Miss Earnshaw teaches us math.
☞ **Similar:** coach, educate, instruct, train

Tt

u

teacher
NOUN teachers
A teacher is someone who helps people to learn about things.

v
w
x
y
z

technology
NOUN
Technology is science and machines that people use in everyday life.

technology
Say:
tek-nol-o-jee

team
NOUN teams
A team is a group of people who work or play sports together.
☞ **Similar:** band, bunch, gang, group, squad

tear
NOUN tears
Tears are drops of salty water that come from your eyes when you cry.
☞ **Rhymes:** deer

tear
VERB tears, tearing, tore, torn
When you tear paper or cloth, you make a hole or split in it.
☞ **Rhymes:** care

tease
VERB teases, teasing, teased
If you tease someone, you do or say things to annoy them in a playful way.

teddy bear
NOUN teddy bears
A teddy bear is a stuffed toy in the shape of a bear.
☞ **Word history:**
The teddy bear was named after President Theodore Roosevelt after he refused to shoot a bear cub. Teddy is a short form of the name Theodore.

teenager
NOUN teenagers
A teenager is a young person between the ages of 13 and 19.

teeth
Teeth is the plural of **tooth**.

telephone
NOUN telephones
A telephone is a machine that you use to talk to people who are far away. Telephone is often shortened to **phone**.
☞ **Word history:** The word **telephone** was made up by putting together the Greek words *tele*, meaning "far away" and *phone*, meaning "sound."

telescope
NOUN telescopes
A telescope makes things that are far away look bigger. You can look through a telescope to look at the stars and planets.

televise
VERB televises, televising, televised
If an event is televised, it is filmed and broadcast on television.

television

NOUN televisions
A television is a machine that receives signals that are broadcast and turns them into pictures and sound. Television is often shortened to **TV**.

Who is the
teddy bear
named
after?

Look around the page to find the answer.

tell

VERB tells, telling, told
If you tell someone something, you speak to that person about it or give them information about it.
*He won't **tell** us where the treasure is!*

temper

NOUN tempers
1 A person with a bad temper gets mad easily.
2 A temper tantrum is a fit someone has when they can't control their anger.
*Tired children often have **temper** tantrums.*
☞ **Similar:** fury, rage, tantrum

temperature

NOUN temperatures
When you measure temperature, you measure how hot or cold something is.
☞ **Say:** temp-er-a-cher

temple

NOUN temples
A temple is a building where people go to worship.
*That is a Buddhist **temple**.*

tender

ADJECTIVE
1 Food that is tender is soft and easy to chew.
☞ **Opposite:** tough
2 If a part of your body is tender, it hurts when you touch it.
☞ **Similar:** bruised, painful, sensitive, sore
3 Someone who is tender is gentle and loving.
*He gave his girlfriend a **tender** kiss.*
☞ **Similar:** caring, gentle, kind, loving, warm

tennis

NOUN
Tennis is a game in which you use a racket to hit a ball over a net and score points if your opponent cannot hit it back.

tent

NOUN tents
A tent is a shelter that is made of cloth and supported with poles and ropes. You sleep in a tent when you go camping.

terrestrial

ADJECTIVE
Terrestrial means happening on land rather than in water or in the air. Terrestrial television is broadcast on Earth, not through satellites.

terrible

ADJECTIVE
Something that is terrible is very bad or horrible.
*We had a **terrible** vacation.*
☞ **Similar:** awful, dreadful, rotten

terrified

ADJECTIVE
If you are terrified, you are very scared.
*Lucy was **terrified** of the big dog when it began to bark.*
☞ **Similar:** frightened, petrified, scared

terror

NOUN
Terror is very great fear.
☞ **Similar:** dread, fright, horror, panic

a
b
c
d
e
f
g
h
i
j
k
l
m
n
o
p
q
r
s
Tt
u

*It is warm and dry in the **tent**.*

tent

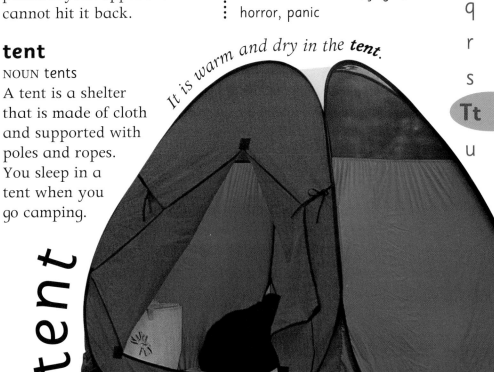

a
b
c
d
e
f
g
h
i
j
k
l
m
n
o
p
q
r
s
Tt
u
v
w
x
y
z

test
NOUN tests
1 When you take a test, you answer questions to show how much you know.
VERB tests, testing, tested
2 If you test something, you try it or use it to see what it is like.

text
NOUN texts
A text is a piece of writing.

text message
NOUN text messages
A text message is a message that you send to someone using a mobile phone.

thank
VERB thanks, thanking, thanked
If you thank someone, you say you are grateful to them for something they have done.
*I **thanked** everyone for their presents.*

thaw
VERB thaws, thawing, thawed
When something that is frozen thaws, it melts.
*The snow started to **thaw** in the sunshine.*

theater
NOUN theaters
A theater is a building where people perform plays and shows for other people to watch.
☞ **Say: thee**-a-ter

theme
NOUN themes
A theme is an idea or subject.

thermometer

theory
NOUN theories
A theory is an idea about how or why something happens.
☞ **Say: theer**-ee

thermometer
NOUN thermometers
You use a thermometer to measure temperatures.
☞ **Word history:** The word **thermometer** includes the Greek word *therme* meaning "heat," so a thermometer is a device for measuring heat.
☞ **Say: thur-mom**-it-er

*I checked the temperature with a **thermometer**.*

thesaurus
NOUN thesauruses or thesauri
A thesaurus is a book that lists groups of words with similar meanings.
☞ **Say: thi-sor**-rus

thick
ADJECTIVE thicker, thickest
1 Something that is thick is wide.
*Zahavit cut a **thick** slice of brown bread.*
☞ **Opposite:** thin
2 Someone who is thick is stupid.
☞ **Similar:** brainless, dim, slow, unintelligent
Opposite: quick-witted

thief
NOUN thieves
A thief is a person who steals things.
☞ **Rhymes:** beef
Similar: burglar, pickpocket, robber, shoplifter

thigh
NOUN thighs
Your thighs are the top parts of your legs.
☞ **Rhymes:** sky

thin
ADJECTIVE thinner, thinnest
1 Something that is thin is not very wide.
*The walls are **thin** so we can hear everything they say.*
☞ **Opposite:** thick
2 Someone who is thin is not very fat.
☞ **Similar:** bony, skinny, slender, slim, underweight
Opposite: fat

thing
NOUN things
A thing is an object or product.

think
VERB thinks, thinking, thought
When you think, you use your mind to have ideas or opinions.
*She **thought** about what she would eat for lunch.*

thirsty
ADJECTIVE thirstier, thirstiest
If you are thirsty, you want to drink something.

thirsty

*Jackie was so **thirsty**, she finished her drink in one gulp.*

thorn
NOUN thorns
A thorn is a sharp spike on a plant.
*Roses have sharp **thorns**.*

thought
NOUN thoughts
A thought is an idea that you have in your mind.
☞ **Say: thawt**

thoughtful
ADJECTIVE
If you are thoughtful, you are kind and think about other people's feelings.
*It was **thoughtful** of you to remember my birthday.*
☞ **Say: thawt-ful**
Similar: caring, helpful, kind, unselfish

thousand
NOUN thousands
A thousand is ten hundreds (1,000).

thread
NOUN threads
A thread is a thin string that you use for sewing.
☞ **Say: thred**

threaten
VERB threatens, threatening, threatened
If you threaten to do something unpleasant, you say you will do it.
*Sam's mother **threatened** to send him to bed early if he didn't behave.*
☞ **Say: thret-en**

threw
Threw is the past tense of the verb **throw**.

thrilled
ADJECTIVE
If you are thrilled about something, you are very pleased about it.

thrilling
ADJECTIVE
Something that is thrilling is very exciting.

throat
Say:
throwt
*My **throat** is sore.*

throat
NOUN throats
Your throat is the back of your mouth, where you swallow.

throne
NOUN thrones
A throne is a special chair that a king or queen sits on.

throw
VERB throws, throwing, threw, thrown
When you throw something, you hold it in your hand and then let go and push it through the air.
☞ **Similar:** chuck, fling, hurl, lob, sling, toss

thumb
NOUN thumbs
Your thumb is the short, thick finger on the side of your hand.
☞ **Say: thum**

thump
VERB thumps, thumping, thumped
If you thump someone, you hit them hard.
☞ **Similar:** beat, knock, punch, smack, strike, whack

thunder
NOUN
Thunder is the loud, rumbling sound that you hear during a storm.

throw

*She **threw** the ball a long way.*

a
b
c
d
e
f
g
h
i
j
k
l
m
n
o
q
r
s
Tt
u
v
w
x
y
z

215

a
b
c
d
e
f
g
h
i
j
k
l
m
n
o
p
q
r
s

Tt

u
v
w
x
y
z

Time

Telling the time

We measure time in **hours**, **minutes**, and **seconds**. Most traditional clocks have two hands to tell us the time. The **little hand** tells us the hours; the **big hand** tells us the minutes.

Digital clock

Digital clocks tell us the time in numbers. The numbers before the dots tell you the hour. They go from 1 to 12. The numbers after the dots tell you the minutes. These go from 1 to 60.

There are 60 minutes in one hour.

On the hour is **o'clock**.

There are five minutes between each number on a clock face.

nine **o'clock**

09.00

midnight *day*

morning a.m.

12:00 01:00 02:00 03:00 04:00 05:00 06:00 07:00 08:00

thunderstorm

NOUN thunderstorms
A thunderstorm is a storm that has thunder and lightning.
Emily and Rachael hid under the bed covers during the **thunderstorm**.

ticket

NOUN tickets
A ticket is a piece of paper that shows that you have paid to do something.
He bought four **tickets** *for the concert.*

tickle

VERB tickles, tickling, tickled
When you tickle someone, you touch their skin lightly and make them laugh.

tide

NOUN tides
The tide is the change in the level of the sea that happens twice a day.
It's best to go swimming in the sea when the **tide** *is in.*

tidy

VERB tidies, tidying, tidied
1 When you tidy a room, you put everything away in its place.
Mr. Jones **tidied** *up the garage to make space for a new car.*
ADJECTIVE tidier, tidiest
2 If a place is tidy, it is neat and everything is in its proper place.
Jo's bedroom is always **tidy**.
☞ **Opposite:** untidy

tie

NOUN ties
1 A tie is a thin strip of material that you wear around your neck, under the collar of a shirt.
VERB ties, tying, tied
2 When you tie something, you fasten it with a knot or bow.
She **tied** *a ribbon in her hair.*
☞ **Similar:** attach, fasten, knot
3 When two people tie in a game, they score the same number of points.

tiger

NOUN tigers
A tiger is a large, fierce, striped animal that lives in Asia. Tigers belong to the cat family and hunt at night for their food.

tight

ADJECTIVE tighter, tightest
A tight piece of clothing fits your body closely.
These pants are too **tight**.
☞ **Say:** tite
Similar: firm, secure
Opposite: loose

tights

NOUN
Tights are a piece of clothing that women and girls wear over their legs and hips.

timber

NOUN
Timber is wood that has been cut into pieces so that it can be used for building or making things.
☞ **Similar:** wood

15 minutes **past** the hour is a **quarter past**.

quarter past nine

09.15

30 minutes **past** the hour is **nine thirty**.

nine **thirty**

09.30

15 minutes **to** the hour is a **quarter to**.

quarter to ten

09.45

noon afternoon **p.m.** evening night midnight

09:00 10:00 11:00 12:00 1:00 2:00 3:00 4:00 5:00 6:00 7:00 8:00 9:00 10:00 11:00 12:00

time

NOUN times

1 Time is all the hours, days, and years in the past, present, and future.
*Do you know what **time** it is?*

2 The number of times that you do something is how often you do it.
*I go swimming three **times** a week.*

3 One number times another number is the two numbers multiplied together.
*What's three **times** four?*

timid

ADJECTIVE

Someone who is timid is not very brave.
*The bird was **timid** and flew away when I moved.*

☞ **Similar:** afraid, nervous, scared, shy
Opposite: bold

tin

NOUN

Tin is a light, silver-colored metal.

tiny

ADJECTIVE tinier, tiniest

Something that is tiny is very small.
*The newborn baby is **tiny**.*

☞ **Similar:** little, miniature, small, teeny-weeny
Opposite: huge

tip

NOUN tips

1 The tip of something is its narrow, pointed end.
*He had a spot of ink on the **tip** of his nose.*

2 A tip is a little piece of advice that helps you to do something.
*The coach gave us a lot of **tips** on how to win.*

3 If you give someone a tip, you give them a small, extra amount of money when they have done something for you.
*We left the waiter a **tip**.*

VERB tips, tipping, tipped

4 If you tip something, you move it so that it is not upright.
*He **tipped** the bucket over.*

tiptoe

VERB tiptoes, tiptoeing, tiptoed

To tiptoe, you walk slowly and quietly on your toes.

tire

NOUN tires

A tire is a circle of rubber with air inside it around a wheel on a car or bicycle.

tired

ADJECTIVE

If you feel tired, you feel that you want to sleep.

☞ **Similar:** drowsy, sleepy

tissue

NOUN tissues

A tissue is thin paper that you use for blowing your nose.

☞ **Say:** tish-oo

title

NOUN titles

1 The title of a book, movie, or painting is what it is called.

2 Someone's title is the part of their name that shows their rank or job.

a
b
c
d
e
f
g
h
i
j
k
l
m
n
o
p
q
r
s
Tt
u
v
w
x
y
z

toad

NOUN toads

A toad is an animal that looks like a large frog. Toads are amphibians but usually live on land.

toast

NOUN

Toast is bread that has been grilled on both sides until it is crisp and brown.

today

Today is this day.
*I'm going to the zoo **today**.*

toe

NOUN toes

Your toes are the five separate parts at the end of each foot.

toffee

NOUN

Toffee is a type of chewy candy.

together

ADVERB

When people do something together, they do it with each other.
*Let's walk to school **together**.*

toilet

NOUN toilets

A toilet is a large bowl that you use for getting rid of waste from your body.

told

Told is the past tense of the verb **tell**.

tomato

NOUN tomatoes

A tomato is a soft, juicy, red fruit that you can eat raw or cooked.

Tomatoes are often used in salads.

tomorrow

Tomorrow is the day after today.
*We're going on vacation **tomorrow**.*

tongue

NOUN tongues

Your tongue is the part inside your mouth that you can move and that you use for talking and for tasting food.
☛ **Say: tung**

tonight

Tonight is the evening and night of today.
*We're performing our school concert **tonight**.*

took

Took is the past tense of the verb **take**.

tool

NOUN tools

A tool is something that you hold in your hand and use to do a job.

*He used his **tools** to mend the shed.*

tooth

NOUN teeth

1 Your teeth are the hard, white things inside your mouth that you use for biting and chewing. **2** The teeth on a comb or saw are the pointed parts.

toothbrush

NOUN toothbrushes

A toothbrush is a small brush that you use for cleaning your teeth.

toothpaste

NOUN

Toothpaste is a special cleaner that you use for brushing your teeth.

top

NOUN tops

1 The top of something is the highest part of it.
*It's a long way to the **top** of the mountain.*
☛ **Similar:** peak, summit, tip
Opposite: bottom
2 A top is a lid.
*Do you have the **top** to the ketchup bottle?*
☛ **Similar:** cap, cork, stopper
3 A top is a piece of clothing that you wear on the top part of your body.
☛ **Similar:** blouse, shirt, sweatshirt, T-shirt

topic

NOUN topics

A topic is a subject that you learn about or talk about.
*Our history **topic** for this week is the Romans.*

topple

VERB topples, toppling, toppled
If something topples over, it falls over.

Is a **tomato** a **fruit** or a **vegetable**?

Look around the page to find the answer.

tore

Tore is the past tense of the verb **tear**.

tornado

NOUN tornadoes or tornados
A tornado is a violent, whirling wind that causes great damage to land and buildings.
☞ **Say:** tor-**nay**-doh
Word history: The word **tornado** comes from the Spanish word *tronada*, meaning "thunderstorm."

tortoise

NOUN tortoises
A tortoise is an animal with a hard shell that moves slowly and hides inside its shell when it is in danger.
☞ **Say:** tort-tus

toss

VERB tosses, tossing, tossed
1 When you toss something, you throw it into the air.
*Steven **tossed** the ball to me.*
☞ **Similar:** chuck, fling, hurl, sling
2 When you toss a coin, you throw it into the air and guess which side will face upward when it lands.

total

NOUN totals
1 The total is the amount that you get when you add numbers together.
*The **total** of two, three, and four is nine.*
ADJECTIVE
2 Total means complete.
*We were left in **total** darkness.*
☞ **Say:** toe-tal

touch

VERB touches, touching, touched
When you touch something, you put your hand on it.
*Please do not **touch** any of the paintings.*
☞ **Similar:** feel, handle, pat, rub, stroke
Say: tuch

tough

ADJECTIVE tougher, toughest
1 Something that is tough is strong and will not break easily.
*Crash helmets are made of **tough** plastic.*
☞ **Similar:** durable, hard, solid, strong, sturdy
Opposite: weak
2 Something that is tough is difficult.
*We had to do some **tough** math problems.*
☞ **Opposite:** easy

tough
Say:
tuff

tourist

NOUN tourists
A tourist is a person who travels and visits places for pleasure.

tow

VERB tows, towing, towed
To tow a vehicle means to pull it along behind another vehicle.
*The truck **towed** the car to the garage.*
☞ **Say:** toe

*The **tortoise** moved slowly along the ground.*

tortoise

a
b
c
d
e
f
g
h
i
j
k
l
m
n
o
p
q
r
s
Tt
u
v
w
x
y
z

219

towel

NOUN towels

A towel is a piece of soft material that you use for drying your body.

tower

NOUN towers

A tower is a tall, thin building.

☞ **Rhymes:** our

town

NOUN towns

A town is a place with houses and other buildings, where people live, work, and shop. A town is smaller than a city but larger than a village.

toy

NOUN toys

A toy is something that you play with.

trace

VERB traces, tracing, traced

When you trace a picture, you copy it by putting a sheet of thin paper over it and drawing around the outline.

track

NOUN tracks

1 A track is a mark that a person or animal leaves as they walk along.

*The fox left **tracks** in the snow.*

2 A track is a path or rough road.

*They drove up a bumpy **track**.*

3 A track is a piece of ground that has lines marked on it so that it can be used for races.

*They did four laps around the running **track**.*

tractor

NOUN tractors

A tractor is a vehicle that people use on farms.

☞ **Word history:** The word **tractor** comes from the Latin word *tractus*, meaning "pulled," because a tractor is used for pulling other vehicles or machines on a farm.

tradition

NOUN traditions

A tradition is something that people have done in the same way for many years. Something that people do as a tradition is **traditional**.

*It is a **tradition** to celebrate the New Year with a party.*

tradition Say:
tra-dish-un

traffic

NOUN

The traffic on a road is all the cars, buses, trucks, and other vehicles on it.

*There was a lot of **traffic** on the bridge.*

traffic light

NOUN traffic lights

A traffic light is a set of differently colored lights that tell drivers when they must stop and when they can go.

trail

NOUN trails

A trail is a narrow path.

We followed a nature trail through the woods.

train

NOUN trains

1 A train is a vehicle that travels on railroad lines.

VERB trains, training, trained

2 When you train, you practice sports skills.

*She **trains** for three hours a day.*

3 When you train someone, you teach them to do something.

*He **trained** the parrot to talk.*

☞ **Similar:** coach, educate, instruct, teach

trainer

NOUN trainers

A trainer is someone who teaches specific skills.

*A **trainer** taught my dog to sit.*

trampoline

NOUN trampolines

A trampoline is a piece of equipment that you can bounce on.

☞ **Say: tram**-po-leen

transport

VERB transports, transporting, transported

To transport people or things means to take them from one place to another.

☞ **Similar:** bring, carry, move, ship, take

transportation

NOUN

Transportation is carrying goods or people from one place to another. Different methods of transportation are used to travel on land, on water, and in the air.

Transportation

h**O**t
\air/
balloon

This collection of words will be helpful on any journey.

In the air... airplane, aircraft, glider, jet

helicopter helicopter helicopter helicopter helicopter helicopter

BOAT

On water... canoe, dinghy, ferry, sailboat, ship, water skis, windsurfer, yacht

bus

Train... diesel, electric, high-speed, steam

RML 2603

s t r e t c h l i m o u s i n e
drive, go, journey, ride, speed, travel

pollution, smoke

TAXI

sports car

Journeys may be... boring, bumpy, exciting, relaxing, tiring

m**O**t**O**r cycle
– *fast*
– *rapid*
– *speedy*

bicycle bicycle bicycle bicycle

On land ... bike, bus, car, coach, taxi, trailer, train, truck, van

a
b
c
d
e
f
g
h
i
j
k
l
m
n

trap

NOUN traps

1 A trap is a machine or trick that you use to catch someone.

VERB traps, trapping, trapped

2 When you trap a person or animal, you catch them and hold them so that they cannot get away.

travel

VERB travels, traveling, traveled

When you travel, you go from one place to another. *We **traveled** through the country on vacation.*

tray

NOUN trays

A tray is a flat board that you use for carrying food and drinks.

*Leaves fall off the **trees** in the fall.*

tree

tread

VERB treads, treading, trod, trodden

When you tread on something, you put your foot on it. *Be careful not to **tread** on a thorn.*

☞ **Say:** tred
Similar: stamp, trample, walk

treasure

NOUN

Treasure is a large amount of gold, jewels, or other valuable things. *The map showed us where the buried **treasure** was.*

treat

NOUN treats

1 A treat is something special that someone gives you or does for you. *It was a birthday **treat**.*

VERB treats, treating, treated

2 The way you treat someone is the way you behave toward them, for example whether you are kind or nasty to them. *She **treats** her pet hamster well.*

3 To treat someone means to try to make them better when they are ill or hurt.

☞ **Say:** treet

treatment

NOUN

Treatment is something that a doctor gives you or does to you to make you better.

☞ **Similar:** care, first aid, medicine, surgery

tree

NOUN trees

A tree is a tall plant with a trunk, branches, and leaves.

tremble

VERB trembles, trembling, trembled

When you tremble, you shake because you are cold or afraid.

☞ **Similar:** quake, quiver, shake, shiver

How many sides does a triangle have?

Look around the page to find the answer.

tremendous

ADJECTIVE

Something that is tremendous is very good.

☞ **Similar:** excellent, fantastic, wonderful

trendy

ADJECTIVE trendier, trendiest

Trendy clothes are modern and fashionable.

triangle

NOUN triangles

1 A triangle is a shape that has three straight sides. Something that is the shape of a triangle is **triangular**.

2 A triangle is a musical instrument in the shape of a triangle, which you hit with a small metal bar.

trick

NOUN tricks

1 A trick is something clever or skillful that you do to entertain people.
*Louis is good at magic **tricks**.*
2 If you play a trick on someone, you tell them something untrue for fun.
VERB tricks, tricking, tricked
3 If you trick someone, you tell them something untrue for fun.
☞ **Similar:** cheat, deceive, fool

tricycle

NOUN tricycles

A tricycle is a vehicle with three wheels that you ride by turning the pedals with your feet.
☞ **Word history:** The word **tricycle** comes from the Greek words *tri* and *cycle*, meaning "three wheels."

tricycle Say:
try-sik-ul

*I rode my **tricycle** to the park.*

trim

VERB trims, trimming, trimmed
When you trim something, you cut the edges off of it to make it neat.
*My sister **trimmed** my hair.*

trip

NOUN trips

1 A trip is a journey.
*We went on a school **trip**.*
VERB trips, tripping, tripped
2 If you trip, you catch your foot on something and fall over.
☞ **Similar:** slip, stumble

triumph

NOUN triumphs

A triumph is a great success.
☞ **Say: try**-umf
Similar: achievement, success, victory

trivial

ADJECTIVE

Something that is trivial is not at all important or serious.

trombone

NOUN trombones

A trombone is a large, brass musical instrument. You make different notes by sliding a long tube backward and forward.

trophy

NOUN trophies

A trophy is a cup, medal, or other prize that you receive when you win a competition.
☞ **Say: trow**-fee

tropical

ADJECTIVE

Tropical means from the hot, wet part of the world near the Equator.

trot

VERB trots, trotting, trotted
To trot means to run slowly.
☞ **Similar:** jog, run

trouble

NOUN troubles

When there is trouble, people get angry and bad things happen.
*If you smash that window, you'll be in **trouble**!*
☞ **Say: trub**-ul

trout

NOUN trout

A trout is a type of fish that people often eat.

truck

NOUN trucks

A truck is a vehicle that people use for carrying goods.

true

ADJECTIVE

Something that is true really happened and is not made up.
☞ **Similar:** accurate, correct, honest, right
Opposite: false, untrue

trumpet

NOUN trumpets

A trumpet is a small, brass musical instrument. You make different notes by pressing down different buttons.

a
b
c
d
e
f
g
h
i
j
k
l
m
n
o
p
q
r
s
Tt
u
v
w
x
y
z

trunk
NOUN trunks
1 The trunk of a tree is the main part that grows up out of the ground.
2 An elephant's trunk is its long nose.
3 A trunk is a large box that you can keep things in.

trust
VERB trusts, trusting, trusted
If you trust someone, you believe that they are honest and will not steal from you or lie to you.

truth
NOUN
The truth is things that are true.
*Do you always tell the **truth**?*

truth
Say:
trooth

try
VERB tries, trying, tried
1 If you try to do something, you make an effort to do it.
*He **tried** to climb up the tree but it was too difficult.*
☞ **Similar:** aim, attempt
2 If you try something, you use it or test it to see if it works.
*Can I **try** your skateboard?*
3 If you try something, you eat or drink some of it to see if you like it.
*Would you like to **try** one of my cookies?*

T-shirt
NOUN T-shirts
A T-shirt is a shirt with a round neck, short sleeves, and no buttons.

tube
NOUN tubes
1 A tube is a hollow pipe.
2 A tube is a narrow container for cream or paste. You squeeze the tube to get the cream or paste out.

tuck
NOUN tucks, tucking, tucked
1 When you tuck clothes in, you push them neatly inside another piece of clothing.
***Tuck** your shirt into your pants.*
2 If you tuck someone into bed, you cover them up so that they are warm and comfortable.

tug
VERB tugs, tugging, tugged
If you tug something, you pull it roughly.
*My sister was **tugging** at my sleeve.*
☞ **Similar:** jerk, pull, yank

tumble
VERB tumbles, tumbling, tumbled
If you tumble, you fall down and roll over.
*She **tumbled** down the hill.*
☞ **Similar:** fall, roll, topple

tummy
NOUN tummies
Your tummy is your stomach.

Sean's favorite T-shirt is red.

tune
NOUN tunes
A tune is a set of musical notes that go together nicely.
*I played the **tune** on the piano.*

tunnel
NOUN tunnels
A tunnel is an underground passage.

turkey
NOUN turkeys
A turkey is a type of large bird that is kept on farms for its meat.
☞ **Word history:** Turkeys were named after the country, Turkey, because they looked like another bird, the guinea fowl that first came from Turkey.

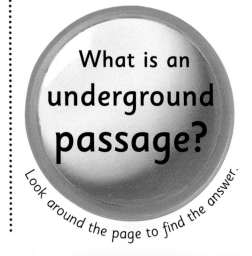

What is an **underground passage?**

Look around the page to find the answer.

turn

NOUN turns

1 If it is your turn to do something, you are the person who must do it next.
*It's your **turn** to do the dishes.*
VERB turns, turning, turned

2 When something turns, it moves around.
*The watch hands **turn** clockwise.*
☛ **Similar:** revolve, rotate, spin, whirl

3 When you turn, you change the direction you are looking or going in.
*He **turned** to see what was happening behind him.*

4 To turn means to become.
*His fingers **turned** blue from the cold.*

turnip

NOUN turnips
A turnip is a round, white vegetable.

tusk

NOUN tusks
Tusks are the long, pointed teeth that stick out of the mouths of some animals, such as elephants.

TV

NOUN TVs
A TV is a television.

twice

ADVERB
If you do something twice, you do it two times.
*He rang the bell **twice**.*

twig

NOUN twigs
A twig is a very small branch of a tree.

twin

NOUN twins
Twins are two children who are born to the same mother at the same time.

twinkle

VERB twinkles, twinkling, twinkled
If something twinkles, it shines and sparkles.
*The stars **twinkled** in the sky.*

The baker twisted the bread before he put it in the oven.

twist

VERB twists, twisting, twisted
If you twist something, you turn or rotate it.
*He **twisted** the top off the jar.*

type

NOUN types

1 One type of thing is one sort of thing.
*They sell two **types** of skateboard.*
☛ **Similar:** kind, sort
VERB types, typing, typed

2 When you type, you write something by pressing down the letters on a typewriter or computer keyboard.

type

typhoon

NOUN typhoons
A typhoon is a violent tropical storm.
☛ **Word history:** The word **typhoon** comes from the Chinese words *da feng*, meaning "great wind."

typical

ADJECTIVE
Something that is typical is like all other things of the same kind, and is not unusual or different.
*They lived in a **typical** city street.*
☛ **Say: tip**-i-kul
Similar: average, normal, ordinary, usual
Opposite: unusual

tyrant

NOUN tyrants
A tyrant is somebody who rules over others in a harsh and cruel way.

*Nisha **typed** a letter to her friend.*

a
b
c
d
e
f
g
h
i
j
k
l
m
n
o
p
q
r
s
Tt
u
v
w
x
y
z

225

U

upside
uʍop

ugly
ADJECTIVE
Something that is ugly is not nice to look at.
☞ **Say: ug**-lee
Similar: hideous, horrible, plain, unattractive
Opposite: beautiful

Uu umbrella
NOUN umbrellas
An umbrella is a cover that you hold over your head to keep you dry when it rains.
☞ **Word history:** The word **umbrella** comes from the Italian word *ombrella*, meaning "a little shade." The first umbrellas were used to protect people from the sun.

umpire
NOUN umpires
An umpire is someone who makes sure that players follow the rules of a game or sport.
☞ **Similar:** judge, referee

unable
ADJECTIVE
If you are unable to do something, you cannot do it.

unbelievable
ADJECTIVE
If something is unbelievable, it is so strange that it is difficult to believe it is true.
☞ **Similar:** amazing, impossible, incredible

uncle
NOUN uncles
Your uncle is the brother of one of your parents, or the husband of your aunt.

uncomfortable
ADJECTIVE
1 If you are uncomfortable, your body hurts or does not feel relaxed.
*He felt **uncomfortable** on the hard chair.*
2 Something that is uncomfortable causes you pain or does not feel nice on your body.
*These shoes are really **uncomfortable**.*
☞ **Opposite:** comfortable

u m b r e l l a

*My **umbrella** keeps me dry in the rain.*

unconscious
ADJECTIVE
1 If you are unconscious, you are in a very deep sleep and people cannot wake you up. People sometimes become unconscious after they have been hit on the head.
2 An unconscious action is one that you do without thinking about it.
☞ **Say:** un-**kon**-shus
Opposite: conscious

uncover
VERB uncovers, uncovering, uncovered
When you uncover something, you take off a thing that has been covering it, so that people can see it.
*The archaeologists **uncovered** a Roman mosaic.*

undercover
ADJECTIVE
If you do something in an undercover way, you do it secretly, without telling people what you are doing.
*The police were working on an **undercover** investigation.*

underground
ADJECTIVE
Underground means below the ground.
*A secret **underground** tunnel connects the two houses.*

undergrowth
NOUN
The undergrowth in a forest is all the bushes and plants that grow under the trees.
*It was hard to walk in the thick **undergrowth**.*

underline

VERB underlines, underlining, underlined
When you underline something, you draw a line under it.
*Don't forget to **underline** the title of your story.*

underneath

ADJECTIVE
Something that is underneath is below another thing.

understand

VERB understands, understanding, understood
If you can understand something, you know what it means or how it works.
*Did you **understand** the question?*
☞ **Similar:** comprehend, figure out, grasp

underwater

ADJECTIVE
Underwater animals and plants live in seas and rivers.

underwear

NOUN
You wear underwear next to your skin, under your other clothes.

What is the **opposite** of **ugly?**
Look around the page to find the answer.

undo

VERB undoes, undoing, undid, undone
When you undo something, you untie it.
*It was difficult to **undo** the knot in the rope.*
☞ **Say:** un-**doo**
Similar: detach, loosen, unfasten, untie, unwrap

undress

VERB undresses, undressing, undressed
When you undress, you take your clothes off.
☞ **Opposite:** dress

unemployed

ADJECTIVE
Someone who is unemployed does not have a job.
☞ **Opposite:** employed

uneven

ADJECTIVE
Something that is uneven is not smooth or level.
☞ **Similar:** bumpy, lumpy, rough
Opposite: even

uneventful

ADJECTIVE
If something is uneventful, nothing exciting or interesting happens.
*It was an **uneventful** day.*
☞ **Similar:** boring, dull, ordinary, quiet

unexpected

ADJECTIVE
If something is unexpected, you did not expect it to happen.
*Everyone left the beach because of the **unexpected** rain.*
☞ **Opposite:** expected

unfair

adjective
If something is unfair, some people are treated better than others or given more of something than others.
*That's **unfair**—she got three candies and I only got two!*
☞ **Opposite:** fair

a
b
c
d
e
f
g
h
i
j
k
l
m
n
o
p
q
r
s
t
Uu
v
w
x
y
z

*Fish blowing bubbles **underwater***

underwater

a b c d e f g h i j k l m n o p q r s t **Uu** v w x y z

unfit

ADJECTIVE

If you are unfit, you are not very healthy and not used to doing exercise.
*Some of the children were too **unfit** to take part in the race.*
☞ **Similar:** unhealthy, unwell, weak
Opposite: fit

unfortunate

ADJECTIVE

If something is unfortunate, it happens because of bad luck.
*It was **unfortunate** that it rained on sports day.*
☞ **Similar:** ill-fated, jinxed, unlucky
Opposite: fortunate

unhappy

ADJECTIVE unhappier, unhappiest

If you are unhappy, you are sad about something.
*She is **unhappy** because she failed the exam.*
☞ **Similar:** depressed, downhearted, miserable, sad
Opposite: happy

unhealthy

ADJECTIVE

1 If you are unhealthy, you are ill.
*You need to get some rest—you look **unhealthy**.*
☞ **Similar:** frail, ill, infirm, sick, unfit, unwell
2 Things that are unhealthy are bad for you.
*It's **unhealthy** to eat snacks all the time.*
☞ **Say:** un-**hel**-thee
Opposite: healthy

unicorn

NOUN unicorns

A unicorn is a mythical animal that looks like a horse and has one long horn on its forehead.
☞ **Say: yoo**-ni-korn
Word history: The word **unicorn** comes from the Latin words *uni* and *cornu*, meaning "one horn."

unicycle

NOUN unicycles

A unicycle is a bicycle with only one wheel, which people use for performing acrobatic tricks.
☞ **Say: yoo**-ni-sye-kul

*Rebecca looks well-dressed in her band **uniform**.*

uniform

uniform

NOUN uniforms

A uniform is a set of clothes that people wear to show that they belong to a certain school or group or that they do a certain job.
☞ **Say: yoo**-ni-form

unique

ADJECTIVE

If something is unique, it is the only one of its kind and there is no other that is exactly like it.
*Every snowflake is **unique**.*
☞ **Say:** yoo-**neek**

unisex

ADJECTIVE

Unisex means for both men and women.
☞ **Say: yoo**-nee-sex

unit

NOUN units

A unit is an amount that you use to measure how big or how heavy something is.
*A meter is a **unit** of length.*

unite

VERB unites, uniting, united

If people unite, they join together to do something.
*The children **united** against the school bully.*
☞ **Say:** yoo-**nite**

Universe

NOUN

The Universe is all of space, and everything in it. The Universe includes the Earth, the other planets, and all the stars.
☞ **Word history:** The word **universe** comes from the Latin word *universum*, meaning "turned into one," because when we think of the Universe we are thinking of all the different stars and planets as one thing.

university
NOUN universities
A university is a place where students can go to study after they have left high school.

university
Say:
yoo-ni-vur-si-tee

unkind
ADJECTIVE
Someone who is unkind is cruel to other people and does mean things to them.
*She was **unkind** to her little sister.*
☛ **Similar:** cruel, malicious, mean, nasty, spiteful, unpleasant
Opposite: kind

unknown
ADJECTIVE
If something is unknown, people do not know about it.
*Highways were **unknown** in the 19th century.*

unleaded
ADJECTIVE
Unleaded gasoline does not have any lead in it, and so is not so bad for the environment.
*My car takes **unleaded** gas.*
☛ **Say:** un-**led**-id

unlikely
ADJECTIVE
If something is unlikely, it will probably not happen.
*It is **unlikely** that they will win the competition twice in a row.*
☛ **Opposite:** likely

unload
VERB unloads, unloading, unloaded
When you unload things from a vehicle, you take them out.

unlock
VERB unlocks, unlocking, unlocked
When you unlock something, you open the lock on it.
*He **unlocked** the door.*
☛ **Similar:** open, unbolt, unfasten
Opposite: lock

unlock

unlucky
ADJECTIVE unluckier, unluckiest
1 If you are unlucky, something bad happens to you.
*How **unlucky** to break your arm!*
2 Something that is unlucky brings bad luck.
*It's thought to be **unlucky** to walk under ladders.*
☛ **Opposite:** lucky

unnecessary
ADJECTIVE
If something is unnecessary, you do not need to do it.
*It's **unnecessary** to wear your coat inside.*
☛ **Say:** un-**nes**-i-sair-ee
Opposite: necessary

unpack
VERB unpacks, unpacking, unpacked
When you unpack things, you take them out of a suitcase or box.
☛ **Opposite:** pack

unpleasant
ADJECTIVE
Something that is unpleasant is not nice.
☛ **Similar:** disgusting, foul, horrible, nasty, offensive, revolting
Opposite: pleasant

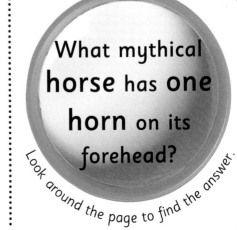

*I **unlocked** my bike lock.*

What mythical **horse** has **one horn** on its forehead?
Look around the page to find the answer.

a
b
c
d
e
f
g
h
i
j
k
l
m
n
o
p
q
r
s
t
Uu
v
w
x
y
z

a
b
c
d
e
f
g
h
i
j
k
l
m
n
o
p
q
r
s
t
Uu
v
w
x
y
z

unscrew

VERB unscrews, unscrewing, unscrewed
When you unscrew something, you loosen it by turning it or by undoing screws on it.
*She **unscrewed** the numbers from the door.*

untidy

ADJECTIVE untidier, untidiest
If a place is untidy, it is in a mess.
*Her room was always **untidy**.*
☛ **Say:** un-**tie**-dee
Similar: cluttered, littered, messy
Opposite: tidy

untie

VERB unties, untying, untied
When you untie rope or string, you undo the knots in it.
*She **untied** the rope and rowed away.*
☛ **Similar:** loosen, undo, unfasten
Opposite: tie

untrue

ADJECTIVE
If something is untrue, it is not true.
*His story about finding buried treasure was **untrue**.*
☛ **Similar:** false, incorrect, made-up, wrong
Opposite: true

unused

ADJECTIVE
Something that is unused has never been used.
☛ **Say:** un-**yoozd**

unusual

ADJECTIVE
Something that is unusual is not normal or ordinary.
*It is **unusual** to have snow in July.*
☛ **Similar:** abnormal, bizarre, odd, strange, weird
Opposite: usual

unwell

ADJECTIVE
If you are unwell, you are ill.
☛ **Similar:** ailing, ill, sick
Opposite: well

unwilling

ADJECTIVE
If you are unwilling to do something, you do not want to do it.

unwise

ADJECTIVE
Something that is unwise is not a good or sensible thing to do.
*It is **unwise** to swim in the very deep part of the ocean.*
☛ **Similar:** foolish, rash, reckless, silly, stupid

unwrap

VERB unwraps, unwrapping, unwrapped
When you unwrap something, you take the wrapping or covering off it.
☛ **Say:** un-**rap**
Opposite: wrap

upbringing

NOUN
Your upbringing is the way that your parents raise you.

upright

ADVERB
Something that is upright is sitting or standing up straight.
*The dog stood **upright** on its hind legs.*
☛ **Say:** **up**-rite

uproar

NOUN
If there is an uproar, there is a lot of noise and confusion.

upset

VERB upsets, upsetting, upset
1 To upset someone means to make them feel unhappy.
*The other children **upset** Emma by not letting her play with them.*
☛ **Similar:** distress, hurt, worry
2 If you upset something, you knock it over.
*The cat **upset** the vase of flowers.*
ADJECTIVE
3 If you are upset, you feel unhappy.
☛ **Similar:** distressed, hurt, miserable, sad

unwrap
*Tom **unwrapped** the toffees.*

upside-down

ADVERB

When something is upside-down, it is the wrong way up and the top part of it is where the bottom should be. *He hung the picture* **upside-down**.

upstairs

ADVERB

If you go upstairs, you go to a higher floor in a building. *She went **upstairs** to her bedroom.*

☞ **Opposite:** downstairs

upward

ADVERB

If you go upward, you go toward a higher position. *She let go of the balloons and they drifted **upward**.*

☞ **Opposite:** downward

urge

NOUN urges

1 If you have an urge to do something, you want to do it or need to do it. *She had a sudden **urge** to giggle.*
VERB urges, urging, urged
2 If you urge someone to do something, you try to persuade them to do it. *He **urged** them to be careful when playing by the river.*

☞ **Similar:** encourage, persuade

urgent

ADJECTIVE

If something is urgent, you need to do it immediately. *I need to talk to you—it's **urgent**.*

☞ **Say:** ur-jent
Similar: crucial, important

use

NOUN uses

1 If something has a use, you can do something with it. *This penknife has many **uses**.*
2 If something is in use, someone is using it. *Steam trains are still in **use** in some areas.*

☞ **Say:** yooss

use

VERB uses, using, used

When you use something, you do a job with it. *May I **use** your pen, please?*

use Say: yooze

useful

ADJECTIVE

If something is useful, it can help you to do something. *Scissors are **useful** in the classroom.*

☞ **Similar:** effective, helpful, valuable
Opposite: useless

useless

ADJECTIVE

If something is useless, you cannot use it and it does not help you at all.

☞ **Opposite:** useful

What do you use a utensil for?

Look around the page to find the answer.

usual

ADJECTIVE

Usual means normal. *I left school at the **usual** time.*

☞ **Similar:** normal, ordinary, standard, typical
Opposite: unusual

utensil

NOUN utensils

A utensil is a tool that you use for cooking and eating food.

☞ **Say:** yoo-**ten**-sil

utensil

Utensils are used to prepare and cook food.

a
b
c
d
e
f
g
h
i
j
k
l
m
n
o
p

Uu

v
w
x
y
z

231

V

a b c d e f g h i j k l m n o p q r s t u v w x y z

Vase

vaccination
NOUN vaccinations
When you have a vaccination, a doctor gives you an injection that stops you from getting a disease. The substance the doctor injects is called a **vaccine**.

vacuum cleaner
NOUN vacuum cleaners
A vacuum cleaner is a machine that cleans floors by sucking up dirt.

vaccination Say:
vak-si-nay-shun

vain
ADJECTIVE vainer, vainest
1 People who are vain think that they are very clever or beautiful.
☛ **Similar:** arrogant, big-headed, boastful, conceited, proud
Opposite: modest
2 A vain attempt to do something does not work. *They made a **vain** attempt to put out the fire.*

valley
NOUN valleys
A valley is an area of low land between hills, often with a river or stream flowing through it.
☛ **Similar:** canyon, dale, dell

valuable
ADJECTIVE
1 Something that is valuable is worth a lot of money. *These paintings are **valuable**.*
☛ **Similar:** expensive, precious, priceless
2 Something that is valuable helps you in some way. *He gave us some **valuable** advice.*
☛ **Similar:** helpful, useful
Say: val-yoo-bul

van
NOUN vans
A van is a small truck that people use for carrying goods.

vandal
NOUN vandals
A vandal is someone who deliberately breaks or damages things.
☛ **Similar:** hoodlum, hooligan

vanilla
NOUN
Vanilla is a sweet flavoring that you add to food. It is made from the pods of a tropical plant.

vanish
VERB vanishes, vanishing, vanished
To vanish means to disappear suddenly. *The magician waved his wand and the rabbit **vanished**.*

various
ADJECTIVE
Various means of several different kinds. ***Various** people have visited our school this year.*

vase
NOUN vases
A vase is a jar that you put flowers in.
☛ **Say: vayz**

vast

ADJECTIVE

Vast means very big.
☛ **Similar:** enormous, gigantic, huge, large

vegetable

NOUN vegetables

A vegetable is a plant that people grow for food.
☛ **Say: vej**-tab-bul

vegetarian

NOUN vegetarians

A vegetarian is someone who does not eat meat or fish.
☛ **Say:** vej-it-**tair**-ree-an

vehicle

NOUN vehicles

A vehicle is something that people travel in or use to transport goods.

Word history:
The word **vehicle** comes from the Latin word *vehiculum*, meaning "something that carries," because a vehicle carries people or goods.

veil

NOUN veils

A veil is a piece of thin cloth that women sometimes wear over their heads or faces.
*The bride wore a **veil** during the wedding.*

verb

NOUN verbs

A verb is an action word such as "run," "speak," or "jump" that tells you what someone or something does.

verse

NOUN verses

1 A verse is one part of a poem or song.
*We'll sing the first **verse** again.*
2 Verse is a general name for poetry.
*He wrote a book of **verse**.*

very

ADVERB

Very means extremely.
*My father was **very** angry.*
☛ **Similar:** exceedingly, extremely, really, terribly

vest

NOUN vests

A vest is a sleeveless, waist-length garment, often worn under a suit coat.

vet

NOUN vets

A vet, or veterinarian, is a person who is trained to treat sick animals.

vicious

ADJECTIVE

1 A vicious animal is fierce and might attack people.
☛ **Similar:** ferocious, fierce, savage, wild
2 Someone who is vicious is cruel or unkind.
☛ **Similar:** brutal, cruel
Say: vish-us

victory

NOUN victories

A victory is when you win a competition or battle.
*The race-car driver was thrilled with his **victory**.*
☛ **Opposite:** defeat

video

NOUN videos

A video is a recording of a film that you can watch on a television screen.
☛ **Word history:** The word **video** comes from the Latin word *videre* meaning "to see," because a video is a recording that you can see.

a b c d e f g h i j k l m n o p q r s t u **Vv** w x y z

233

a
b
c
d
e
f
g
h
i
j
k
l
m
n
o
p
q
r
s
t
u

w
x
y
z

village

NOUN villages

A village is a place in the country where people live. Villages are usually smaller than towns.

violent

ADJECTIVE

1 Something that is violent breaks or damages things. *The **violent** storm threw cars across the street.*
2 A violent person often hits or attacks other people.
☛ **Similar:** aggressive, brutal, vicious

*Chloe plays the **violin**.*

violin

NOUN violins

A violin is a musical instrument that you hold under your chin and play by pulling a bow across the strings.

virtual

ADJECTIVE

A virtual place is one that you see on a computer screen and that feels real because you can feel as if you are moving around in it.

virus

NOUN viruses

1 A virus is a type of germ that can make you ill.
2 A virus is a set of instructions that someone puts into your computer to make it go wrong.
☛ **Say:** vye-rus

visible

ADJECTIVE

If something is visible, you can see it.
*The mountain was **visible** for miles.*
☛ **Opposite:** invisible

visit

VERB visits, visiting, visited

When you visit someone, you go to see them. When you visit a place, you go there.
*I went to **visit** her in the hospital.*

violin

visitor

NOUN visitors

A visitor is someone who visits a person or place.

vitamin

NOUN vitamins

Vitamins are chemicals that exist in food and help to keep us healthy.
*Oranges contain a lot of **vitamin** C.*

voice

NOUN voices

Your voice is the sound that comes out of your mouth when you speak or sing.
*Can you sing in a high **voice**?*

voicemail

NOUN

Voicemail is a way of storing messages on a telephone.

volcano

NOUN volcanoes

A volcano is a mountain that that has been created by liquid rock from inside Earth.
☛ **Word history:** The word **volcano** comes from the name of Vulcan, the Roman god of fire.

volleyball

NOUN

Volleyball is a game in which people hit a ball over a high net using their hands.

volume

NOUN volumes

1 A volume is a book which is one of a series.
2 The volume of a sound is how loud it is.
*Please turn up the **volume**!*

vote

VERB votes, voting, voted

When you vote, you choose one person or thing from a list.

vowel

NOUN vowels

The five vowels in English are the letters **a**, **e**, **i**, **o**, and **u**.
☛ **Rhymes:** owl

W

wipe

wade
VERB wades, wading, waded
When you wade through water, you walk through it.

*A flamingo **wades** across the lake.*

w a d e

waist
NOUN waists
Your waist is the part of your body around your middle.

wait
VERB waits, waiting, waited
When you wait, you stay in a place and do not do anything until someone arrives or something happens.

wake
VERB wakes, waking, woke, woken
When you wake up, you stop sleeping.
*I'll try to **wake** up early tomorrow.*

walk
NOUN walks
1 If you go for a walk, you go somewhere on foot for pleasure.
VERB walks, walking, walked
2 When you walk, you move along on foot.
*We usually **walk** to school.*
☛ **Similar:** amble, stroll

wall
NOUN walls
A wall is a structure built from stone or brick. Walls are used to hold up the roof of a building or to separate one piece of land from another.
*There is a high **wall** around the yard.*

wallet
NOUN wallets
A wallet is a small case that you carry money in.
☛ **Say: wal**-it

wand
NOUN wands
A wand is a special stick that people use when they are performing magic tricks. In fairy tales, magic wands are used for casting magic spells.

wand Say:
wahnd

wander
NOUN wanders, wandering, wandered
When you wander, you walk around without going in any particular direction.
*We spent the afternoon **wandering** around the mall.*
☛ **Say: wahn**-der
Similar: drift, ramble, roam

What small case can you carry your money in?
Look around the page to find the answer.

want
VERB wants, wanting, wanted
1 If you want something, you would like to have it.
*I **want** a puppy for my birthday.*
☛ **Similar:** desire, wish for
2 If you want to do something, you would like to do it.
*I **want** to go horseback riding.*

a
b
c
d
e
f
g
h
i
j
k
l
m
n
o
p
q
r
s
t
u
v
Ww
x
y
z

a
b
c
d
e
f
g
h
i
j
k
l
m
n
o
p
q
r
s
t
u
v
Ww
x
y
z

war

NOUN wars
When there is a war, people fight against each other. Often the two sides are from different countries.
☞ **Say: wore**

wardrobe

NOUN wardrobes
A wardrobe is a cupboard for keeping clothes in.

warm

ADJECTIVE warmer, warmest
1 If something is warm, it is somewhat hot but not very hot.
The hot-water bottle felt nice and warm.
☞ **Similar:** hot, lukewarm, tepid
Opposite: cool
2 If the weather is warm, the sun is shining and it feels hot.
☞ **Similar:** hot, mild, pleasant, summery, sunny
Opposite: cool

warn

VERB warns, warning, warned
If you warn someone about a danger or problem, you tell that person about it before it happens.
The man warned us that it was dangerous to walk on the thin ice.
☞ **Say: worn**

warning

NOUN warnings
If you give someone a warning about a danger or problem, you tell that person about it before it happens.
There were warnings posted everywhere about the approaching hurricane.

wash

VERB washes, washing, washed
1 When you wash something, you clean it with water and soap.
Who will help me wash the dishes?
☞ **Similar:** clean, mop, rinse, scrub, wipe
2 When you wash, you clean your body with water and soap.
Did you remember to wash behind your ears?

washing machine

NOUN washing machines
A washing machine is a machine that you use for washing clothes.

wasp

NOUN wasps
A wasp is an insect with a black-and-yellow striped body. Wasps can sting you.

waste

VERB wastes, wasting, wasted
If you waste something, you use more of it than you need to, or you do not use it in a sensible way.
Don't waste electricity!
☞ **Similar:** squander

watch

NOUN watches
1 A watch is a small clock that you wear on your wrist.
VERB watches, watching, watched
2 When you watch something, you look at it for a long time.
The teacher watched the children playing.

*Will you **water** my plants while I'm away?*

water
NOUN
1 Water is a clear liquid that falls as rain and forms streams, rivers, lakes, and oceans.
*Would you like a glass of **water**?*
VERB waters, watering, watered
2 When you water plants, you pour water onto them so that they can live.

waterfall
NOUN waterfalls
A waterfall is a place where a river falls over a steep cliff.

waterproof
ADJECTIVE
If something is waterproof, water cannot get through it or into it.
*Remember to bring a **waterproof** coat with you.*

What striped insect stings?
Look around the page to find the answer.

waterski
VERB waterskis, waterskiing, waterskied
When you waterski, you are pulled along behind a boat while you stand on two skis.
*Have you ever tried **waterskiing**?*

wave
NOUN waves
1 When there are waves in water, the surface moves up and down or from side to side.
*The children were playing in the **waves**.*
☞ **Similar:** ripple, surf, swell
VERB waves, waving, waved
2 When you wave to someone, you move your hand or arm to tell that person something.
*She **waved** goodbye as the ship sailed away.*
3 When something waves, it moves backward and forward.
*The branches of the tree **waved** in the strong wind.*
☞ **Similar:** flap, flutter, stir

wax
NOUN
Wax is a solid, oily substance that melts when it is heated. Wax is used to make candles.

way
NOUN ways
1 The way to a place is the direction you go in to get there.
*The sign showed the **way** to the village.*
2 The way you do something is how you do it.
*What is the right **way** to use this video camera?*

weak
ADJECTIVE weaker, weakest
Someone who is weak is not very strong.
*He was too **weak** to lift the box.*
☞ **Similar:** delicate, feeble, frail, puny
Opposite: strong

weapon
NOUN weapons
A weapon is a gun, knife, or anything else that you can use to hurt someone.
☞ **Say:** wep-on

wear
VERB wears, wearing, wore, worn
When you are wearing clothes, you have them on your body.

j
k
l
m
n
o
p
q
r
s
t
u
v
Ww
x
y
z

Weather

Come rain or shine, there are many words to describe the weather.

sunny
baking, boiling
humid, roasting
cloudless, dry, pleasant
bright, clear, warm

blast, breeze,
hurricane, tornado, **wind**

THUNDER
and
lightning
boom!
crash!

storm
flash!

rainbow
beautiful, colorful, lovely

Cloudy, dull, gray
foggy
misty, gloomy

snow

typhoon

rain

strike!

snowy
icy
frosty

raindrops
r a i n d r o p s

hail

cold fresh

raining
pouring
shower
splashing spitting

freezing

238

weather

NOUN

The weather is what is happening in the sky and air around us, for example, if it is cold or hot, dry or raining.
☞ **Say: weth**-ur

web

NOUN webs

A web is a fine net of sticky threads that a spider makes to catch flies.
*Spiders' **webs** covered the entrance to the cave.*

website

NOUN websites

You go to a website on the internet to find information about something.

wedding

NOUN weddings

When there is a wedding, two people get married.

week

NOUN weeks

A week is a period of seven days.
*There are two **weeks** left until the end of school.*

weekend

NOUN weekends

The weekend is Saturday and Sunday, the days when many people do not go to school or work.

weep

VERB weeps, weeping, wept
When you weep, you cry.
*She **wept** for hours when she lost her cat.*
☞ **Similar:** bawl, blubber, cry, sob, wail

weigh

VERB weighs, weighing, weighed
1 When you weigh something, you measure how heavy it is.
2 The amount that something weighs is how heavy it is.
*How much do you **weigh**?*
☞ **Say: way**

weight

NOUN weights
1 The weight of something is how heavy it is.
2 Weights are pieces of metal that people use for measuring how heavy things are.
☞ **Say: wayt**

weird

ADJECTIVE weirder, weirdest
Something that is weird is very strange.
*People dressed in **weird** and wonderful costumes at the halloween party.*
☞ **Say: weerd**
Similar: bizarre, mysterious, odd, strange

well

NOUN wells
1 A well is a deep hole in the ground from which people get water or oil.
ADJECTIVE
2 If you are well, you are healthy and not ill.
*Are you **well** today?*
☞ **Opposite:** unwell, sick
ADVERB
3 If you do something well, you do it in a good or suitable way.
*He behaved very **well**.*

went

Went is the past tense of the verb **go**.

wept

Wept is the past tense of the verb **weep**.

west

NOUN

West is one of the four main compass directions. West is the direction in which the Sun sets.

west

*The compass points **west**.*

wet

ADJECTIVE wetter, wettest
1 If something is wet, it is covered with water or soaked in water.
☞ **Similar:** damp, soaking, sopping
2 If the weather is wet, it is raining.
☞ **Similar:** drizzling, pouring, rainy, showery
Opposite: dry

whale

NOUN whales
A whale is a very large sea animal. Whales are mammals and breathe through a hole in the top of their head.

a b c d e f g h i j k l m n o p q r s t u v **Ww** x y z

a
b
c
d
e
f
g
h
i
j
k
l
m
n
o
p
q
r
s
t
u
v
Ww
x
y
z

wheel

NOUN wheels
Wheels are the round parts underneath cars and bicycles that they move along on.

wheelchair

NOUN wheelchairs
A wheelchair is a chair with wheels. People use wheelchairs to move from place to place if they have difficulty walking.

whisker

NOUN whiskers
Whiskers are the stiff hairs that grow near the mouths of some animals.

whisper

VERB whispers, whispering, whispered
When you whisper, you speak in a very quiet voice.
*She **whispered** her secret into his ear.*
☞ **Similar:** murmur, mutter

The referee blew the...

whistle Say: wis-ul

whistle

NOUN whistles
1 You blow into a whistle to make a high sound.
VERB whistles, whistling, whistled
2 When you whistle, you press your lips together and blow to make a high, musical sound.

white

ADJECTIVE
Something that is white is the color of snow.

whole

ADJECTIVE
Whole means complete.
*She ate a **whole** Easter egg at once!*
☞ **Say: hole**

whole wheat

ADJECTIVE
Whole wheat bread is bread that is made from whole grains of wheat.

wicked

ADJECTIVE
Someone who is wicked does very bad or unkind things.
☞ **Similar:** bad, criminal, evil

...whistle to start the game.

wide

ADJECTIVE wider, widest
Something that is wide is a long way from one side to the other.
*The stream was too **wide** to jump across.*
☞ **Similar:** broad, large, thick
Opposite: narrow

width

NOUN
The width of something is how wide it is.
*We measured the **width** of the path.*

wife

NOUN wives
A man's wife is the woman he is married to.

wild

ADJECTIVE wilder, wildest
1 A wild flower or animal lives in its natural environment and is not controlled or looked after by people.
2 If you behave in a wild way, you run around and make a lot of noise.
*The children went **wild** in the amusement park.*
☞ **Similar:** boisterous, excited, noisy, rowdy, unruly
Rhymes: child

will

NOUN wills
1 If you have the will to do something, you have the determination to do it.
*She had the **will** to win.*
VERB
2 If you will do something, you are going to do it.
*I **will** phone you this afternoon.*

willing

ADJECTIVE
If you are willing to do something, you want to do it or are happy to do it.
*Are you **willing** to help in the yard?*
☞ **Similar:** happy, pleased, ready

win
VERB wins, winning, won
If you win a game or competition, you come first.
*She was pleased when she **won** the game.*
☞ **Opposite:** lose

wind
NOUN winds
Wind is air that blows over the Earth.
*The **wind** blew his umbrella inside out.*
☞ **Rhymes:** sinned

wind
VERB winds, winding, wound
1 When you wind something, you turn it around and around.
2 A path or road that winds has a lot of bends and turns in it.
☞ **Rhymes:** find

windmill
NOUN windmills
A windmill is a building with large sails, which uses wind power to turn a machine that grinds grain or pumps water.

window
NOUN windows
A window is a piece of glass in the side of a building that lets light and air into the building.

windshield
NOUN windshield
The windshield on a car is the big window at the front that the driver looks out of.

windsurfing
NOUN
Windsurfing is a sport in which you sail on water, standing on a narrow board with a sail attached.

windy
ADJECTIVE windier, windiest
If it is windy, there is a lot of wind.

wing
NOUN wings
1 The wings on a bird or insect are the parts that it uses for flying.
2 The wings on an airplane are the parts that stick out at the sides.

Windmill

...the windmill's sails.

Wind power turns...

winner
NOUN winners
The winner is the person who wins a game or competition.

winter
NOUN
Winter is one of the four seasons. Winter follows fall and comes before spring. It is the coldest time of the year.

wipe
VERB wipes, wiping, wiped
When you wipe something, you clean it or dry it by rubbing it with a cloth.
*He **wiped** the mirror with a cloth.*
☞ **Similar:** clean, dust, mop, polish, rub, wash

wire
NOUN wires
A wire is a long, thin metal thread. Wires can be used to carry electrical power.

wise
ADJECTIVE wiser, wisest
Someone who is wise knows and understands a lot of things.
☞ **Say:** wize
Similar: clever, educated, intelligent, sensible
Opposite: foolish

a
b
c
d
e
f
g
h
i
j
k
l
m
n
o
p
q
r
s
t
u
v
Ww
x
y
z

a
b
c
d
e
f
g
h
i
j
k
l
m
n
o
p
q
r
s
t
u
v
Ww
x
y
z

wish

NOUN wishes

1 A wish is something that you would like very much. *The fairy granted her wishes.*

VERB wishes, wishing, wished

2 If you wish for something, you would like it very much. *I wish I could dance better!*

witch

NOUN witches

A witch is a woman who uses magic powers.

wizard

NOUN wizards

A wizard is a man who uses magic powers.

wobble

VERB wobbles, wobbling, wobbled

To wobble means to move from side to side and nearly fall over. *He wobbled on his ice skates.*

wolf

NOUN wolves

A wolf is a wild animal that looks like a large dog and lives in cold countries. Wolves live in packs and hunt other animals for food.

woman

NOUN women

A woman is an adult female person.

☛ **Say: wum-an**

The wooden dolls get smaller and smaller and smaller and smaller.

wonder

NOUN

1 Wonder is the feeling you have when you look at something strange and exciting.

VERB wonders, wondering, wondered

2 If you wonder about something, you have questions in your mind about it. *I wonder how she got here?*

wonder

Say: **wun-der**

wonderful

ADJECTIVE

Something that is wonderful is very good or amazing. *We had a wonderful time on vacation.*

☛ **Say: wun-der-ful**

Similar: fantastic, great, marvelous, superb

wood

NOUN

1 Wood is the hard material that we get from trees. Wood is used for making furniture and is also burned as fuel.

2 Woods are trees growing together over a large area.

wooden

ADJECTIVE

Something that is wooden is made of wood.

wool

NOUN

Wool is the soft material that we get from sheep. Wool is used for making clothes and can also be made into carpets.

word

NOUN words

A word is a group of letters and sounds that has a meaning.

work

NOUN

1 Work is a job that you must do.

VERB works, working, worked

2 When you work, you do a job.

3 When a machine is working, there is nothing wrong with it and you can use it.

world

NOUN

The world is the planet Earth and all the people and things on it.

worm

NOUN worms

A worm is a small, thin animal that lives in the ground and has a soft body and no legs.

worried

ADJECTIVE

If you are worried about something, you feel nervous about it or slightly afraid of it.

☛ **Similar:** anxious, concerned, nervous, uneasy

worry

VERB worries, worrying, worried

If you worry about something, you feel nervous about it or slightly afraid of it.

☛ **Say: wur**-ee

worse

ADJECTIVE

A person or thing that is worse than others is less good.

That was bad, but this one is worse.

worst

ADJECTIVE

The worst person or thing is the one that is least good or most unpleasant.

That's the worst of all.

worth

ADJECTIVE

The amount that something is worth is how much money people will pay to buy it.

The jewels were worth a lot of money.

would

VERB

If you would do something, you want to do it but you cannot.

I would go to the movies with you if I had enough money.

☛ **Rhymes:** good

wound

NOUN wounds

A wound is a cut on your body.

☛ **Say: woond**

Similar: cut, gash, graze

wrap

VERB wraps, wrapping, wrapped

When you wrap something, you fold paper around it.

☛ **Say: rap**

wriggle

VERB wriggles, wriggling, wriggled

When you wriggle, you twist and turn from side to side.

☛ **Say: rig**-ul

wrinkle

NOUN wrinkles

Wrinkles are small lines or creases on your clothes or on someone's skin.

☛ **Say: ring**-kul

wrist

NOUN wrists

Your wrist is the part of your body where your hand joins your arm.

☛ **Say: rist**

write

VERB writes, writing, wrote, written

When you write, you put letters and words on paper.

☛ **Say: rite**

wrong

ADJECTIVE

1 Something that is wrong is not correct.

That is the wrong answer.

☛ **Opposite:** right

2 Something that is wrong is bad.

It's wrong to steal.

☛ **Say: rong**

a b c d e f g h i j k l m n o p q r s t u v **Ww** x y z

wrap Sam **wrapped** the presents in colored paper.

a
b
c
d
e
f
g
h
i
j
k
l
m
n
o
p
q
r
s
t
u
v
w
Xx
Yy
Zz

X Y Z

yo-yo

X-ray
NOUN X-rays
An X-ray is a special photograph that shows your bones and the inside of your body.
*The doctor looked closely at the chest **X-ray**.*

X-ray

xylophone
NOUN xylophones
A xylophone is a musical instrument that has wooden bars on a frame. When you hit each bar, it makes a different note.
☞ **Word history:** The word **xylophone** comes from the Greek words *xulon*, meaning "wood" and *phone*, meaning "sound," so a xylophone is an instrument that makes sound from wood.

xylophone
Say:
zye-le-fone

yacht
NOUN yachts
A yacht is a boat with a sail that people use for racing or pleasure.
☞ **Say: yot**

yank
VERB yanks, yanking, yanked
When you yank something, you pull it roughly.
☞ **Similar:** jerk, pull, tug

yap
VERB yaps, yapping, yapped
When a dog yaps, it barks with a high sound.

yard
NOUN yards
A yard is an area outside a building, with a fence or wall around it.
*Steve and Mary are playing in the **yard**.*
☞ **Similar:** courtyard

yawn
VERB yawns, yawning, yawned
When you yawn, you open your mouth and breathe in deeply because you are tired or bored.
☞ **Rhymes:** pawn

year
NOUN years
A year is a period of 12 months.
*I haven't seen Kevin all **year**.*

yell
VERB yells, yelling, yelled
When you yell, you shout loudly.
*He **yelled** at the children to go away.*
☞ **Similar:** bawl, bellow, cry, howl, roar, scream, shout

What is the opposite of young?

Look around the page to find the answer.

yellow
ADJECTIVE
Something that is yellow is the color of the sun.

zipper

*The top has a **zipper** at the collar.*

yesterday
ADVERB
Yesterday is the day before today.
*I went to the zoo **yesterday**.*

yoga
NOUN
When you do yoga, you do special exercises to stretch your body and make you feel relaxed.

yogurt
NOUN
Yogurt is a food that is made from milk and is often flavored with fruit.
*Would you like some **yogurt**?*

yolk
NOUN yolks
The yolk of an egg is the yellow part.
☞ **Say: yoke**

young
ADJECTIVE younger, youngest
Someone who is young is not very old.
*The grandmother held the **young** child in her arms.*
☞ **Say: yung**
Opposite: old

youth
NOUN youths
1 Your youth is the time when you are young.
*In his **youth**, he was a very good baseball player.*
2 A youth is a young man.
☞ **Say: yooth**

yo-yo
NOUN yo-yos
A yo-yo is a toy that spins up and down on a string.

zebra
NOUN zebras
A zebra is an African animal that looks like a horse and has black and white stripes on its body.

zero
NOUN zeros
Zero is the number **0**.
☞ **Similar:** nil, nothing

zest
NOUN
Somebody who has zest has lots of enthusiasm for doing a task.

zigzag
NOUN zigzags
A zigzag is a line that goes from side to side, making sharp points as it changes direction.
*The shirt's pattern has lots of different colors in a **zigzag**.*

zip code
NOUN zip codes
A five-digit zip code identifies each postal area in the United States.

zipper
NOUN zippers
You use a zipper for fastening clothes or bags. It has two rows of teeth, which are pressed together when you close the zipper.

zodiac
NOUN
The zodiac is the 12 sections into which the sky is divided. Each part is represented by a different symbol.
☞ **Say: zoe**-dee-ak

zoo
NOUN zoos
A zoo is a place where wild animals are kept so that people can see them and study them.

zoom
VERB zooms, zooming, zoomed
To zoom means to move very fast.
*A motorcycle **zoomed** past me.*
☞ **Similar:** hurry, hurtle, rush, speed, tear, whizz

a b c d e f g h i j k l m n o p q r s t u v w Xx Yy Zz

245

Spelling tips

If you can't find the word you are looking up, you may have spelled it incorrectly. Here are some spelling tips.

Split long words

To make it easier to look up or spell long words, split them into **syllables**. A syllable is one short sound in a word. Then figure out the order of the letters in each syllable.

For example:
Elephant has three syllables. It seems easier to put the first syllable, "el," into alphabetical order than "elephant."

syllables... **el-e-phant**
1 2 3

How many syllables do these words have? *(Answers on page 256)*

1. **happy**
2. **sad**
3. **expensive**
4. **impossible**
5. **refrigerator**
6. **supercalifragilisticexpialidocious!**

Confusing spellings

Not all words are spelled the way they sound. This can make it hard to look things up. Read these common problem words to help you spell difficult words.

Ph pronounced like an f

al**ph**abet, tele**ph**one, **ph**araoh, ele**ph**ant, **ph**otogra**ph**

Silent letters

clim**b**, com**b**, dou**b**t, **g**host, **g**naw, **h**our, **k**nee, **k**nife, s**w**ord, **w**hole, **w**rap, **w**reck, **w**riggle, **w**rite

Do you know what the missing silent letters are in these words? *(Answers on page 256)*

1. ras_berry
2. lam_
3. s_issors
4. _not

Sound alikes

Some words sound alike but are spelled differently.

sale—Jack bought some new shoes during the **sale**.
sail—It took a day to **sail** from England to France.
ate—Joe **ate** the whole cake.
eight—There were **eight** coins in the bag.
passed—Have you **passed** the spelling test?
past—It is ten minutes **past** three.
brake—She used the **brake** to slow down.
break—They took a **break** from work.
toe—He dropped a book on his big **toe**.
tow—The farmer used his tractor to **tow** the trailer.

Can you figure out what the two words are for each pair of pictures? The words sound the same but are spelled differently. The first letter of each answer is shown as a clue. *(Answers on page 256)*

Sound unalikes

Some words are spelled the same but sound different.

The two words that go with these pairs of pictures are spelled the same, but sound different. Can you figure out what the words are? The first letter of each answer is given as a clue. *(Answers on page 256)*

"I before E, except after C"

This is a general spelling rule (there are a few exceptions). Here are some examples:
i before e... s**ie**ve, p**ie**ce, th**ie**f, rel**ie**f, bel**ie**ve, br**ie**f
... except after c... c**ei**ling, rec**ei**ve

Common abbreviations

ad	advertisement
a.m.	before noon (used with times; from the Latin *ante meridiem*)
a.s.a.p.	as soon as possible
Ave.	avenue
C	Celsius or Centigrade
CD	compact disc
cm	centimeter
Co.	Company (used after the names of some companies)
DJ	disc jockey
Dr.	doctor
DVD	digital video disc or digital versatile disc
e.g.	for example (from the Latin *exempli gratia*)
etc.	and all the rest (from the Latin *et cetera*)
F	Fahrenheit
ft	foot or feet
g	gram
hp	horsepower
ID	identification
in	inch
kg	kilogram
km	kilometer
kph	kilometers per hour
l	liter
lb	pound (from the Latin *libra*)
m	meter or mile
Miss	Mistress (a title that goes before an unmarried woman's name)
mm	millimeter
mph	miles per hour

Mr	Mister (a title that goes before a man's name)
Mrs	Mistress (a title that goes before a married woman's name)
Ms	(a title that goes before a married or an unmarried woman's name)
no	number (from the Italian *numero*)
OK	all correct
oz	ounce
p.	page
PC	personal computer
p.m.	after noon (used with times; from the Latin *post meridiem*)
PO	Post Office
PS	postscript (an extra note written at the end of something, such as a letter; from the Latin *post scriptem*)
RSVP	please reply (used on an invitation to a party, wedding, or other event; from the French *répondez s'il vous plaît*)
St.	Saint, or street
tel.	telephone
3-D	three-dimensional (having height, width, and depth)
TV	television
UFO	unidentified flying object
VIP	very important person
www	World Wide Web
yd	yard

Punctuation

. You put a period at the end of a sentence.
The cat sat on the mat.

, You use a comma to separate parts of a sentence, or divide up a list of things.
There is a bed, table, and cupboard in the room.

: You can use a colon in front of a list.
She packed the following: T-shirts, sandals, swimwear, and sunscreen.

; You use a semicolon as a pause in a sentence, or to separate two different subjects in one sentence.
There wasn't much to do; it had been raining all day.

? You use a question mark at the end of sentences that are questions.
What are you doing tonight?

! You use an exclamation mark at the end of an order, or when the sentence is an exclamation.
Oh dear!

' An apostrophe is used to shorten two words into one, or to show who something belongs to.
That's Jason's pen.

" " or ' ' Quotation marks show where speech begins and ends.
"I'm going home at 2 o'clock," she said.

- A hyphen joins two words together.
I'm right-handed.

— A dash can show a change of subject.
I am going home this afternoon—it's my mother's birthday.

() Parentheses can be used to say something that is not part of the main text.
Pam arrived just in time (the ship was about to set off).

Text messaging

ALOrO	all or nothing
AML	all my love
ASAP	as soon as possible
BBS	be back soon
BF	boyfriend
BFN	bye for now
BTW	by the way
CU	see you
CUL8R	see you later
F2T	free to talk
FYEO	for your eyes only
FYI	for your information
GF	girlfriend
GMTA	great minds think alike
HAND	have a nice day
HTH	hope this helps
H&K	hugs and kisses
IAC	in any case
IDK	I don't know
ILUVM	I love you very much
KIT	keep in touch
LOL	laugh out loud
LTNC	long time no see
MYOB	mind your own business
OIC	Oh, I see
PCM	please call me
QT	cutie
R	are
RU?	are you?
RUOK?	Are you OK?
SIT	stay in touch
SRy	sorry
SWALK	signed with a loving kiss
THNQ	thank you
Thx	thanks
Ti2GO	time to go
U	you
UR	you are
WAN2	want to
WAN2TLK?	want to talk?
WUWH	wish you were here
X	kiss
Xoxoxoxo	hugs and kisses

Facts and figures

Numbers

1 one
2 two
3 three
4 four
5 five
6 six
7 seven
8 eight
9 nine
10 ten

11	eleven
12	twelve
13	thirteen
14	fourteen
15	fifteen
16	sixteen
17	seventeen
18	eighteen
19	nineteen
20	twenty
21	twenty-one
30	thirty
40	forty
50	fifty
60	sixty
70	seventy
80	eighty
90	ninety
100	one hundred
101	one hundred and one
1000	one thousand
10,000	ten thousand
100,000	one hundred thousand
1,000,000	one million

1st	first
2nd	second
3rd	third
4th	fourth
5th	fifth
6th	sixth
7th	seventh
8th	eighth
9th	ninth
10th	tenth
11th	eleventh
12th	twelfth
13th	thirteenth
14th	fourteenth
15th	fifteenth
16th	sixteenth
17th	seventeenth
18th	eighteenth
19th	nineteenth
20th	twentieth
21st	twenty-first
30th	thirtieth
40th	fortieth
50th	fiftieth
60th	sixtieth
70th	seventieth
80th	eightieth
90th	ninetieth
100th	one hundredth
101st	one hundred and first

Fractions

$\frac{1}{2}$ one half

$\frac{1}{3}$ one third

$\frac{1}{4}$ one quarter

$\frac{1}{5}$ one fifth

$\frac{1}{6}$ one sixth

$\frac{1}{7}$ one seventh

$\frac{1}{8}$ one eighth

$\frac{1}{9}$ one ninth

$\frac{1}{10}$ one tenth

Days of the week

Monday
Tuesday
Wednesday
Thursday
Friday
Saturday
Sunday

Months of the year

January
February
March
April
May
June
July
August
September
October
November
December

Seasons

spring
summer
fall
winter

Measurements

Metric measures

Length

10 millimeters = 1 centimeter

100 centimeters = 1 meter

1,000 meters = 1 kilometer

Weight

1,000 grams = 1 kilogram

1,000 kilograms = 1 tonne

Volume

10 milliliters = 1 centiliter

10 centiliters = 1 deciliter

10 deciliters = 1 liter

Imperial measures

Length

12 inches = 1 foot

3 feet = 1 yard

1,760 yards = 1 mile

Weight

16 ounces = 1 pound

100 pounds = 1 hundredweight

20 hundredweight = 1 ton

Volume

16 fluid ounces = 1 pint

8 pints = 1 gallon

Animal families

There are special names for young animals and animal groups.

Young animals

What do you call a baby pig?
Or a young goat? Find out here...

Fox and cub

Rabbit and kitten

Deer and fawn

Goose and gosling

Bear and cubs

Hare and leveret

Goat and kid

Kangaroo and joey

Pig and piglet

Lion and cub

Sheep and lambs

Seal and calf or pup

Elephant and calf

Dog and puppy

Swan and cygnet

Animal groups

Special nouns, called "collective nouns," name groups of animals.

A school of dolphins

A pride of lions

A swarm of bees

A flock of sheep

A gaggle of geese

A litter of kittens

A herd of cows

A school of fish

A flock of swans

A pack of dogs

Map of the world

Asia

Europe

Africa

Indian
Ocean

Atlantic
Ocean

Australia
and
Oceania

Southern Ocean

Antarctica

254

Arctic Ocean

North America

Atlantic Ocean

Tropic of Cancer

Pacific Ocean

Equator

South America

Tropic of Capricorn

Continents and oceans

A **continent** is one of the great divisions of land in the world. There are seven in total. Can you count them on this map? In between the continents, five vast **oceans** swell and flow. Look on the map to find out their names.

Acknowledgments

DK Publishing, Inc. would like to thank the following people for their help in the production of this book:

Additional design assistance
Jacqueline Gooden, Steven Laurie, Laura Roberts, Mary Sandberg, Venice Shone

Additional editorial assistance
Caroline Bingham, Deborah Lock, Anna Lofthouse, Amanda Rayner, Sarah Walker

DK picture library research
Sally Hamilton, Rose Horridge, Sarah Mills

Picture agency credits
The publisher would like to thank the following for their kind permission to reproduce their photographs:

Key: a=above; c=center; b=below; l=left; r=right; t=top.
Allsport: 197bc; Peter Anderson: 90cla; Anglo-Australian Observatory: 195ac; Paul Bricknell: 83ccl, 176tc, 187ca; Geoff Brightling: 86tcr, 183tc, 189cca, 189ccb; British Museum: 149tr; Jane Burton: 96cra, 165br, 190ccb; Peter Chadwick: 179tc; Andrew L Chernack, Springfield, Pennsylvania: 127ca; Bruce Coleman Collection: Pacific Stock 207b, 256b Kim Taylor 100cb; Corbis: © Joseph Sohm; ChromoSohm Inc 241br; Brian Cosgrove: 238; Phil Crabbe: 190cca; Andy Crawford: 89cra, 96tr, 202bc, 224tr; Philip Dowell: 17cal, 83tc, 83clb, 83bcr, 89c; Mike Dunning: 98cla; Fleet Air Army Museum: 207tr; Neil Fletcher: 91tl; Jo Foord: 199ccb; John Garrett: 197clb; Philip Gatward: 196bl; Glasgow Museum: 97c; Paul Goff: 222bl; Steve Gorton: 83cr, 196cbl, 197br, 197bcl, 198cca; Ronald Grant Archive: 50bc; Frank Greenaway: 87c, 89trb, 204cb, 240cb; Derek Hall: 200br; Stephen Hayward: 5-6b, 87br; Anthony Pozner of Hendon Way Motors: 154bl; Hunstanton Sea Life Centre: 178ca, 178crb; The Image Bank / Getty Images: John Kelly 180t; James Jackson: 197bcr; Colin Keates: 84c; Roland Kemp: 176br; Barnabas Kindersley: 5clb, 27, 64tr, 169tr; Dave King: 69tl, 78cl, 83cla, 83cra, 89tl, 89tr, 89bl, 89bcl, 96br, 162cla, 174cl, 182car, 196br, 197crb, 197bcra, 209tr, 232cl; Bob Langrish: 102tl, 103tl; Cyril Laubscher: 72cr; Richard Leeney: 233bl; Mike Linley: 86tcl; Sampson Lloyd: 134l; London Planetarium: 195bl, 195bc; Jane Miller: 252bc; Ray Moller: 196cbr; Michael Moran: 200bl; Tracy Morgan: 252bl, 252bcl, 253br David Murray: 83br; David Murray and Jules Selmes: 50tc, 218tr; NASA: 5tr, 21, 68br, 195cr, 195clb, 195l; NASA/ Finley Holiday Films: 5cr, 195cr, 195acl; N.H.P.A.: Stephen Dalton 92br, 92-93b, 208cl, 208c, 208cr; Martin Harvey 42c; Natural History Museum: 3tr, 17cbr, 47bl, 47bc, 47bcr, 77br, 108tc, 108cra, 109tc, 132clb, 132bl, 132bc, 132bla, 137tc, 137ac, 156c; Ian O'Leary: 83cbr, 83cca, 83tcr; Stephen Oliver: 64tr, 83tl, 93tr, 111bc, 115cl, 121br, 135r, 168tr, 191cr, 191r, 197bcla; Oxford Scientific Films: Max Gibbs 147br; Pa Photos: Michael Stephens 171br; Roger Phillips: 83cal; Photodisc: David Toase 145; The Department of Electrical and Electronic Engineering, University of Portsmouth: 171bl; Susanna Price: 177crb, 193cb, 243br; RNLI: 169tr; Department of Cybernetics, University of Reading: 171tl, 171cl; Tim Ridley: 83ccr, 90tr, 99tr, 99bc, 167crb, 183c, 186bl, 196bc, 242c; Royal Green Jackets Museum: 17cl; Guy Ryecart: 166br, 225br; Science Photo Library: John Chumack 47c, 47t; US Department of Energy 171r; Karl Shone: 89bcr, 103tr, 167tr; Steve Shott: 97br, 103c, 162bl, 173cca, 192cla; South of England Rare Breeds Centre: 67cl; Clive Streeter: 83cb; Telegraph Colour Library / Getty Images: Steve Fitchett 188cb; Colin Walton: 83c; Matthew Ward: 73bc, 73br, 182tr, 182cra, 182tcr; Barrie Watts: 94bl, 94bc, 94br, 95bl, 95br; Laura Wickenden: 167br; Philip Wilkins: 175tc; Jerry Young: 17bl, 35ac, 70c, 86tc, 101bc, 103tc, 103tlb, 116tr, 121c, 137tr, 167cra, 168-169b, 190cla, 196tr, 201tr, 219b.

Jacket: NASA: front tc; National Motor Museum, Beaulieu: front tr; National Oceanic and Atmospheric Administration/ National Geophysical Data Centre: back cra;

Answers

pp 4–5 Alphabetical order
Cupboard chaos: ball, bucket, car, doll, drum, shovel, soldier, teddy, tractor, train
It's nonsense!: **1.** cow; **2.** allow; **3.** copy; **4.** berry; **5.** accent; **6.** belt; **7.** fin
Silly sentence: An astronaut began his incredible journey.

pp 10–11 Find out more
Similar words and Opposites:
hot—similar: boiling, opposite: cold;
lucky—similar: fortunate, opposite: unlucky;
noisy—similar: loud, opposite: quiet.

pp 246-247 Spelling tips
Split long words: **1.** 2; **2.** 1; **3.** 3; **4.** 4; **5.** 5; **6.** 14
Confusing spellings: **1.** p; **2.** b; **3.** c; **4.** k
Sound alikes: **1.** flower and flour; **2.** pair and pear; **3.** hare and hair
Sound unalikes: **1.** bow; **2.** wind; **3.** tear